Designing Randomised Trials in Health,
Education and the Social Sciences

Also by Carole J. Torgerson
SYSTEMATIC REVIEWS

Designing Randomised Trials in Health, Education and the Social Sciences

An Introduction

David J. Torgerson and Carole J. Torgerson
University of York

First published 2008 by
PALGRAVE MACMILLAN
Houndmills, Basingstoke, Hampshire RG21 6XS and
175 Fifth Avenue, New York N.Y. 10010
Companies and representatives throughout the world

PALGRAVE MACMILLAN is the global academic imprint of the Palgrave Macmillan division of St. Martin's Press, LLC and of Palgrave Macmillan Ltd. Macmillan® is a registered trademark in the United States, United Kingdom and other countries. Palgrave is a registered trademark in the European Union and other countries.

ISBN-13: 978–0230–53735–4   hardback
ISBN-10: 0–230–53735–9   hardback
ISBN-13: 978–0230–53736–1   paperback
ISBN-10: 0–230–53736–7   paperback

This book is printed on paper suitable for recycling and made from fully managed and sustained forest sources. Logging, pulping and manufacturing processes are expected to conform to the environmental regulations of the country of origin.

A catalogue record for this book is available from the British Library.

Library of Congress Cataloging-in-Publication Data
Torgerson, David J. (David John), 1960–
    Designing randomised trials in health, education and the social sciences /
        David J. Torgerson and Carole J. Torgerson.
        p. ; cm.
    Includes bibliographical references and index.
    ISBN-13: 978–0–230–53735–4   (hardback : alk. paper)
    ISBN-10: 0–230–53735–9   (hardback : alk. paper)
    ISBN-13: 978–0–230–53736–1   (paperback : alk. paper)
    ISBN-10: 0–230–53736–7   (paperack : alk. paper)   1. Clinical
trials.   2. Social sciences—Research—Methodology.   I.
    Torgerson, Carole.   II. Title.
    [DNLM: 1. Health Services Research.   2. Randomized Controlled
    Trials as Topic—methods.   3. Education.   4. Research Design.   5.
    Social Sciences. W 84.3 T682d 2008]
    R853.C55T67 2008
    610.72′4—dc22   2007052309

10   9   8   7   6   5   4   3   2   1
17   16   15   14   13   12   11   10   09   08

Printed and bound in Great Britain by
CPI Antony Rowe, Chippenham and Eastbourne

Contents

List of Figures, Boxes and Tables

Figures

Boxes

Tables

Preface

The randomised controlled trial (RCT) has long been considered the 'gold-standard' method for establishing effectiveness in health care research. Many hundreds of thousands of health care RCTs have been published. The fiftieth anniversary of the 1948 RCT of streptomycin was widely celebrated by health care researchers in 1998. However, one wonders how many educational or social science researchers are aware of the larger 1931 and 1932 randomised trials of an educational intervention conducted by Walters? And if they had known would the seventy-fifth anniversary, in 2007, of those trials have been a cause for celebration? Relatively few RCTs have been undertaken in the wider social sciences. Many methodological advances in the design of trials have been undertaken in health care, which are directly applicable to other areas. Whilst many social science research methods texts have been published, little attention or detail is given to the design and conduct of the RCT in such texts. In health sciences research several excellent texts describe the RCT, usually from a statistical standpoint, which make them less accessible to the non-statistician or general research methodologist. This book is an attempt to remedy this deficit. We avoid, as far as possible, detailed statistical arguments or formulae. Instead we focus on the importance of trial design.

Since the early descriptions of the RCT there has been a tremendous amount of methodological work, mainly in health care trials. As health trialists have widened their remit away from the placebo controlled drug trial, methodological innovations have been developed to deal with the threat of post-randomisation biases. In this book we detail these threats and describe different trial designs that can as easily be applied to the wider social sciences as they can be to health care trials. Many published trials make elementary mistakes that undermine their validity. By way of example we discuss how to avoid these problems through proper design and thereby, hopefully, develop a design that will produce reliable results. We think that there will be a revived interest in the RCT across the social sciences as politicians and policy-makers begin to crave evidence for 'what works?' The most reliable guide to providing evidence on what works is the RCT. Other approaches, long over-used by researchers and practitioners, are nearly always subject to inherent flaws, which can render their results uninterpretable. In this book we describe the main justification for the RCT, and details of how we should randomise, and information about potential bias. We also look in detail at different trial designs, at how to appraise trial quality and we outline the importance of economic analysis alongside RCTs.

Acknowledgements

We thank Joy Adamson, Martin Bland, Iain Chalmers and Jo Dumville for their helpful comments on earlier draft chapters and Alison Robinson for proof reading the manuscript. We also thank Jo North for her careful copy editing of the book. Any remaining errors are the authors' responsibility. We also thank William Torgerson. We acknowledge support from the ESRC Researcher Development Initiative: Training in pragmatic social interventions.

Glossary of Terms

Active or on treatment analysis – An analytical method whereby only those who comply with their assigned intervention are included in the analysis. Non-compliers may be analysed in the control condition. Method violates randomisation and can introduce bias.

Allocation concealment – This prevents foreknowledge of allocation of an individual by the researcher, participant or practitioner. This is important because random allocation can be undermined if participants are chosen to be in a desired group.

Alternation – A non-random method of forming comparator groups, whereby trial participants are alternately assigned to treatment or to act as controls.

Attrition – Some participants are lost during the study and cannot be included in the analysis. This is termed attrition.

Before and after (pre- and post-test) – The weakest form of quantitative evaluation. Participants are measured at a point in time, given an intervention and then re-measured. Any change is attributed to the intervention. Bias is a strong possibility due to temporal and regression to the mean effects.

Bias – A term denoting that a known or unknown variable is or may be responsible for an observed effect other than the intervention.

Blinding – This denotes that the researcher is masked or 'blinded' to the identity of the group allocation of the participants when undertaking post-tests. This prevents biased assessment. Sometimes participants are also blinded to the true nature of the experiment.

Blocked randomisation – This method of randomisation prevents groups becoming either numerically unbalanced or suffering from chance bias. It does this by randomising in blocks (e.g., block of four). Thus, a block of four can be: ABAB, AABB, BBAA, BABA, ABBA, BAAB. This means that the study will be balanced, although the block size must be kept secret to conceal the allocation sequence.

Case control study – A study where participants are identified with a specific outcome (cases) and then compared with a control group of participants without the outcome.

Campbell Collaboration – Inspired by the Cochrane Collaboration (see below) but aims to synthesise controlled studies in education, crime and justice and social welfare (www.campbellcollaboration.org/).

Cochrane Collaboration – A world-wide collaboration, the aim of which is to collect and review all of the controlled trials in the health care field, to inform clinicians and policy-makers (www.cochrane.org/).

Comprehensive cohort design – A study design whereby participants who do not consent to be randomised, or cannot be randomised, are followed up alongside the randomised groups.

Confidence intervals – A method of expressing sample uncertainty around the estimate of treatment effect. They are usually 95 per cent intervals: if an identical trial is conducted many times then 95 per cent of the trials will have confidence intervals which contain the true estimate of effect.

Confounders – A variable associated with cause and outcome; can mask a true relationship between another variable and outcome.

CONSORT – Consolidated Standards for Reporting Trials is a descriptive method adopted by many medical journals for publication of RCTs.

Cost-benefit analysis – An economic technique that measures both costs and benefits in monetary terms. If costs are lower than benefits then the intervention should be adopted.

Cost-effectiveness analysis – An economic method that measures costs in monetary terms but measures benefits in 'natural' units. When comparing two mutually exclusive alternatives, the intervention with the lowest cost-effectiveness ratio should be adopted.

Cost-utility analysis – A form of cost-effectiveness analysis where the outcomes are measured in units of utility. An intervention should be adopted if the cost-utility ratio is lower than a decision-maker's willingness to pay threshold.

Effect size – This is the difference between two groups described in standard deviation units (i.e., difference divided by the standard deviation), which is termed the effect size.

Factorial design – A trial design where two or more different interventions are evaluated using the same participant sample. Has the advantage that two trials for the price of one can be undertaken. The simplest 2 x 2 factorial design results in four different groups.

ITT analysis – intention to treat analysis – This is where all participants are analysed in their original randomised groups; it is the most robust analytical method.

Minimisation – A non-random method that can form comparator groups. Groups are formed in such a way as to ensure that they are balanced on known covariates. If undertaken properly minimisation is as effective, and often better, at eliminating selection bias as random allocation.

Multi-variate analysis – In an RCT most known and unknown variables affecting outcome will be balanced at baseline. Nevertheless, particularly in small studies, imbalance in prognostic variables can still affect the precision of the results. This is particularly the case with the pre-test variable, which will strongly predict outcome. A more precise estimate of the effect size (i.e., with smaller confidence intervals) can be obtained by undertaking a multivariate analysis with the pre-test score as a covariate as well as the group allocation.

Numbers needed to treat or teach (NNT) – This is a method of converting the effects of an intervention into an easily understood metric. Thus, a NNT of 5 means that five people need to be taught in order that one extra person passes an important threshold (e.g., an exam).

Observational data or study – Data generated from a non-randomised study where estimates of effectiveness are gathered by comparing people exposed to an intervention with those unexposed.

Paired randomisation – Participants are formed into matched pairs on the basis of important covariates (e.g., gender). Once the study group has been formed into pairs a random member of each pair is allocated to the intervention.

Pairwise randomisation – A method of allocating participants that ensures numerical balance within a centre but avoids the problem of predictability that occurs with blocked randomisation. Randomisation takes place only when two participants are eligible and then one is selected, at random, for the intervention.

Participant preference – A type of trial where preferences of participants are recorded and sometimes only participants with no preference are randomised.

Pilot study – A type of study that precedes the definitive trial; can be an internal or external pilot. Characteristics are: small sample size and or incompletely developed intervention.

Per-protocol analysis – Participants not complying with the treatment protocol are excluded from the analysis. Violates randomisation and can lead to bias.

Placebo – Commonly used in drug trials for the control treatment. The placebo is an inert substance that looks and tastes like the real drug and blinds or masks the participant, doctor and assessor as to the treatment group.

Power – Given a pre-specified hypothesised difference between intervention groups the power of a study relates to the chances of observing any difference between groups as being statistically significant if it exists. Power is commonly set at either 80 per cent or 90 per cent.

Preference trial – A trial design that takes participants' preferences into account by either asking them before randomisation (fully randomised preference design) or by only randomising those who do not have a preference and letting those with a preference have their preferred treatment.

Quasi-alternation – A biased method of constructing group membership that uses some characteristic of the participant, such as month of birth, first letter of surname to determine allocation.

Quasi-randomisation – Usually used to refer to alternation or other systematic methods of forming comparator groups, such allocating by date of birth.

Random sampling – A sampling method to allow an estimation of a parameter within a stated population. This allows generalisation of parameter estimates. Sometimes confused with randomisation.

RCT – Randomised controlled trial. This is where groups have been formed through random allocation (or a similar method). This is the main method that ensures that allocation bias is eliminated at baseline.

Regression analysis – A statistical method that is sometimes used on trial data to adjust for chance imbalances between two groups and to improve the precision of estimates of any treatment effect.

Regression discontinuity design – A quasi-experimental alternative to the RCT. This design selects people into their intervention groups on some pre-test variable with a pre-defined cut-off; if properly implemented this approach can produce unbiased estimates of effect sizes – albeit less efficiently than an RCT.

Resentful demoralisation – Participants who have a preference for an intervention and who are assigned to the opposite intervention may become demoralised and this may bias the trial's results.

Selection bias – This occurs when groups are formed by a process other than randomisation and important factors that are associated with outcome differ between the groups *before* they are exposed to the intervention.

Significance – This can be statistical, clinical, educational, economic. Statistical significance is usually 5 per cent (p = 0.05) or 10 per cent (p = 0.10) and relates to replication of a trial. Replication of an identical trial, where there is no treatment effect, many times will result in 5 per cent of the trials showing a difference as being statistically significant if the 5 per cent level is adopted. Other forms of significance relate to whether or not a difference between groups is worth having in terms of policy or practice.

Simple randomisation – This is the easiest form of randomisation akin to tossing a coin. A disadvantage with simple randomisation is that with small studies (<100) there is a high probability of having large chance imbalance between the groups. More importantly, there can be imbalance in important covariates. Restricted forms of randomisation are often used to prevent this.

Stratification – This is a process whereby randomisation is restricted (e.g., by blocking) such that any important known confounders are balanced between the groups.

Zelen's method – A trial design whereby participants are randomised *before* consent to take part in the study is obtained. The single consent method is where consent is only sought from those allocated to the novel intervention.

1
Background to Controlled Trials

1.1 Background

A key reason for undertaking any research is to increase certainty in an uncertain world. We all directly or indirectly consume research. We hope the treatment we are prescribed by our doctor will be effective in improving our condition. We want to know which educational interventions, curricular innovations and teaching methods are effective in increasing knowledge, skills and understanding. Policy-makers and practitioners are interested in the relative effectiveness of crime and justice interventions, for example rehabilitation programmes and sentencing policies.

Health and social science research can provide the knowledge that enables us to determine what does and does not work. The 'gold-standard' research method for addressing the 'what works?' question in 'evidence-informed' policy-making and practice is the randomised controlled trial (RCT).

The aims of this book, therefore, are: to introduce the RCT; to describe its methodology and design, focusing on when and how to undertake an RCT; to describe examples of high quality and weak application of the method; and to introduce critical appraisal of published RCTs. We do not include in the book detailed statistical justification for using the RCT or describe detailed statistical approaches for its analysis. Statistical theory and analysis are more than adequately covered by other authors (e.g., Altman, 1991; Bland, 2000). If the research design of an RCT is adequate and applied rigorously, then relatively simple statistical analysis is required. Even the most heroic form of statistical analysis cannot compensate for a poorly designed, poorly conducted trial. Consequently, it is the design aspect of a trial that is the most important issue relating to an RCT, and this is the focus of the book.

The randomised controlled trial (RCT) is a simple research method of elegant design. Two or more groups are formed through random allocation; one or more of the groups is exposed to an intervention (experimental group), while the other group(s) receive(s) an alternative treatment or no treatment (comparison or control group). The effects of the intervention are observed by comparing the outcomes of both groups. If the groups assembled through randomisation are sufficiently large, we can be confident that any differences observed between the groups will be a consequence of the intervention, rather than a result of some other known or unknown variable.

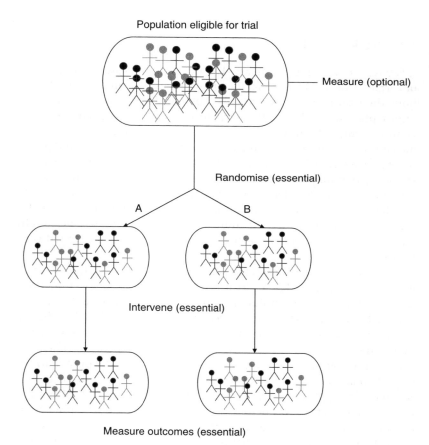

Figure 1.1:   Schematic outline of a randomised trial

In Figure 1.1 we show the basic outline of the randomised trial. In essence the design is as follows: we assemble a population for whom the intervention is appropriate (this population may then be measured, although this step is not a pre-requisite); we then allocate the participants to two or more groups and apply the intervention(s) to the groups formed by randomisation; at some pre-specified time in the future we measure the groups in terms of their outcome – if there is a difference between the groups, and assuming that the difference and the sample size are sufficient, we can infer a causal relationship between our intervention and the group differences.

1.2 The randomised trial

Social interactions in the fields of health care, education, crime and justice, and other social sciences involve complex phenomena, including relationships between doctors and patients, teachers and students, social workers and clients. The best method for evaluating any proposed changes in health care, education, crime and justice, and other areas of public policy is the RCT, because it is able to deal adequately with the level of complexity inherent in these fields (Sheldon and Oakley, 2002) by 'teasing out' from the background 'noise' whether or not an intervention is actually effective.

The RCT has developed considerably since its inception in the middle of the last century. Whilst some disciplines use the method more often than others (health care research compared with, for example, educational research), the breathtaking simplicity of the design means, for questions of effectiveness, it could be used more often in place of other less rigorous evaluative approaches.

In this book we use a variety of examples to illustrate the design of trials. Due to historical reasons, many of these examples are from health care research; however, we include examples from other disciplines, in particular education and crime and justice. This is primarily because, as health care researchers have applied the RCT away from drug trials, they have had to grapple with numerous problems that threaten its internal validity, including how to deal with participants' strong preferences for a given treatment. Education and other social science researchers, whilst dealing with similar problems, have undertaken fewer RCTs in recent years. Health care trial research is funded more generously than in other areas, allowing more methodological research activity to take place in the design and use of the RCT. Nevertheless lessons from the design and conduct of trials in education and other social sciences (e.g., the development of cluster or group randomised trials) have been enthusiastically adopted by health care researchers.

The RCT has long been recognised as the 'gold-standard' research method in health care research (Pocock, 1983), although this has not always been the case. Silverman (2004) described entrenched opposition he encountered from both clinicians and clinical researchers to the use of the method in the 1940s and 1950s. It is still sometimes argued, even in health care, that issues of effectiveness can be resolved through the use of other research methods, such as basic science, qualitative enquiry or through before and after approaches (Penston, 2007). However, the use of other methods to infer causality has led, and continues to lead, to the implementation of ineffective or harmful interventions.

1.3   Health care disasters

At this point it is worth noting some deadly examples from health care research of inappropriate implementation of interventions not previously having been adequately exposed to a randomised trial. Mistakes in health care research can be counted in mortality or morbidity, and this has led to the realisation that, morally and ethically, patients need to be protected from potentially hazardous new treatments by first evaluating the treatments in RCTs. In contrast, in other areas, for instance social welfare, any potentially hazardous effect of an intervention does not manifest itself with such direct or obvious consequences.

One of the earliest health care disasters involved administering oxygen to premature infants. In the 1940s and 1950s the incidence of blindness seemed to be increasing among premature babies. The cause of this was not discovered until an RCT evaluating the 'routine' practice of supplementing premature babies with oxygen showed that babies allocated to oxygen supplementation had significant increases in blindness, compared with un-supplemented infants (Silverman, 1977, 1997). Similarly, in the late 1940s and early 1950s, and on the basis of evidence from case reports, some premature babies were given prophylactic antibiotics. It was only later, during a randomised trial published in 1954, that this routine practice was shown to lead to brain damage and death in significantly more babies than those who had received an alternative treatment (Silverman and Altman, 1996).

One of the biggest catastrophes in terms of actual numbers of deaths was the routine use of anti-arrhythmia drugs for post-myocardial infarction patients. Many cardiologists were opposed to the use of RCTs on

---

Box 1.1:   The CAST trial

From about 1978, hundreds of thousands of patients were given flecainide and other, similar anti-arrhythmia drugs. In 1987 an adequately
powered trial was begun. In 1989 the trial was terminated abruptly
due to *increased* deaths in the active treatment groups.

All cause death was 7.7 per cent in the treatment group compared
with 3.0 per cent in the placebo group (relative risk of death of
taking active treatment = 2.5, 95 per cent confidence interval 1.6 to
4.5) (Cardiac Arrhythmia Suppression Trial (CAST) Investigators,
Preliminary Report, 1991).

It has been estimated that tens of thousands of people died as a
result of uncontrolled use of these agents (Silverman, 1997).

---

ethical grounds. They believed that such drugs were beneficial and that
to withhold them, therefore, would be unethical (see Box 1.1).

Trials were eventually started in the 1980s, but stopped early because
of significantly increased mortality among patients allocated to the
active treatment (CAST Investigators, 1991). Indeed, the trialists were so
confident the anti-arrhythmia drugs would prove to be beneficial or, at
worst, have no effect, that the trial was designed to enable early stop-
page once an important benefit had been found. Instead, the interim
analysis found that mortality was significantly elevated in the active
treatment groups. As these drugs had not previously been evaluated
using large RCTs, it has been estimated that tens of thousands of
patients died through their unrestricted use in routine clinical practice
(Silverman, 1997).

In another disaster, thousands of pregnant women were given a synthetic hormone to prevent miscarriage. Randomised trials later failed to
show that this treatment – diethylistilboestrol (DES) – was effective.
Unfortunately, it transpired that some female children whose pregnant
mothers were exposed to DES later developed rare vaginal cancers and
other serious health conditions (Oakley, 2000).

In 2004 a randomised controlled trial evaluating a 'standard' therapy
for head injured patients (high dose steroids) was terminated half way
through (CRASH Trial Collaborators, 2004). After recruiting half of the
20 000 participants across the world it was found that two-week mortality was significantly elevated among the steroid-treated patients. It has
been estimated that the failure to evaluate this treatment promptly
probably caused the deaths of more than 10 000 people (Sauerland and

Maegele, 2004). In the field of head injuries alone, several 'standard' treatments still remain unevaluated (CRASH Trial Collaborators, 2004).

A systematic review and meta-analysis of all the trials of antioxidants (e.g., betacarotene, vitamins A, C, E and selenium) showed that vitamins A and E and betacarotene supplementation can actually *increase* mortality (Bjelakovic et al., 2007). For vitamin C and selenium supplementation no evidence was found for harm or benefit.

Medical regulators now require evidence from properly conducted randomised controlled trials before drug treatments are implemented. Non-tested older drug treatments, vitamins, herbal supplements, 'natural' remedies and many non-pharmaceutical treatments (e.g., novel surgical therapies) can still be given to patients.

It is important to note that clinicians who have used harmful interventions probably did so with the best of intentions. Silverman, himself an early advocate of the use of RCTs in paediatric medicine, describes the case of a premature infant under his care. On the basis of data derived from animal experiments, he gave the child a drug treatment to prevent blindness only to discover later (from an RCT) that this drug increased mortality among infants and did not prevent blindness (Silverman, 2004).

Whilst new treatments are often seen as better than old interventions or 'standard care' this may not be necessarily true. In a review of RCTs comparing the efficacy of new drugs for childhood cancers with usual care it was found that in around half the trials the new drug was superior and in half it was inferior (Kumar et al., 2005). It is important, therefore, that all novel interventions are tested in rigorous RCTs.

1.4   Social science trials

Education and other social science trialists are able to point to fewer clear examples of adverse effects accruing through the lack of an RCT, to counter the arguments of those who oppose the wider use of trials. Despite this, however, these areas are not without their equivalent of anti-arrhythmia disasters and one is the 'Scared Straight' programme.

'Scared Straight' is a widely used intervention in North America. Juvenile offenders are taken to meet long-term prisoners in order to deter them from further crime. A recent version being offered in the UK is to take juvenile drug users to prisons to meet jailed drug offenders. A series of RCTs from North America was undertaken and summarised in a systematic review. The review demonstrated that the 'Scared Straight' programme actually *increased* the risk of offending in the juveniles in the

---

Box 1.2:   Scared straight (Petrosino et al., 2002)

This initiative originated in the USA in the 1970s. The aim was to take juvenile offenders and expose them to presentations from prisoners serving life sentences, in order to deter them from further offending behaviour. Uncontrolled evaluations (i.e., before and after studies) suggested it had had a 94 per cent success rate of preventing juveniles from recidivism and the programme was widely implemented in the USA. Similar programmes have been used in the UK, Australia, Norway and Canada.

A systematic review of the randomised trials of Scared Straight found that all but one indicated a harmful effect of the programme and *increased* offending among participants. A meta-analysis of the trials showed that the odds of offending were 1.68 (95 per cent CI 1.20 to 2.36) for juveniles allocated to the intervention group.

---

intervention group compared with juveniles in the control group (Petrosino et al., 2002) (see Box 1.2).

Similar examples include a trial, undertaken in the UK, testing the effectiveness of social work supervision of school truants, which showed an increase in the risk of truancy compared with no supervision (Berg et al., 1978). In the USA a trial was undertaken to look at the use of routine arrests for people who were suspected of intimate partner abuse (Hirschel et al., 1992). Contrary to expectations, arrests did not lead to a reduction in future partner abuse.

An interesting example is the use of driver education among older school children to reduce vehicle accidents among young drivers on the basis of survey evidence. However, a systematic review of RCTs showed that, contrary to expectations, driver education programmes led to an *increase* in young driver deaths and road accidents (Cochrane Injuries Group Driver Education Reviewers, 2001).

1.5   Conclusions

The randomised controlled trial is the most effective method of assessing causality. Other approaches can give misleading results, and there are many examples, particularly from health care research, where practitioners and policy-makers have implemented ineffective or harmful interventions on the basis of evidence derived from non-randomised study designs. Whilst the basic format of the randomised trial (Figure 1.1) is exceedingly simple, there are many variations on the basic design, which allow us to answer different effectiveness questions. For instance, rather than randomising individual people we may wish to randomise institutions such as schools or hospitals, in a so-called cluster design. Despite these variations, however, the basic principle remains the same: we assemble our groups through random allocation and this allows us to make causal inferences. Other study designs do not allow us to do this with the same degree of robustness. In the following chapter we examine the weaknesses of the before and after study or pre- and post-test design, which is one of the most widely used study designs to infer causality, a role, we will argue, for which it is not suitable.

1.6   Key points

- The RCT is the 'gold-standard' research method for addressing effectiveness questions in health, education and social policy.
- The essence of the RCT is *random* allocation of individuals or groups of people into two (or more) groups to form experimental and control groups.
- This method leads to the control of all known and unknown variables in order that a causal relationship between an intervention and outcome(s) can be established.

2
The Limitations of Before and After Designs

2.1 Background

Quasi-experimental research methods widely used in health and social science research are often used to make causal inferences. Yet (with certain exceptions, for example, the regression discontinuity design, Cook and Campbell, 1979) their designs are often not sufficiently reliable to do so. Many quasi-experiments cannot 'design-out' potential bias, unlike randomised controlled trials. In this chapter we discuss the particular problems of the before and after study.

2.2 Pre- and post-test design

> 'It is incident to physicians, I am afraid, beyond all other men, to mistake subsequence for consequence.' Samuel Johnson (1734)

The basic design of the pre- and post-test study (or before and after study) is as follows. First, a problem is observed through a pre-test, which may take a number of forms, for example, high blood pressure in a patient, low test scores, increases in crime incidence. After identification and measurement of the problem an intervention is implemented. The participants are re-tested (post-test). Any differences between the pre- and post-test measures are sometimes then ascribed to the intervention. For example, if patients with high blood pressure are given a medication to reduce their blood pressure and on re-measurement the blood pressure is reduced, a causal connection is sometimes assumed. Similarly, a group of students with the lowest test scores in an exam are given extra tuition and then re-tested. Again, if the test results have increased sometimes a causal inference is made. Another example could be to identify distinct geographical areas with a high street crime rate, devote extra policing resources to these areas and then re-measure the incidence of crime. Cook and Campbell (1979) have deemed this evaluative approach to be the weakest 'quasi-experimental' method, because it is subject to several flaws.

2.3   Temporal changes

The first problem with a pre- and post-test design is one of temporal trends. Many acute illnesses tend to be self-limiting, and recovery will occur in the absence of any intervention – a point Dr Johnson made in the eighteenth century. Similarly, in the field of education, children tend to improve in knowledge, understanding and skills irrespective of any intervention but simply through increased maturity during the passage of time. Furthermore, within an educational, health care or judicial setting, when people are exposed to a routine intervention this often appears to have a positive effect. Disentangling this effect from any addition or change due to a novel intervention is virtually impossible using a pre- and post-test design. These temporal effects, however, can be further exaggerated by the statistical phenomenon of 'regression to the mean'.

2.4   Regression to the mean

The regression to the mean (RTM) phenomenon is widespread, and affects nearly all fields of endeavour (Morton and Torgerson, 2003). The phenomenon occurs when a group of individuals, schools, hospitals, etc., is measured or tested. If, for example, a group of schools is measured in terms of performance in public examinations a spread of values will be observed, ranging from high to low. The majority of the schools, however, will cluster around the average. If the schools are measured again twelve months later, the schools with low initial scores will tend to 'regress' upwards towards the mean, whilst the schools that initially scored very well will tend to decline towards the mean. Similarly, when a group of children or patients is measured with a test and then re-measured with either the same test or a different one, the individuals with 'extreme' high or low scores on the first test (i.e., the outliers) will tend to regress to the mean. If an intervention focuses on individuals who score below a certain test threshold this statistical phenomenon ensures that, as a group, the individuals will improve whether or not the intervention is actually effective. Note that regression to the mean is a 'group' phenomenon. Within the group some individual values will not change between tests, or even become more extreme. Regression to the mean does not guarantee that all extreme values will regress to the mean, only that most will (Morton and Torgerson, 2003). Importantly, it is impossible to identify from a group of extreme values those that will or will not regress without any intervention.

Due to lack of understanding about regression to the mean many people assume that, because an intervention among people with 'extreme' low values has been followed by a consequent improvement, the intervention has been effective.

Misunderstanding of this phenomenon is widespread in many fields.

> I suspect that the regression fallacy is the most common fallacy in the statistical analysis of economic data. (Friedman, 1992)

Tversky and Kahneman (1974) described misinterpretation of the phenomenon by pilot instructors, who noted that trainee pilots' good landings accompanied by praise invariably led to poor landings on subsequent flights. Conversely poor landings (and chastisement) seemed to lead to 'improved' landing skills (Tversky and Kahneman, 1974). This was misinterpreted as the praise encouraging pilots to be lulled into complacency and chastisement improving their performance, when, in fact, the actual explanation for the subsequent change in landings was the regression to the mean effect. For every landing appraisal there is an element of error. Measurement of single landings among a group of pilots will identify some that have landed heavily and others that have landed well. Regression to the mean occurs on re-measurement of the next landing.

Another classic example of the regression to the mean phenomenon is change in road safety policy after an increase in road traffic accidents (Campbell and Ross, 1968). A sudden increase in road accidents often provokes a police response of cracking down on drink driving, for example. Because of regression to the mean it is highly likely that in the following year the accident rate will fall, irrespective of the effectiveness or otherwise of the intervention.

Regression to the mean occurs when there is a measurement error due to a number of possible factors: for example, a test may not measure the 'true' value of a student's knowledge and understanding; the student may make mistakes and perform unexpectedly badly; the test itself may not be an accurate measure of all the necessary knowledge and skills; or the test marker may make mistakes. A student with an extreme value (high or low) will, on average, have a greater error value attached to their 'true' score result compared with a student who achieves an average value.

If we then re-measure the student with an extreme value the second test will tend to move towards the true value because, by chance, a proportion of the observed first result was erroneous.

Where there is little measurement error, regression to the mean has little influence. For example, if we measure the height and weight of a sample of people and then re-measure them an hour later on the same scales those at the extremes of the height and weight distribution will tend to remain constant, as there is usually little measurement error associated with such scales. There will be some difference in measurements, but these will only be in the order of a few millimetres or grams. On the other hand, if we measure the blood pressure of the same group of people and then re-measure this an hour later we will find that the blood pressure measurements of those with initial high blood pressure have, on average, tended to decrease and the blood pressure measurements of those with initial low blood pressure have, on average, increased. This is because measurement of blood pressure has a high error value, unlike measurement of height and weight.

In an educational example of regression to the mean let us consider two RCTs in literacy learning (Foster et al., 1994). In the first experiment children 'with PAT scores greater than 20 (67 per cent) were not included in the study' (Foster et al., 1994). On the basis of a single test the authors chose the children at the bottom of the distribution to be included in the study. Consequently we would expect an increase in their scores due to regression to the mean effects. In this experiment, the children in the control group improved their scores by about 0.5 of a standard deviation, whilst the children in the intervention group improved their scores by 1.8 standard deviations. The improvement attributable to the intervention is about 1.3 standard deviations (i.e., 1.8 − 0.5). In the second study the authors tested another group of children and 'children with the highest and lowest scores on this test were eliminated from the sample'. In this instance we would expect there to be little or no regression to the mean effects, and the change in the control group was indeed much lower compared with the first experiment at about −0.15 of a standard deviation (Foster et al., 1994).

In Figure 2.1 the regression to the mean phenomenon is demonstrated by a graphical representation of the assessments of fifteen students' essays 'blind' marked by two markers. This was the first time the two markers had marked together (which would increase the error value of the test). In the figure, the difference in marks between the two markers is plotted against the first marker's mark on the x-axis. Note that for those students who scored between 50 per cent and 60 per cent with the first marker (i.e., around the average) there was high agreement between markers. For those students who scored a high mark with the first marker, the second marker tended to disagree more and score them lower. The corresponding plot of these marks shows a classic symptom of regression towards the mean, where there is a correlation between the difference in pre- and post-test scores (in this instance first and second markers) and pre-test scores.

Regression to the mean *will* confound any education, health or public policy strategy based on selecting groups of people or hospitals, prisons or schools that have performed particularly badly or well on a measure. Regression to the mean will explain why so many 'action research' or 'clinical audit' projects appear to be successful. A problem is identified through using some form of measurement (e.g., an increase in poor student behaviour, or increase in hospital infections), some change is implemented and there is a fairly good chance that the regression to the mean effect will produce an improvement. One of us (DJT) heard of an audit of a cervical screening programme which resulted in a ranking of cytologists with those with low false positive rates at the top of the ranking and those with high false positive rates at the bottom. Examining cervical smears under a microscope is not error-free, and consequently, by chance, some cytologists will have a relatively high error rate and call back more women than necessary for a re-smear. In this instance those at the bottom of the table were sent for 'retraining' and the next audit found that they had improved, just as we would expect through regression effects.

Government policy initiatives are affected by regression to the mean effects. For instance, the policy of identifying poorly performing schools, hospitals or police forces and 'naming and shaming' them in a league table will tend to appear to work, as these 'extreme' or outlying values

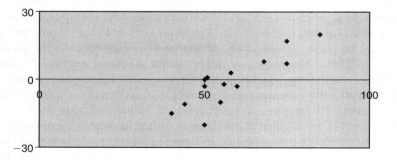

Figure 2.1:   Correlation between two test scores

will tend to regress back to the group mean. To simulate such an effect, one of us (CJT) analysed the performance among education authorities with respect to percentage changes in pass rates in public exams (Torgerson, 2001). The authorities were ranked from highest to lowest in their change in exam pass rates between 1998 and 1999. The top 5 per cent of authorities increased their pass rate by 7.1 per cent, compared with the average of 2 per cent, whilst the pass rate of the bottom 5 per cent declined by 1.8 per cent. In the following year, however, the bottom 5 per cent increased their pass rate by 4.7 per cent, whilst the top 5 per cent only increased theirs by 1.2 per cent. The difference in percentage pass rates between authorities at the top and the bottom of the 'league' table was entirely predictable due to regression to the mean effects. If the government had initiated some educational policy programme aimed at the bottom 5 per cent of education authorities in 1999 then it would have seen a gratifying increase in examination pass rates in the subsequent year. Of course this finding would have been completely confounded by regression to the mean effects.

The UK government measured burglary rates around the country and then initiated a burglary prevention programme among areas of high crime. An evaluation appeared to show it had worked, but the results were entirely consistent with the regression to the mean phenomenon (Marchant, 2005).

Regression to the mean effects can also explain the 'placebo' phenomenon. In many placebo-controlled trials the placebo group often exhibits an apparent treatment effect. This has been observed in, for example, placebo-controlled trials of hormone replacement therapy (HRT). Karlberg et al. (1995) undertook a placebo-controlled trial of HRT to improve quality of life among women going through the menopause. They found that women on the placebo treatment, whose average symptom score was 26 at the start of treatment, went on to experience a seven-point improvement after six weeks of placebo therapy (HRT produced a 17-point improvement). The improvement in the placebo group would be partly, if not solely, attributable to regression to the mean effects. This is because many quality of life measures are not accurate measures of the 'true' quality of life of a person, but contain an element of error within the measurement. For example, measurement of menopausal symptoms will be prone to error: generally women who are eligible for trials of HRT are selected on the basis that they have higher menopausal symptom scores than average and consequently it is likely that, on re-testing such women, their scores will tend to regress towards the population mean.

The placebo effect is controversial. A systematic review of three-armed trials (placebo, active and open control studies) found little evidence for a placebo effect (Hrobjartsson and Gotzsche, 2001). Much of what is termed the 'placebo effect' will simply be due to the regression effect although this does not exclude the possibility of there being a true placebo phenomenon.

2.5   Discussion

The pre- and post-test method will consistently over-estimate any benefit of an intervention because of regression to the mean effects and temporal changes. A tertiary review (i.e., a review of reviews) of studies of psychological, educational and behavioural treatments has shown that before and after studies consistently over-estimate effectiveness by an average of 61 per cent compared with studies with a control group (Lipsey and Wilson, 1993). Therefore, the use of a concurrent control group is absolutely essential in order to control for temporal changes and regression to the mean effects.

Many social science interventions are evaluated using before and after designs. For an example of an evaluation that demonstrated the need for a contemporaneous control group, consider an experiment examining different interventions to prevent men from assaulting their female partners (Dunford, 2000). Three different interventions were evaluated and the re-assault rate was examined. Eighty-three per cent of the men in the intervention groups did not re-injure their partner – one of the highest rates reported in the literature. However, the control group, which did not receive any intervention, had very similar rates (i.e., 79 per cent). The difference was not statistically significant, demonstrating an absence of evidence that any of the three interventions was more effective than no intervention (Dunford, 2000). If a control group had *not* been included in this evaluation, then one may have concluded, erroneously, that the three interventions were all effective. There are probably a number of reasons to explain why the majority of men did not re-injure their partners. Firstly, regression to the mean effects may have been partly responsible. For a proportion of the men the spousal abuse was an unexpected event and unlikely to happen again, at least in the short term, that is, their behaviour was 'extreme' and on re-measurement there was a regression to the long-term mean of non-violent behaviour. Secondly, all of the men were brought to the attention of the authorities and this 'intervention' alone may have had some effect. The addition of counselling may not have added any benefit. Finally, temporal changes could explain some of the changes in behaviour. For example, some of the men may have gained employment due to an upturn in the economy, which in turn could have lowered their levels of stress and made them less likely to assault their partners. Importantly, because this study contained a contemporaneous control group, all of these effects would have affected all groups equally.

It is possible to evaluate an intervention without a control group and make a causal inference in some cases. Once diagnosis of some diseases has been made we know the outcome, with almost certainty. Once clinical symptoms of rabies appear death is virtually inevitable. Consequently, any treatment which results in the recovery of even a few patients can be deemed to be effective. Another example where a trial is, arguably, unnecessary, is the use of the 'Mother's kiss' technique to dislodge foreign objects from a child's nasal passage (Glasziou et al., 2007). In this technique the parent of a child with the object in the nostril occludes the opposite nostril and blows in the child's mouth. Within ten seconds this will usually remove the offending object. Because the effect is dramatic and the object did not dislodge itself in the preceding hours, we can be confident that this is an effect of treatment and therefore does not warrant testing in an RCT. However, the circumstances where this occurs are relatively rare, especially in the wider social sciences. This is due to the myriad of potentially alternative explanations for change, and consequently we need an untreated control group, preferably formed by random allocation, to control for these confounders.

The need to use contemporaneous control groups when trying to estimate effectiveness has been recognised for some considerable time. In the next chapter we consider the historical perspective of the controlled trial.

2.6   Key points

- One group before and after designs are widely used research methods (e.g., action research, audit, design experiments).
- Such single before and after designs are biased through temporal and regression to the mean effects.
- Regression to the mean occurs when a single test with an error component is used to categorise groups and then another similar test is used as follow-up.
- Control groups are needed to control for regression to the mean and temporal effects.

3
History of Controlled Trials

3.1 Background

The problems of using pre- and post-test designs have been recognised by researchers from different disciplines for many years. The need for a concurrent control group has been recognised for at least 150 to 200 years (Chalmers, 2001).

3.2 Trials in the twentieth century

Most modern randomised controlled trials in the social sciences can trace the history of their design to the 1920s and 1930s when R. A. Fisher, a statistician, formalised random allocation within experimental agriculture (Fisher, 1971). The influence of agricultural experiments is still to be found in the terminology of RCTs in health and the social sciences. For example, 'blocked' randomisation originally related to blocks of land, whilst 'split-plot' design related to splitting a plot of land into different areas. In the 1940s, Lindquist (1940) wrote a book 'translating' Fisher's texts on agricultural statistics into the field of educational research. He described several randomised designs appropriate for the use of evaluating educational interventions in school settings. In particular, he described how confounding could be avoided in educational trials if whole classes or schools were randomised (i.e., cluster or group randomisation) (Lindquist, 1940). Furthermore, he described the appropriate statistical methods for analysing cluster trials, an area neglected by health researchers for about fifty years.

Oakley reports (2000) that randomised experiments in the field of literacy instruction for children with learning difficulties were conducted around the beginning of the twentieth century, although it is difficult to ascertain how the control groups in some of these studies were formed, and they may not have used true random allocation (Forsetlund et al., 2007). Forsetlund and colleagues (2007) have described their search for the first RCT of social interventions. The earliest study they found that unequivocally used randomisation was published in the early 1930s (Forsetlund et al., 2007). Two studies by the same author looked at the effect of counselling on students' performance (Walters, 1931, 1932). In the trial described by Walters (1932), 994 freshman, or first-year undergraduate students, were 'divided into three equal groups by random sampling'. The aim of the study was to assess whether counselling students by older peers or tutors resulted in better progress than no counselling. However, the author referred to a smaller study he published in the previous year where 'the 220 delinquent freshmen were divided into two groups by random sampling' (Walters, 1931). In this short report Walters noted that the 'delinquency in the counselled group had decreased 34 per cent, while that of the control group had fallen only 13 per cent, a net saving of 21 per cent' (Walters, 1931).

An earlier trial that looked at interventions to increase voting behaviour may have also been randomised (Gosnell, 1926), and this pre-dated Walters' experiments by about five years. The key passage was as follows:

> In order to set up this experiment it was necessary to keep constant, within reasonable limits, all the factors that enter into the electoral process except the particular stimuli which were to be tested [list of factors]. The method of random sampling was used to control these factors during the testing of the particular stimuli used in the experiment. (Gosnell, 1926)

It seems likely that Gosnell was describing the following process: 6000 adults were identified and then a random half of the sample was given an intervention leaving the other half-sample to act as the control group. Although the paper refers to random *sampling*, as do the reports by Walters, it seems that the paragraph above describes random *allocation*.

A more widely known randomised trial of a social science intervention was the Cambridge-Somerville experiment in 1937. In this trial 'delinquent' boys were allocated into two groups by the toss of a coin: one group received the intervention (social worker attention) and the other acted as a control group (Oakley, 2000). Follow-up in this experiment continued until the 1970s when the boys were middle-aged men. The intervention ultimately proved to be unsuccessful, as those who received the social work intervention were more likely to have been imprisoned than those who did not. Indeed, all the study outcomes favoured the control group rather than the intervention group. It has been argued that an unfortunate consequence of the Cambridge-Somerville experiment was to make the social work profession abandon the use of controlled trials as the gold-standard method of evaluation as it did not produce the 'correct' results (MacDonald, 1997).

The Medical Research Council's 1948 streptomycin trial (Medical Research Council, 1948) is often perceived as the first 'properly' randomised controlled trial in health care research; nevertheless there are reports of other controlled trials before this experiment. In 1944 an RCT of a substance called patulin was undertaken to test its effectiveness for the treatment of the common cold (Medical Research Council, 1944). Based on numerous anecdotes and some poor quantitative evidence, patulin was seen as an effective treatment for the common cold. To test this belief in a rigorous fashion, nearly 1500 workers from a number of factories were randomised to receive either patulin or a placebo. The trial failed to demonstrate that patulin was an effective treatment for the common cold. Historically, this study is often overlooked possibly because it had a null result.

The 1948 streptomycin study to treat pulmonary tuberculosis (TB) established its effectiveness. The impetus of the trial was the need to ration a scarce resource (streptomycin). Patients with pulmonary TB were enrolled into the study, and those with infection of the meninges of the brain were excluded, as such infection invariably proved to be fatal. The trial demonstrated a significant benefit of treatment; however, it also showed that a substantial proportion of untreated patients improved.

In 1954 the largest RCT ever to have taken place was performed in the USA where 750 000 children were randomised to receive either polio vaccination or placebo vaccination (there was an additional observational cohort of children). This trial provided evidence of the efficacy of polio vaccine. The study also noted a volunteer bias: those who declined to take part in the trial had a lower incidence of polio than those in the control groups. Jonas Salk, the originator of the vaccine, was not particularly sympathetic to the idea of RCTs:

> I found but one person who rigidly adhered to the idea of a placebo control and he is a bio-statistician who, if he did not adhere to this view, would have had to admit his own purposelessness in life. (Salk, quoted in Rosenburger and Lachin, 2002)

Today we can learn important lessons from such a large trial. Many of the current arguments about, for example, the safety of measles vaccination, could be resolved if we undertook an RCT with millions of participants instead of pursuing current policy: an uncontrolled experiment on all children.

3.3   Trials before the twentieth century

There is compelling evidence of experiments in medicine using similar methods to randomisation to form control and treatment groups predating the streptomycin and patulin trials. Chalmers recently described several such experiments (Chalmers, 2001), including, for example, an experiment undertaken by a surgeon in the Peninsular war in the early nineteenth century. One-third of 366 sick soldiers were allocated to being routinely bled whilst the other two-thirds were allocated to not being bled. Of the soldiers allocated to bleeding thirty-five (29 per cent) subsequently died; in contrast, of those allocated to the no bleeding group only six (2.5 per cent) died.

> It had been so arranged, that this number was admitted, alternately, in such a manner that each of us had one third of the whole. The sick were indiscriminately received, and were attended as nearly as possible with the same care and accommodated with the same comforts. One third of the whole were soldiers of the 61st Regiment, the remainder of my own (the 42nd) Regiment. Neither Mr Anderson nor I ever once employed the lancet. He lost two, I four cases; whilst out of the other third [treated with bloodletting by the third surgeon] thirty five patients died. (Milne and Chalmers, 2006)

In 1747 James Lind (www.jameslindlibrary.org/) used an experimental method to investigate the treatment of scurvy through the use of lemons and oranges. In that experiment twelve sailors suffering from the disease were allocated to receive lemons and oranges or an alternative such as vinegar or salt water. The lemons and oranges treatment was so successful that the two sailors allocated to it were well enough to nurse the other victims of the disease or to return to duty (Pocock, 1983). Like the army, however, the navy did not take notice of the results of this experiment and another generation was to pass before routine scurvy prevention, using citrus fruits, was introduced into the navy (Rodger, 2005).

3.4   Conclusions

Controlled trials have been undertaken for some considerable time. Randomisation was only formally adopted within the last 100 years, starting in agriculture. The Medical Research Council adopted random allocation for some major studies in the 1940s, which brought it into wider use within health care. Since then the number of RCTs in health care has exploded, with over half a million controlled trials. Although the number of RCTs in health care has been growing at an exponential rate since the 1940s, there is a worrying trend that since 2000 the number of new trials being reported has declined (Gluud and Nikolova, 2007). This may be partly due to increased regulation, such as the European Clinical Trials Directive.

The USA and UK dominate as countries that undertake the most health care trials, with about 22 per cent of all trials being undertaken in the USA and 12 per cent of all trials being of UK origin (Gluud and Nikolova, 2007). Interestingly, however, when the number of trials per million of the population is calculated then Sweden, Denmark and New Zealand have undertaken the most trials, with the UK only eighth in the league table and the USA trailing a distant eighteenth (Gluud and Nikolova, 2007). Other large European countries, such as France and Germany, appear to conduct relatively few RCTs in the health care field.

Controlled trials were developed because it was widely recognised that uncontrolled evaluations are susceptible to a number of biases that cannot be addressed unless a contemporaneous control group is included in the evaluation. A contemporaneous control group may prevent temporal changes affecting the results. Whilst such control groups can be identified or created by methods other than randomisation, these are inferior to designs using random allocation which can also control for regression to the mean and selection effects. In the next chapter we discuss the importance of randomisation.

3.5   Key points

- Randomised trials have been described since the 1940s: by Lindquist in education, and the MRC in health care.
- Two of the first randomised trials of the twentieth century were undertaken in the 1930s in educational research.
- Controlled studies of some kind have been undertaken for several hundred years.
- Many hundreds of thousands of patients may have died or been injured because of failure to undertake RCTs early enough.
- Many treatments used routinely today may be hazardous due to lack of evidence of effectiveness using the appropriate RCT.

4
What is Special About Randomisation?

4.1 Background

The main difference between other study design methods and the randomised controlled trial is that in the latter two or more groups are formed by *random* allocation. Randomisation is the best approach to dealing with and controlling for selection bias, regression to the mean and temporal changes. Other issues, such as blinding, or the use of placebos, may be associated with some types of randomised trial but their use is neither a necessary nor a sufficient condition for a study to be identified as a randomised trial.

4.2 Non-randomised controlled trials and selection bias

Control groups must be formed through a process of random allocation, or a similar method, in order to eliminate selection bias. Selection bias occurs when the intervention/treatment group has an imbalance in a variable that is associated with outcome compared with the control group. For example, early non-randomised evaluations of computer technology in schools compared technology resource-rich schools with technology resource-poor schools (Torgerson and Elbourne, 2002). The problem with this approach was that schools with large numbers of computers were likely to be systematically different from schools with lower numbers of computers. For instance, it is likely that technology-rich schools have more pupils from higher socio-economic groups compared with schools that are technology-poor. Because socio-economic status is heavily correlated with educational performance any difference between the 'high' and 'low' usage schools could merely have been a reflection of differences in the socio-economic backgrounds of the children attending the schools rather than differences in the technology resources in the schools. The best way of avoiding this kind of selection bias is to form intervention and control groups through random allocation. In this instance, we could have randomised schools to receive more resources to spend specifically on computers, whilst the control schools could have received the same resource with the proviso to spend it on other activities.

It is possible to control statistically for some selection biases. For example, if the socio-economic backgrounds of children within schools could be measured accurately, this could be used to 'control' or 'adjust' for mean differences in this variable between the groups. However, whilst one can legitimately adjust for known variables using the statistical technique of multiple regression analysis, it is impossible to adjust statistically for unknown variables that might affect outcome. For example, if the teachers in schools with computers were different in some other un-measured variable from teachers in the control schools, we could not control for this variable in any analysis.

Even if we know that a certain variable (for example socio-economic background) will influence outcome, often it is difficult to measure the variable accurately. Any measurement of socio-economic background is a proxy marker of its 'real' characteristic. Consequently we cannot control for its effects properly through a statistical analysis. For incompletely measured variables we can only deal with any relationship with outcome through the process of randomisation. Randomisation also controls for the unknown variables that may affect outcome, in addition to known, partially measured variables. The beauty of randomisation is that it controls for the known, measurable variables, the known unmeasured variables and, most importantly, the unknown and unmeasured variables that could affect outcomes.

> As we know, there are known knowns. There are things we know we know. We also know there are known unknowns. That is to say we know there are some things we do not know. But there are also unknown unknowns, the ones we don't know we don't know. (Donald Rumsfeld, 12 February 2002, Department of Defense news briefing)

In non-randomised studies selection bias can produce unreliable results. For example, hormone replacement therapy (HRT) has been shown to be associated with lower risks of cardiovascular disease and stroke. These observations were derived from comparing the outcomes of women using HRT with the outcomes of women not using it (Grady et al., 1992). Women using HRT have consistently been shown to experience fewer heart attacks and strokes when compared with women of a similar age not using HRT. Because the comparison groups in these observations were not assembled using randomisation or similar techniques, the potential for selection bias is great. For instance, HRT users tend to be of a higher socio-economic group, to exercise more and to eat a better diet than non-users. All of these variables are associated with lower incidence of cardiovascular disease and strokes. When a large RCT was undertaken it reported that HRT actually *increased* heart disease and strokes compared with placebo users (Writing Group, 2002). Similarly, non-randomised data have appeared to show that supplements of anti-oxidant vitamins (e.g., vitamin E, beta-carotene, vitamin C) can protect against heart disease (Khaw et al., 2001). When a large RCT was undertaken to test this widespread belief no evidence was found of any benefit, although there was a slight, not statistically significant, increase in mortality in the supplemented group (MRC/BHF Heart Protection Study, 2002). Vitamin E supplementation has even been shown (in an RCT) to *increase* the incidence of colds and other infections among older people (Gratt et al., 2002). Indeed, a meta-analysis of vitamin E trials demonstrated that the most commonly used dose of vitamin E (i.e., in excess of 800 IU per day) actually significantly *increases* the risk of mortality compared with no vitamin E supplements (Miller et al., 2005), with a more recent review confirming this risk of harm (Bjelakovic et al., 2007). These examples show how rigorously conducted RCTs can overturn the results based on non-randomised evidence.

In the examples cited above, selection bias created an association that turned out not to be true. Sometimes, however, we note an association, which is actually causal, and make the false assumption with regard to the direction of causality. For example, the use of dummies (pacifiers) is associated with cessation of breast-feeding. In an effort to promote breast-feeding the World Health Organisation (WHO) recommended that nursing mothers should avoid the use of dummies (Kramer et al., 2001). In an RCT Kramer and colleagues tested an intervention that reduced the use of dummies from 39 per cent to 16 per cent. However, at three months the percentage of babies still being breast-fed was exactly the same in both groups (i.e., 82 per cent). When the researchers compared the mothers who used dummies with those who did not they found 25 per cent of mothers using dummies had given up breast-feeding compared with 13 per cent who did not use dummies. In this instance, the decision to give up breast-feeding *caused* the dummy use (not the other way around). Therefore, the WHO advice, based on non-randomised evidence, was simply erroneous.

As mentioned above, the RCT is the best way of ascertaining the effectiveness of some potential interventions by disentangling the myriad of potentially confounding variables. For example, young people living in a deprived area are more likely to undertake criminal activities than young people living in a more affluent area. To ascertain the best policy response to this problem Kling et al. (2005) undertook an RCT in the USA. Three groups were formed: a control group; an experimental group where participants were offered housing vouchers redeemable for rental properties only in affluent areas; and a third group where participants were given vouchers redeemable anywhere. The results showed a significant reduction in crime among females, a lower reduction among males, but in both cases *only* among those families which *moved out* of the deprived neighbourhoods. For families in the voucher-control group, that is, the group which received housing vouchers, redeemable anywhere, there was no effect on incidence of crime among the young people. This suggests, therefore, that it was the influence of the neighbourhood rather than poverty *per se* that increased the incidence of crime in the young people. Interestingly, there was no impact on educational outcomes (Kling et al., 2005).

Some studies reported as randomised trials are actually not randomised trials. Before we discuss how random allocation ensures that, on average, the groups formed are equivalent, we first describe a number of 'quasi-random' methods of allocating participants to treatment groups, and demonstrate why these can lead to bias.

4.3   Quasi-random methods of forming comparison groups

The quasi-random method most frequently used to form the experimental groups is probably 'alternation'. Alternation is a deterministic method of forming groups and can produce equivalent groups as effectively and sometimes more effectively than simple randomisation. However, it is generally considered inferior to true random allocation, the main reason for which is that alternation is usually predictable. Researchers can, consciously or unconsciously, schedule participants leading to a biased allocation. Another reason why randomisation is preferable to alternation is that most statistical tests are based upon mathematical theories of 'randomness'. It is possible, though unlikely, that alternation can lead to a correlation in covariates between members of the groups and this will have the effect of making subsequent statistical tests less conservative (Chalmers, 2001). In the following we will describe alternation.

Potential participants are 'alternated' between treatments. In 'trickle' or sequential recruitment, where participants are recruited as they arrive at a clinic, for example, then we would randomly assign the first partici-pant to, say, treatment A, the next to treatment B, the third to treatment A and so on until we have recruited all of our sample. The description of the bloodletting experiment in the nineteenth century as described earl-ier appeared to use alternation. Alternatively, in 'block' recruitment, such as a list of school children to be allocated to an educational experi-ment, we would take a list of participants, rank them in some way, per-haps alphabetically, and allocate the first on the list to, say, treatment A and then the second to treatment B, third to treatment A, fourth to B and so on until all participants have been allocated. As long as there is *no* interference in this schedule of allocation the resulting groups will, on average, be equivalent in known and unknown variables. If partici-pants are ranked by a variable, such as age, then alternation will produce more equivalent groups than simple randomisation, as such an approach automatically leads to stratification, which is where randomisation is constrained, so as to ensure balanced groups (see later). The problem that arises with alternation is that the allocation sequence can usually be known in advance and participants can be withheld from the alterna-tion schedule. If the alternation is not adhered to, this can lead to the formation of groups that are not equivalent. Thus, selection bias is intro-duced, making the results of the experiment unreliable.

Another quasi-random method (which is sometimes considered to be ordinary alternation) is 'quasi-alternation'. This is where participants are allocated according to month or year of birth, day of the week, alpha-betically or using some similar approach. An example of quasi-alternation would be where all people with a surname beginning with A would be allocated to one group and all those with a surname beginning with B would be allocated to the other group. A similar example would be where all participants born in January would be in the same group, as would all participants born in February. This method of allocation not only leads to predictability, which is the main weakness of ordinary alternation, but can also lead to selection bias in its own right. If, for some reason, outcome is correlated with month of birth, for example, then differences may be attributed to this rather than to the interven-tion. For example, in the English education system, children born in August tend, on average, to be educationally disadvantaged because they are always 'young' in the school year compared with others in their peer group; for children born in September, on average, the converse is the case. Similarly, alphabetical alternation is likely to produce biased groups as clearly some ethnic groups have surnames that favour certain letters of the alphabet and therefore tend to predominate in one of the comparator groups. As an example of quasi-alternation consider the following experiment. In this study the authors wanted to see if using a lottery ticket increased response rates to a questionnaire survey. They allocated the potential respondents into three groups in the following way:

> Before mailing, recipients were randomized by rearranging them in alphabetical order according to the first name of each person. The first 250 received one scratch ticket for a lottery conducted by the Norwegian Society for the Blind, the second 250 received two such scratch tickets, and the third 250 were promised two scratch tickets if they replied within one week. (Finsen and Storeheier, 2006)

In this instance they found an imbalance between males and females between the allocated groups. There were statistically significantly fewer females in the control group compared with the other two groups. This is because, presumably, female Norwegian names favour letters towards the beginning of the alphabet compared with male names. Consequently this study is likely to suffer bias in its results, particularly if men and women respond differently to the use of lottery tickets when completing a questionnaire. It is interesting to note that the authors (and the journal referees) of this paper, thought that this was a randomised trial.

Although systematic methods, such as the one described above, sometimes appear to be alternation, they are in fact substantially inferior as they can introduce bias in their own right even if rigorously undertaken.

Because alternation is predictable it should, in general, be avoided. However, uncritical bias towards alternation may lead to the classification of some studies as being weak when, in fact, they are sound. For example, a systematic review of trials looking at different questionnaire designs for improving response rates noted that many probably used alternation (Edwards et al., 2002). Nevertheless, the reviewers rightly concluded that in this instance alternation would not have led to bias in the trials because those mailing out questionnaires would not have had foreknowledge of the characteristics of respondents, which is necessary for alternation to be subverted. Alternation is used occasionally when groups of people are being allocated. For example, in a controlled trial of fitting dogs with an insecticide dog collar to reduce the incidence of the sand fly transmitted disease (Leishmania infantum) to children in Iran, eighteen villages were matched in incidence of disease and then alternated to intervention and control groups (Gavgani et al., 2002). By using this approach the trialists probably made the groups more comparable than if they had used simple randomisation. Nevertheless, the circumstances where alternation is permitted are rare, and even if scientifically justified, will tend to lead to the study being classed as methodologically weak by others. It is therefore usually best avoided.

There are other non-random methods that should be avoided. One quite widely used method involves the use of an identification number. We might for instance allocate people on the basis of their hospital number or their social security/national insurance number: odd numbers might form one group and even numbers the other. The major problem with this approach is that it invites subversion, or sabotage, of the allocation process. Because we know that odd numbers will receive a given intervention we can, if so minded, withhold the intervention to selected participants. This can introduce selection bias. For example, Jones and colleagues (2002) allocated participants into their study on school retention in the following way:

> Assignment to study group was based on the last digit in their social security number . . . At the start of each month all San Diego County welfare recipients were examined for eligibility and, if eligible, were randomly assigned to a study group. (Jones et al., 2002)

The problem with this approach is that whoever determines eligibility for the trial will *know* by simply looking at the social security number which assignment group a potential participant will fall into. This means that consciously or unconsciously decisions about possible eligibility can be driven by foreknowledge of group assignment. Consequently it is possible that the allocation process can be susceptible to selection effects. Note also that the authors thought that they were randomly allocating participants to their study.

Allocation using identification numbers is not only a theoretical possibility as one of us (DJT) heard of a social science study in England that used allocation based on National Insurance numbers, and later it transpired that those recruiting the participants appeared not to have followed the allocation as they should have done, which would not have happened if concealed randomisation had been used. Because of the problems of non-random allocation outlined above it is important that, if at all possible, concealed randomisation is undertaken when forming comparison groups.

4.4   True randomisation

Randomisation ensures that, on average, the two or more groups that are formed are similar in all variables that will affect outcome. A quite common mistake is to confuse random *allocation* with random *sampling*.

Random sampling is used to make inferences about characteristics of a sample to the general population. If, for example, one wished to know what the average height of 14-year-old children is in the population, then a random sample of 14-year-olds could be identified and measured. As long as this sample is of a sufficient size then the average height of 14-year-olds could be estimated with sufficient precision, which avoids the need to measure all the 14-year-olds in the population. Thus, a random sample has high external or ecological validity: that is inferences about the sample can be extrapolated to the general population. In contrast, random allocation makes no statement about the external validity of the sample population to the general population.

Random allocation is important for *internal* validity, i.e., whether the results are valid within the sample chosen. If we use other methods of allocation we cannot be sure that selection bias has been eliminated and the results are valid for the intervention.

As mentioned above, random allocation eliminates selection bias (Cook and Campbell, 1979), which is the main threat to internal validity. It is present in many non-random methods of forming comparison groups and occurs when the groups have one or more characteristics that differ and are associated with the outcome of interest.

Random allocation is a simple, elegant concept. Allocation of individuals to two or more groups *at random* will produce groups that have, on average, the same characteristics as each other, for example the same range and spread of socio-economic group, or age, or eye colour, etc. Importantly all the known and *unknown* characteristics that could affect outcome are unbiasedly present in all groups. The presence of *all* variables that could affect outcome, known as confounders or in statistical parlance, covariates, in *all* groups will cancel out their effect in the analysis. Nevertheless, there will, by chance, be some variables that are not exactly the same in both groups. However, usually, these variables will not affect outcome.

4.5   How to randomise

The practicalities of randomisation will vary with respect to how participants are recruited into a trial. Many trials use 'trickle' or 'sequential' recruitment. Patients arriving at a clinic, for example, are asked to take part in the trial. Similarly, in a crime and justice trial of offenders, participants are recruited as they arrive at a prison. Alternatively participants can be randomised in one batch or block. Children attending a school can be recruited at the same time and then randomisation can be undertaken simultaneously for all the participants. Whilst the principles of randomisation are the same for both types of recruitment allocation, when recruitment is ongoing this tends to be more expensive, as secure systems for allocation need to be maintained to ensure fidelity of randomisation over the period of time recruitment takes place.

It is sometimes the case that unequal group sizes are required. For example, we might wish to have twice as many participants in one group compared with another. This would then demand a probability of allocation to one group of one-third, and for the other a probability of two-thirds. An unequal probability does not lead to a biased allocation, as the resulting groups, despite being of unequal size, will contain the same proportion of people with different characteristics as groups of equal size.

There are several different approaches to undertaking randomisation. The most robust method, in our view, is simple randomisation.

4.6   Simple randomisation

The simplest form of randomisation is to use a random number table or computer generated list of random numbers to make the allocation. The strength of simple randomisation is its very simplicity: it is difficult for it to go wrong. More complex randomisation methods are disadvantaged by the fact that they can suffer technical bias (an inadvertent error can result in biased allocation). This potential problem should not be under-rated. Simple randomisation is very easy to undertake. Most computers contain a program that produces random numbers (e.g., spreadsheet program or statistical software). Alternatively, most statistical textbooks contain lists of random numbers. If we were planning a two-armed trial with equal numbers then we could simply produce a random list of numbers, assign participants to the numbers and decide whether those assigned to odd numbers comprised the intervention or the control group. For example, in a trial to test the efficacy of a computer assisted instruction program in a prison setting, Batchelder and Rachal (2000) described the procedure for randomly assigning inmates to either the experimental or the control group.

> A random digit table was used to assign all inmates who entered the program to either the experimental group or a control group. As each inmate entered the program, he was matched with the next consecutive number on the random digit table. If the number was even, the inmate was assigned to the control group; if the number was odd he was assigned to the experimental (CAI) group. (Batchelder and Rachal, 2000)

Although this approach is fine in theory, it is probably best to use a secure system to prevent whoever is responsible for the allocation from potentially subverting the process.

Simple randomisation is not without perceived problems, which is why many researchers use alternative approaches. When the overall sample size is small, one problem is that the two groups may be numerically unbalanced. In a trial of, say, 30 individuals it is very unlikely that simple randomisation will produce exactly two groups of 15 each. If simple randomisation produces two groups of, say, 20 vs 10 then the power of the study will fall by 5 per cent. This in itself would not be of great concern, but with small sample sizes simple randomisation can produce allocation schedules of greater imbalance, which will result in significant loss of power (e.g., 23 versus 7). This could be a particular problem in cluster, group or class randomised trials. In these instances, groups of individuals (e.g., schools, GP practices, prisons, hospital wards) are randomly allocated. Usually the number of clusters tends to be small and consequently this risks large chance imbalances which will reduce the statistical power of the study.

Even when the sample size is large enough to make any numerical imbalance very slight compared with the total sample size of the trial, simple randomisation can still lead to an imbalance between groups in an important key variable. For example, phonemic awareness (PA) is known to be an important predictor of outcome in literacy interventions to improve reading ability (Ehri et al., 2001). Simple randomisation could lead to a large imbalance in two groups of students randomised in a reading intervention trial, with an imbalance in the numbers of children in each group with 'high' and 'low' abilities in phonemic awareness. If most children with low phonemic awareness abilities were allocated to one or other of the groups then the groups would be unbalanced in an important factor by chance (chance imbalance) and this could affect the outcome of the experiment.

In trials that recruit from many different centres, where there may be only a few participants per centre, it is often thought to be important to include participants from each centre in the control and intervention treatments. If, for example, we have a number of centres that recruit only four or five participants, the use of simple randomisation could lead to all of the participants in those centres receiving only one treatment. If this occurs it then becomes impossible to control for any possible centre effects on outcomes. Sometimes simple randomisation results in a long string of allocations that favours one of the groups. If a trial is recruiting slowly, for instance, and we have, by chance, a string of allocations over a summer period that favours one of the groups, we may not be able to balance for any seasonal effects and there will be a potential for the introduction of temporal bias (insufficient participants will be available to be recruited to end the chance string of allocations favouring one group).

A similar problem can occur when we want to preferentially randomise in favour of one group. If, for instance, we are using unbalanced randomisation in order to limit or increase access to a service under evaluation, simple randomisation may lead, on occasions, to the service being under- or over-utilised, which may interfere with the practical arrangements for conducting the study.

Another perceived problem is that using simple randomisation may result in some 'cosmetic' imbalances. Thus, the sample size will not be exactly equivalent and there may be some differences between the groups. All of these cosmetic problems are not real issues and can be corrected quite easily in a regression analysis. However, many researchers worry that because of chance differences their trial may not be considered to be methodologically rigorous. These problems can be reduced through the use of other randomisation techniques that restrict the randomisation.

4.7   Blocked randomisation

Blocked randomisation is one of the most widely used methods to reduce the possibility of chance imbalances. If we assume that a variable is a very important predictor of outcome we would like to have equal proportions of participants with high and low values of the variable in all treatment groups. To ensure that there are equal proportions we use a process known as stratification. To do this we generate two or more randomisation schedules using random blocks of numbers. The smallest block is usually a block of four. In a two-armed trial this produces the following allocations: ABAB; AABB; BABA; BBAA; ABBA; BAAB. The randomisation procedure is as follows. A block of four allocations is randomly selected from the six possible sets of blocks, the next block is selected randomly, and so on until there is a long enough string of blocks to allow all the possible participants to be randomised.

In Table 4.1 we can see an example of blocked allocation. If a participant has high value he or she would be allocated using blocks in the first row; however, if the participant has a low value he or she would be allocated according to the blocks in the second row.

In the blocking schedule above with 24 participants evenly divided between high and low values we could guarantee that there would be 6 participants with a high value in group A and 6 participants in group B.

Table 4.1: Stratified randomisation by blocking

Variable (e.g., age)	Allocation schedule										
High	A	A	B	B	A	B	A	B	A	B	B	A
Low	B	B	A	A	A	A	B	B	B	A	A	B

We can stratify by more than one variable, although a problem with increasing the number of stratifying variables is that the number of pathways rapidly increases and can become unmanageable. For example, in a trial evaluating a school drop-out prevention intervention, Sinclair and colleagues (2005) sought to stratify on six variables (disability, ethnicity, eligibility for free school meals, gender, adult with whom youth resided and high school). In a two-armed trial this would result in 128 different categories! By stratifying in this manner the trialists increased their chances of having large numerical imbalances. Therefore, it is advisable not to use more than two stratifying variables. Note that stratified randomisation must also use blocked randomisation. If we stratify groups and then use simple randomisation, this results in the same outcome as using simple randomisation without stratification. Failure to block along with stratification is not uncommon. For example, in a trial published in the *Lancet*, Durelli (2002) and colleagues stated:

> Randomisation was done centrally by the coordinating centre. Randomisation followed computer generated random sequences of digits that were different for each centre and for each sex, to achieve centre and sex stratification. Blocking was not used.

Other examples of this misunderstanding of the nature of stratified randomisation can be found in Hewitt and Torgerson (2006).

By using blocked randomisation the overall group sizes can never be greatly unbalanced within the strata. Many people mistakenly think that the main reason for stratified or 'constrained' randomisation is to maintain equivalent group size. If we use blocked randomisation our groups cannot be unbalanced more than by half the block size within the strata. So, for example, when using a block of four, one group cannot be larger than the other than by a maximum of two participants, if we do not stratify. If we stratify on several variables then we can get numerical imbalances across the trial in total. This occurs because, by chance, we might have the blocks in several strata starting on the same allocation. If some sites do not recruit many participants then they may only use the first one or two sequences from the block. For instance, Klaber-Moffett et al. (1999) used blocked randomisation with block sizes of four, yet their trial was numerically unbalanced by nine participants. This was because they stratified by GP practice and there were 87 GP practices. Consequently, by chance, many of the practices that had recruited only one or two patients must have started their randomisation using blocks which started with the same allocation. However, within the stratifying variable we cannot be unbalanced by more than half the block size.

Simple randomisation, particularly with a total sample size of above 100, is very unlikely to lead to large numerical group imbalances and, as explained previously, even an imbalance as large as 2:1 only has a small effect on statistical power. More importantly, the main reason for restricted randomisation is to maintain balance in important covariates. If we are stratifying the randomisation by a 'high' or 'low' value then the proportions of participants with a 'high' value will be exactly the same in both groups, which simple randomisation cannot guarantee.

There are significant disadvantages with using restricted randomisation (Hewitt and Torgerson, 2006). Firstly, it adds complexity to the process and can increase the chances of human or technical error leading to biased allocation. Second, if the same block sizes are used this can lead to predictability, which in turn can lead to bias. Predictability can lead to subversion bias, which means that a researcher can allocate participants preferentially into one group or another. We discuss subversion bias in more detail in Chapter 5. However, small block sizes can lead to predictable allocation. For example, if the block size is four we can always predict which allocation will be the fourth in a series. Indeed, we will often be able to predict the last two allocations in a block if the first two are allocated into one group. To reduce this latter problem, different block sizes are commonly used and randomly picked so that subsequent allocations cannot be predicted. Also, to reduce predictability, as well as randomly choosing different block sizes, unequal block sizes will occasionally be inserted into the list of blocks to try and make it even more unpredictable. Even with different, randomly assigned, block sizes, allocations can sometimes still be predicted. This is because blocking will lead to group sizes that are very similar. If one keeps track of the group sizes, once an imbalance starts to appear, then one can be fairly confident that the probability of a subsequent assignment to the smaller group will be high. Also, if constrained randomisation is used, then simply guessing that the next allocation will be the opposite of the previous allocation will always lead to an increased chance of being correct. Scheduling a participant to that assignment could then lead to biased groups. This problem is only really dealt with if we use large block sizes; however, if block sizes increase too much then this negates any benefit of restricting the allocation and we may as well have used simple randomisation.

Whilst blocked randomisation will lead to balanced groups on the appropriate covariate (e.g., gender or age), in trials with a sample size of greater than about 100 it is probably better to use simple randomisation and stratify statistically at the end of the trial (Hewitt and Torgerson, 2006). This is because statistical analysis should usually take into account the stratifying variables. Blocking the random allocation only improves the power if the study is very small (Rosenberger and Lachin, 2002). Consequently, in our view it is better not to increase the risk of subversion by blocking, and deal with important covariates in the analysis.

4.8   Matched randomisation

A method of allocation often used by psychological and educational researchers is 'matched' randomisation. In matched randomisation participants are formed into pairs (or triplets in a three-armed trial) on the basis of one or two important covariates. For example, a child might be paired with someone of a similar age and the same gender. Once the participants have been paired, one of each pair is randomly allocated to the intervention group. This process leads to stratification on the pairing variable, which means the groups will be exactly balanced in terms of that variable. Because stratification is very precisely obtained by using pairing this eliminates most of the extraneous variation due to that confounder and leads to more precise statistical estimates of effect, which in turn requires a smaller sample size. There are a number of disadvantages to the method, however. First, if there are not exactly equal numbers of participants then at least one potential participant will be lost to the study. This is particularly the case if one is pairing on more than one variable: say gender and age. It may be possible to match two people on approximate ages, but they may not also be matched on gender. This again will lead to a loss in sample size. Second, if the variable that the participants are paired on has an interaction with the treatment (that is, treatment is much better or worse within different categories of the matching parameter) pairing eliminates the possibility of undertaking a subgroup analysis. Thirdly, in some circumstances pairing can lead to other reductions in statistical power, particularly in cluster trials when the numbers of pairs are relatively few. Finally, matched randomisation cannot be used for studies that use trickle recruitment as obviously we need to identify a number of participants in advance to enable us to make up a pair or triplet.

4.9   Pairwise randomisation

Another form of randomisation that does not have the disadvantages of restricted randomisation but allows numerical balance is 'pairwise' randomisation (Daniels et al., 2004). As noted above, we might want to achieve numerical balance in the trial as we recruit, not just for reasons of power but to avoid other problems, such as temporal bias, and to allow better prediction of treatment resource utilisation. In some instances treatment resources are very scarce and both simple and blocked random allocation will, at times, under-utilise treatment resources and sometimes over-use them. For example, in a surgical trial treatment slots may have to be arranged some time in advance. Simple randomisation may lead to either too many or too few patients being allocated to a surgical treatment. One way around this is to recruit participants in pairs. Once two eligible participants have been recruited one is randomised to the intervention and the other is allocated to the control group. Note this is not paired randomisation as described above. We are not attempting to match the pairs on any characteristic. We are simply randomising in pairs for practical reasons to ensure that treatment resources are used to their maximum efficiency. Therefore, the two participants identified may have very different characteristics to each other, unlike when using matched randomisation. This approach to randomisation does not allow stratification by an individual covariate, although it does allow stratification by centre. Therefore, it is a safe way of allowing centre stratification; it prevents temporal bias, and also allows for efficient utilisation of treatment resources.

We might extend this idea to the use of unequal allocation and identify three potential participants and then randomly select one to go into a group where we wish to ensure complete resource utilisation. This approach has an advantage over blocked randomisation in that it is as unpredictable as simple randomisation. Consequently it preserves some advantages of restricting the randomisation without the downside of increasing the predictability of the next assignment. On the other hand, a drawback to this approach is that if the trial is recruiting slowly then some time may elapse between the first participant giving consent and then recruiting a second individual to the study. This may make it infeasible for some treatments that need to be delivered as soon as a participant presents to the recruiting researcher. We might, however, use a combination of pairwise and simple randomisation if there is a danger of this occurring. For instance, when we have two or more participants available for randomisation we might use a pairwise approach; however, if we only have one participant they could be allocated using simple randomisation. This compromise can lead to predictable allocation in the sense that we can predict that available treatment resources will be efficiently used, but the predictability of an individual allocation is equivalent to simple randomisation.

There are other types of randomisation, such as adaptive randomisation, but these are probably less frequently used than those methods described above. In adaptive randomisation the allocation schedule is altered as the trial proceeds in order to correct any numerical or covariate imbalances that arise during recruitment. The most extreme form of this, and it is not strictly randomisation, is minimisation.

4.10   Minimisation

The main non-random method of forming comparable groups, which some have claimed is superior to randomisation, is minimisation (Treasure and MacRae, 1998). Minimisation is an alternative to stratified random allocation in that it prevents numerical and covariate imbalance. Usually a computer program is required to implement minimisation. The process is as follows. The first five or ten participants are allocated at random. Thereafter, as the groups are built up, minimisation deliberately allocates participants to a group depending on the characteristics of those already allocated. As an example let us consider a cluster-randomised trial of the use of incentives for adult learners (Brooks et al., 2008). In this trial 29 classes were randomised with the intervention group receiving a payment to attend evening classes, whilst the control group received no incentive. In Table 4.2 28 classes have been allocated using minimisation. In this instance the trialists wanted to be make sure the trial groups were balanced on: type of institution (FE or other); location (rural or urban); size of class (8+ or <8); and prior use of incentives.

The twenty-ninth class to be randomised had the following characteristics: it was not an FE college; it was in an urban area; it was large; and previous incentives had not been used. Minimisation will now allocate this class to the group that has the lowest score on these characteristics. In Table 4.2 we sum up the characteristics of the existing allocated classes. Thus, the figures in bold represent the existing totals of the classes already allocated. These are summed and the smaller total, in this case 33, for the

Table 4.2:   Example of minimisation

Covariate	Intervention	Control
FE	6	8
Other	8	6
Rural	5	6
Urban	9	8
8+	5	6
<8	9	8
Incentive	2	1
No	12	13
Sum	34	33

Class 29 = not FE, urban, large, no previous incentives = for
Intervention 8 + 9 + 5 + 12 = 34 for Control 6 + 8 + 6 + 13 = 33.

control group receives the twenty-ninth class. Had the totals been the same then we would have allocated the twenty-ninth class by randomisation.

Minimisation is not a random process; therein lies one of its weaknesses – it can lead to predictability. If someone wished to subvert the allocation schedule they could keep a record of the groups' characteristics (as indeed the computer program must) and, on the basis of a potential participant's characteristics, predict their likely allocation. To avoid this some researchers introduce a random element to minimisation. Instead of an individual always being allocated to the group with the lowest score, a probability (say 0.80) might be assigned so that they still might be allocated to the group with the higher score. The other potential problem of minimisation is its complexity, which can lead to technical problems (e.g., more complex computer programming can increase the possibility of programming errors).

4.11   Practical randomisation

Randomisation can be achieved through tossing of a coin, which has been used extensively in the past. However, this method does not work for trials that require more than two groups or for trials that need one group to be larger than the other, and the method is easily subverted. Alternative methods include using random number tables: these are published in most statistical textbooks; also many statistical packages produce random number lists.

It is important, however, that the process of randomisation is concealed from those entering participants into the trial. This is because there is good evidence to show that researchers and others can and will subvert the allocation sequence, which produces biased groups. The traditional method of preventing foreknowledge of the allocation sequence is to use sealed, sequentially numbered, opaque envelopes. When a participant has agreed to take part in the study, the person enrolling the participant opens a sealed envelope with the allocation. This method has recently fallen into disrepute, as it is not tamper proof. A more rigorous method is to use forms of distance randomisation where someone completely separate from the recruitment process is contacted to give the allocation to the researcher. Thus, for example, the researcher will contact the randomisation service, often by telephone but it can be by fax or through the internet, and give the key characteristics of the participant to be randomised. The researcher undertaking the randomisation then produces the allocation and informs the participant recruiter of the allocation. This process makes it more difficult to tamper with the allocation schedule than by simply using envelopes.

As an aside we note that 'random' numbers produced by a computer are not truly random. They are 'pseudo-random' as the computer has to use some deterministic mechanism within it, such as its clock speed, to produce the random numbers. However, in order to try and predict the allocation sequence one would need very detailed knowledge of the individual computer, consequently such computer generated pseudo-random numbers are generally held to be as good as true random numbers.

Distant randomisation methods need not be expensive. For example, a small trial concealed allocation from researchers undertaking participant recruitment by asking them to telephone the local hospital switchboard where the switchboard operator wrote down the patients' names and details in a book and pulled out an allocation from an urn under her desk. Similarly a trial in the crime and justice field asked staff who were allocating offenders to their groups to telephone a secretary at another department who held the randomisation list and she revealed the allocation only after she had noted the details of the study participant (Davis and Taylor, 1997).

The first, and most crucial, step when randomising is to ensure that a third party (independent of the research team) undertakes the randomisation. In Chapter 5 we discuss at length the problem and potential subversion of the randomisation process, which is a threat to the integrity of the trial. Consequently it is important to identify someone who will be considered independent by a critical referee. World-wide there are many providers of independent randomisation services. If you select such a service, ensure that a backed-up computer service is provided which allows an audit of the randomisations at a later date if this proves necessary.

After identifying a secure randomisation procedure, the next step is to decide on the kind of randomisation. If the trial is large we would suggest the use of simple allocation, as described previously. If a restricted form of randomisation is used, the variables for stratification need to be selected. In a multi-centred trial it is usual to choose 'centre' as a stratifying variable. In other words, a separate block of randomisations is produced for each centre. This is because 'centre effects' (e.g., differences in skilled personnel, differences in types of participants) may affect outcome. However, stratifying by centre is probably best avoided as this increases the possibility of sabotage, by increasing the chance that the block size used in the allocation will be deciphered. On the other hand, one could use pairwise randomisation, which would control for centre effects but eliminate the possibility of subversion.

The choice of stratifying variables should be driven by knowledge of what is an important predictor of outcome. Pre-test score, for example, is usually a very powerful predictor of post-test values. Therefore, it would seem sensible to stratify the randomisation on the pre-test variable. Note, however, if a pre-test score is chosen it must be calculated before the randomisation takes place, and sometimes pre-test scores can be complex and time consuming to produce, which may not allow sufficient time for use as a stratifying variable. If it is possible to collect pre-test data, then setting up two blocking streams for above and below the median will allow the allocation to be balanced on pre-test scores. Note, it is important to measure pre-test variables *before* random allocation if at all possible to avoid subversion. As noted previously, it is possible to stratify on more than one variable but this will increase the complexity of the task. In a trial that involves trickle or sequential recruitment it is important to keep the block sizes concealed from those recruiting the participant, to reduce the risk of bias.

4.12   Regression discontinuity

In this chapter we have argued that randomisation is the best method for eliminating selection bias. Another approach to dealing with selection bias that, in theory, can produce unbiased estimates is the regression discontinuity design (Cook and Campbell, 1979; Shadish et al., 2002; Linden et al., 2006). In a regression discontinuity design, participants are selected for the intervention on the basis of some known and measurable variable. For instance, in some states in the USA children who fail to achieve a certain threshold score in tests can either be retained – that is kept behind – or obliged to attend summer schools (Jacob and Lefgren, 2004). In this instance the threshold that determines eligibility for summer school or being retained is a standardised test. Similarly, some income supplements may be given to families that fall below a certain threshold income level and not given to those above a threshold. Clinically we might give a new blood pressure drug to patients who have blood pressure above a certain threshold where it is deemed they have hypertension and if they fall below this threshold they will get no anti-hypertensive treatment. If we then follow up a cohort of people, including those above and below the threshold, we can plot outcomes against initial baseline values. If the intervention is ineffective then there will be a linear relationship between baseline measurement values and outcomes. Should the intervention be effective, however, then at the threshold point we would expect to see a break or 'discontinuity' in any regression line. For example, in the evaluation of attendance at summer schools or being retained using a regression discontinuity design (Jacob and Lefgren, 2004) the performance of children, on a post-test reading score, was plotted against the pre-test reading score, which was used to select children for the summer school. If the summer school had an effect on reading acquisition we would expect to see a break in the regression line when plotting the pre and post-test reading scores. Using this approach Jacob and Lefgren (2004) concluded that summer schooling did improve literacy acquisition by children.

Regression discontinuity methods can be combined with an RCT to support a causal relationship. The method can be used when it is not ethical or practical to withhold an intervention. Nevertheless this design is inferior to an RCT in a number of aspects. First, even if it is implemented perfectly we require significantly greater numbers of participants compared with an RCT as the power of the design is much lower. Even if the threshold chosen is in the median of the distribution we require approximately 2.75 times the sample size to achieve the same statistical power as an RCT (Cook and Wong, 2007).

A second potential problem with the design is that researchers or practitioners must comply with the threshold point, or else the break becomes 'fuzzy' and may be indistinguishable from random noise in the data. However, one could argue that this is a similar problem encountered with the RCT, which only works *if* people respect the random allocation. Finally, there may be a 'natural' discontinuity at the same point chosen by the researchers and this could potentially confound the results.

4.13   Discussion

Random allocation or minimisation creates comparable groups. Other methods of forming comparison groups, apart from the regression discontinuity approach, are susceptible to bias *at the time of recruitment to the study.* Non-randomised trials are probably more prevalent in social science research than randomised studies. The former will always be susceptible to selection bias and consequently their results need to be treated very cautiously.

There are a number of approaches to randomisation. In our view, as long as there is a reasonable sample size, the best method is simple randomisation. Given sample sizes of over 100, it will produce identical results when combined with regression analysis, compared with stratified randomisation. Nevertheless, certainly within health care research, this is a minority viewpoint. In a review of 232 trials published in major medical journals Hewitt and Torgerson (2006) found that only 9 per cent (21) appeared to have used simple randomisation: all of the remaining trials used some form of restricted randomisation or did not clearly describe (34 per cent) how they randomised. Interestingly, there was no relationship between the size of the trial and whether or not the trialists used restricted randomisation. From a statistical theoretical viewpoint we would expect larger trials to be less likely to use restricted randomisation; however, this was not the case.

Restricted allocation methods do have a role in specific circumstances, such as when relatively few participants can be allocated or when recruitment might be slow and sporadic. For small samples, such as cluster trials, minimisation is a useful alternative to randomisation. Note, however, for minimisation some drug regulatory authorities do not recognise this as a legitimate method of forming unbiased groups.

Randomisation will *not* ensure that there is complete balance between the groups within a single trial. In a *population* of RCTs there will be balance. Randomisation gives us the best method of ensuring that the variable that we do not know about or cannot measure will be balanced between the groups. Because an individually randomised trial might, by chance, be unbalanced on a major variable it is best to use a systematic review of randomised controlled trials to inform policy and practice (Torgerson, 2003) as this allows the occasional trial that is unbalanced – by chance – to be balanced out by other trials included in the review (see Chapter 16). Although random allocation deals with the problems of selection bias, regression to the mean and temporal effects, it can be susceptible to the introduction of bias after allocation has occurred. In the next chapter we look at these. However, note that most of these threats to validity also occur in non-randomised studies, which are also subject to baseline selection bias. In the next chapter we discuss in more detail sources of bias that can affect the RCT.

4.14   Key points

- Randomisation ensures internal validity, not external validity. Random allocation is not the same as random sampling.
- For sample sizes exceeding 100, simple randomisation followed by regression analysis is virtually equivalent to restricted randomisation and is less complex.
- For small trials, particularly cluster randomised trials, restricted randomisation followed by regression analysis will produce more statistical power than simple randomisation.
- In small trials minimisation may be better than blocked randomisation.
- When trials are not possible the best alternative is the regression discontinuity design.

5
Sources of Bias Within Randomised Trials

5.1   Background

> A careful look at randomized experiments will make clear that they are not the gold standard. But then, nothing is. And the alternatives are usually worse. (Berk, 2005)

Bias can give an incorrect estimate of effect; therefore, it is essential to minimise the threat of bias, and this is the main reason for using randomisation. Three main forms of bias that can affect non-randomised studies are: selection bias, temporal changes and regression to the mean effects. The use of random allocation, or a similar method, minimises these threats to the internal validity of a study. Nevertheless, other forms of bias can occur *after* randomisation, and these can threaten the integrity of the trial. It is important to be aware of and acknowledge potential for such biases, and, as far as is possible, to minimise their occurrence and then take steps to deal with them adequately. Most of these biases are forms of selection bias introduced at the time of random allocation or afterwards, although most of them are not unique to randomised trials: they occur as frequently, if not more so, in non-randomised trials. In this chapter we consider the main sources of bias that threaten randomised controlled trials.

5.2   Subversion or sabotage bias

We know that some researchers and practitioners have subverted the randomised trial in which they were participating. There are many possible reasons for this, some of which we have mentioned earlier. One probable reason is simply ignorance. The practitioners or researchers may not realise that non-adherence to the randomisation sequence can potentially render a trial uninterpretable and/or produce misleading results.

Subversion of a randomised trial can occur in one of two ways. First, researchers can allocate participants in a non-random fashion to the groups, which can lead to bias. Subversion of health trials has been reported from soon after the RCT was used in this field. Second, the researcher, clinician, teacher or other worker can implement the intervention with the control participants, thereby obliterating any difference in effect. For example, as mentioned in Chapter 1, a trial in the late 1940s investigated the value of giving premature babies oxygen. At that time oxygen supplementation was widespread, but some researchers suspected a link between this unevaluated treatment and an increase in blindness among premature babies, so a trial was undertaken. A number of the nurses involved in the study administered oxygen to the control group babies, thereby delaying the finding that increased supplemental oxygen to premature babies does, indeed, cause blindness (Silverman, 2004). The nurses did this because they mistakenly believed that the babies would benefit from the oxygen supplementation, and thought that it was unethical of the researchers to randomly deprive them of the oxygen supplementation.

Some studies have demonstrated that in trials where there is a potential to subvert the randomisation schedule different results are obtained from those in which there is no possibility, or only a small possibility of subversion (Schulz et al., 1995; Schulz and Grimes, 2005).

Typically, trials are subverted because a 'novel' method is 'known' to be more effective than a standard method (e.g., oxygen for premature infants). An empirical demonstration of subversion bias was reported in 1999 by the MRC Laparoscopic Groin Hernia Repair Group. In a surgical trial 227 patients were allocated using sealed envelopes; 99 of these had to be excluded (44 per cent) due to the possibility that the randomisation envelopes had been opened in advance of randomisation. An earlier report of a multi-centred surgical trial showed that three separate clinical centres, out of five, subverted treatment allocation. Thus, for the three centres, older patients were deliberately allocated to the control condition (i.e., the mean ages for three centres were: 57 years vs 72 years, $p < 0.01$; 33 vs 69 years, $p < 0.001$; 47 vs 72 years, $p = 0.03$ for experimental and control conditions respectively) (Kennedy and Grant, 1997). In this instance, it appears that several sealed envelopes were opened in advance, and older patients were allocated to the control treatment.

In a survey of 25 clinicians who were recruiting participants to trials that used restricted or blocked allocation, four (16 per cent) admitted to keeping a 'log' of previous allocations, which could then be used to help to guess future allocations (Brown et al., 2005). Although 16 per cent does not seem a great proportion we must look at this in the context that most trials are designed to avoid a 'false positive' rate of 5 per cent. Thus, in 100 well-designed and rigorously conducted trials, five will suggest that the intervention works, when in truth it does not. On the other hand, if 16 per cent of our trials are being subverted such that the subversion favours a particular treatment, and then of the remaining 84 per cent another 4 per cent are false positives, we can see that about 20 per cent of our trials may have false positive results, rather than the 5 per cent we originally anticipated. Therefore, if subversion of randomisation is practised on a scale of 16 per cent of all trials, this may produce very large numbers of false positive or false negative results. The problem of potential subversion or sabotage is very worrying and all efforts must be made to design systems to avoid it occurring.

A review by Hewitt and colleagues of all trials published in four major medical journals in 2002 found more evidence for subversion bias (Hewitt et al., 2005). The authors examined all the retrieved RCTs and categorised them into three groups by the adequacy of allocation concealment: adequate, inadequate or unknown. Trials with adequate concealment had, on average, higher p values than trials that were inadequate or unknown. This suggests that some of the trials in the inadequately concealed group were subverted such that participants with characteristics that predicted poorer outcomes were placed in the control groups (Hewitt et al., 2005).

This association (it is not proof) might lead one to believe that, where allocation can be subverted, it is sometimes done to favour the treatment group. An alternative explanation for this phenomenon, however, is that trialists who use inadequate allocation methods are more likely to evaluate interventions that are effective compared with those who use the most robust approaches to random allocation.

In the review by Hewitt and Torgerson (2006) some instances were reported where the allocation methods did not match the data shown in the report of the trial. This included a study reported in the *British Medical Journal* (Kinley et al., 2002). In this study the authors claimed to have used block randomisation:

This was a block randomised study (four patients to each block) with separate randomisation at each of the three centres. Blocks of four cards were produced, each containing two cards marked with 'nurse' and two marked with 'house officer.' Each card was placed into an opaque envelope and the envelope sealed. The block was shuffled and, after shuffling, was placed in a box.

Recall how in Chapter 4 we illustrated that a trial that uses blocked randomisation cannot be unbalanced by more than half the block size within its stratifying variable. In this instance the trialists were using a block of four and stratifying by centre. Therefore, each centre should have had, at most, a numerical disparity of only two participants. Note that, in this instance, two of the three centres had a numerical disparity of 11, suggesting that either blocked allocation was not used or that the allocation sequence had not been adequately followed (Table 5.1).

Interestingly, an earlier report of the same study gave a slightly different account of how randomisation was undertaken:

Randomisation was accomplished using a balanced block design (four patients to each block) with a separate randomisation process at each of the three centres. A separate series of consecutively numbered, opaque sealed envelopes was administered at each research centre. (Kinley et al., 2001)

Note that, in this instance, the envelopes were consecutively numbered. This description is difficult to reconcile with the subsequent description of shuffling the envelopes as described in the report; otherwise the envelopes would have been out of sequence.

A similar problem occurred in another trial of using dietetic assistants to improve the outcome of patients with hip fracture (Duncan et al., 2006):

Randomisation was by sequentially numbered, opaque, sealed envelope method in blocks of 10, prepared by a member of staff not directly involved in the trial. (Duncan et al., 2006)

In this instance the maximum numerical disparity between the two groups should have been only five. However, 165 participants were allocated to the control group and 153 were allocated to the intervention

Table 5.1:   Numerical disparity in a blocked randomised trial

Southampton		Sheffield		Doncaster	
Doctor	Nurse	Doctor	Nurse	Doctor	Nurse
500	511	308	319	118	118

group. This could not have happened if the authors had undertaken the allocation method that they described in their methods section.

Health care researchers are not alone, however, in having problems with their trials. Evidence of problems in health care trials may be more apparent because many health journals now insist that authors report details of the allocation procedures, which allows readers to note such discrepancies (as above). However, in a non-health context, Boruch (1997) cited a trial of an intervention to reduce or eliminate domestic violence, where it appeared that police officers responsible for the assignment may have violated the randomisation procedure.

An example of a discrepancy in randomisation in an educational trial is from a study by Baker et al. (2000). In this study evaluating the use of volunteers to help children to read, randomisation was reported as follows:

> Pairs of students in each classroom were matched on a salient pretest variable, Rapid Letter Naming, and randomly assigned to treatment and comparison groups.

It appears from this sentence that the authors used paired or matched randomisation, which should have ensured that there were exactly equal numbers in both groups. However, a little later in the paper the authors stated:

> The original sample – those students were tested at the beginning of Grade 1 – included 64 assigned to the SMART program and 63 assigned to the comparison group.

Clearly if paired randomisation had been used then there should have been exactly equal numbers in both groups. As with the previous examples the authors could not have used the randomisation process they described in their methods, or if they did, they must have dropped one member of the pair at the beginning. None of the examples quoted above demonstrates that the trials were actually compromised, they only demonstrate that the authors were not clear about how the random allocation process was undertaken, or that they did not follow precisely the allocation method described.

To avoid the potential problem of subversion of randomisation, the procedure needs to be separated from the researcher who is recruiting the participants. Recently, many health care trials have used a dedicated telephone randomisation service, whereby the researcher undertaking recruitment telephones the independent randomisation service for the allocation number. The randomisation service notes down the details of the participant and then gives the allocation. Whilst using a telephone randomisation service usually is best, even this approach can have potential problems. A colleague once remarked that when working on a trial using telephone allocation the operator offered to give the next four allocations to avoid the trial co-ordinator having to telephone back. Clearly, in this instance, despite using a telephone system, the study was not immune from potential problems of subversion. Another example of possible subversion of telephone randomisation occurred in an evaluation of post-operative care for patients with fractured neck of femur (Turner et al., 2006). This study used blocked telephone randomisation. The authors noted that when two or more patients were available for randomisation, 'staff had the opportunity to influence the order in which they went to theatre' (Turner et al., 2006). This could only be done if the staff had broken the block sequence and therefore could predict the allocation order. If simple randomisation had been used, this problem should not have occurred.

The issue of possible subversion has been recognised as an important validity threat in disciplines other than health care research. For example, in an RCT evaluating a police and social worker intervention to prevent domestic violence, distance randomisation was explicitly used to:

> protect overrides of group assignment by the staff, who might have a concern that some cases receive home visits regardless of the outcome of the assignment process. (Davis and Taylor, 1997)

Therefore, once a domestic violence incident had been reported, a project worker telephoned the research department and gave details of the case to a research secretary who then revealed the allocation.

One of the strengths of randomisation is that, when properly undertaken, it leads to unpredictability, and, if it is separated from the person undertaking participant recruitment, subversion is difficult to achieve. In contrast, in other procedures, such as alternation, subversion is more easily achievable. Unfortunately few trials outside health care research give detailed and adequate descriptions of how participants were randomised. There are notable exceptions. For example, Hirschel and colleagues (1992) described in detail how participants were randomised. It is worth reproducing their description here in full as an example of good practice:

> The procedures for the random assignment used the police department's Computer Assisted Dispatch system. When any call for the

services was received at the police department the complaint-taker brought up a format on the computer that is stamped with the time when the person makes the initial contact. The time field is a five-digit number representing the cumulative seconds at that time for the day and was used to generate the random treatment assignments. Dividing the time field by 3 and adding 1 to the remainder produced a digit of 1, 2, or 3, which represented the code for the assigned treatment response. This is based on the time a call is received and was not subject to manipulation because the time stamp occurred automatically before the telecommunication operator was informed of the reason for the call. There were no problems encountered in implementing the randomization process. By removing the process from human decision-making, this aspect of the experiment was carried out exactly as designed. (Hirschel et al., 1992)

Note how the procedure prevents any manipulation or potential subversion of the random allocation.

5.3   Technical bias

Technical bias is when there is an error in the allocation schedule that leads to bias. This can occur when complex allocation methods are used. For instance, a large trial in health care (the COMET study) used an RCT to evaluate a new epidural anaesthetic for women in labour. This trial used a complex computer randomisation schedule which contained a software error (COMET Study Group, 2001) which led to most participants in the study over the age of 25 years being allocated to one arm of the trial. The fault was only discovered towards the completion of the trial after 1000 women had been 'randomised', and it had to be re-started at great expense. Indeed, potential computer problems with allocation schedules have been reported as far back as the 1970s when Cook and Campbell described an RCT evaluating children being allocated to 'magnet' schools (Cook and Campbell 1979). In the first year of the experiment the randomisation was effective; however, in subsequent years a faulty computer program produced biased groups of children. Cook and Campbell (1979) have also described other forms of randomisation errors. For example, in an urn-based allocation system where all the names of potential participants were placed in a bowl, names towards the end of the alphabet had been placed in last and were more likely to be drawn, because the pieces of paper in the urn had not been sufficiently shuffled. The possibility of technical bias can be minimised by using simple methods of randomisation. The programming requirements for simple randomisation, as opposed to block randomisation or minimisation, are less demanding and consequently less likely to go wrong. For any form of randomisation it is best to run through a series of 'dummy' allocations to check the system is working before using it on participants.

5.4 Attrition bias

Unfortunately, many trials lose participants, and, unless the attrition rate in a trial is random, it can lead to the possibility of selection bias. Participants that leave one arm of the trial may be systematically different (e.g., younger or older) from those who remain. If the drop-outs are different in a known covariate (such as age, as above) this is less worrying than the possibility that the drop-outs may differ on unknown covariates which cannot possibly be compensated for in the analysis through statistical adjustment. Even if the *rate* of attrition is the same in both trial arms bias can still result.

The possibility of bias, however, is minimised, but never eliminated, if attrition rates are similar between the arms of the trial. Attrition bias is minimised if assiduous follow-up methods are applied to all randomised participants. It is also important to try and retain participants even when they do not wish to have the intervention any longer. Often participants are happy to continue to be part of the trial even if they do not wish to continue with the intervention. It is important, therefore, that when a participant wishes to leave the trial it is confirmed that they are also refusing to allow outcomes to be measured. It may be that they will continue to give consent to gather outcomes via a third party, for example, their teacher, doctor or social worker. Whilst including 'non-active' participants will appear to dilute the treatment effects, this is preferable to other, more serious, forms of bias. Dilution bias tends to underestimate the effectiveness of a treatment, giving a more conservative estimate of the benefits or adverse effects of treatment: it cannot overturn the direction of effect. In contrast, attrition bias, which is a form of selection bias, can change the direction of effect, leading the analyst to conclude a treatment was beneficial, when it was actually harmful, or vice versa.

Another approach to reducing attrition is to have a treatment run-in period. In most trials the bulk of the attrition occurs in the early stages as the participants change their minds or find the treatment or therapy no longer suits them. In some studies it is possible to put everyone on the placebo for a few months *before* randomisation. Or alternatively, in non-placebo trials, there might be an observational run-in period.

During this time, hopefully, the bulk of the attrition should occur. Participants are then randomised after the run-in period. For example, in a trial of vitamin treatments nearly a third of the participants dropped out during the run-in period (MRC/BHF Study Group, 2002). Importantly, this occurred before randomisation and, therefore, reduced attrition during the trial. An added benefit of using a run-in period is that if the participants are being selected on the basis of initial pre-test results we might then re-measure them at the end of the run-in period, before randomisation; those who had an erroneous value due to chance will regress back to their normal value and will not then be included in the study.

Having a run-in period may not always be helpful. When using a placebo run-in the subsequent trial may give an over-optimistic estimate of effectiveness as the intervention is applied to a non-trial population. This is because, even with a placebo, a proportion of participants will stop taking the treatment. Pragmatic estimates of effectiveness will include the diluted effects of people who stop taking their treatment for whatever reason. Including a run-in period will exclude 'poor compliers' from effectiveness estimates (Pablos-Mendez, 1998). For example, it has been estimated that having a run-in period for an aspirin trial resulted in a 90 per cent compliance rate over five years, which gave a reduction in myocardial infarction of 0.56; however, had a run-in *not* been used, then the effectiveness of the intervention might have only been a 0.71 reduction (Pablos-Mendez, 1998). However, it is likely that this latter effectiveness is the 'true' effect of the intervention in an average clinical setting. Including a run-in period also increases the cost and complexity of the study.

Paired randomisation is a method sometimes proposed to deal with attrition bias (see for example, Farrington and Walsh, 2005). If participants are paired and one of the pair is lost to follow-up some may consider dropping the remaining member of the pair to deal with any bias caused by attrition. This, however, is a mistake. Removing the surviving member of the pair will correct for differences in *observed* variables, but will not deal with imbalances that occur for *unmeasured* confounders. As an example, consider Tables 5.2, 5.3 and 5.4

This study is balanced (Table 5.2) on gender (an observable characteristic) through matching, whilst an unknown confounder or covariate has been balanced due to the randomisation process. Thus in each group we have three girls and three highs. Let us suppose we lose one of the participants, as shown in Table 5.3.

Table 5.3 shows that now the trial is not balanced on gender as the intervention group now has more girls than the control group.

Table 5.2: Paired randomisation of ten pupils paired on gender

Control (unknown covariate)	Intervention (unknown covariate)
Boy (high)	Boy (low)
Girl (high)	Girl (high)
Girl (low)	Girl (high)
Boy (high)	Boy (low)
Girl (low)	Girl (high)
3 Girls and 3 highs	3 Girls and 3 highs

Table 5.3: Imbalance caused by attrition

Control (unknown covariate)	Intervention (unknown covariate)
Boy (high)	Boy (low)
Girl (high)	Girl (high)
Girl (low)	Girl (high)
Boy (high)	Boy (low)
	Girl (high)
2 Girls and 3 highs	3 Girls and 3 highs

Table 5.4: Attempting to correct for drop-out

Control (unknown covariate)	Intervention (unknown covariate)
Boy (high)	Boy (low)
Girl (high)	Girl (high)
Girl (low)	Girl (high)
Boy (high)	Boy (low)
2 Girls and 3 highs	2 Girls and 2 highs

However, if we attempt to remedy this problem by removing the surviving participant in the pair we can see that, whilst this corrects the problem of gender imbalance, it introduces another bias (Table 5.4).

By removing the surviving participant in the pair we have made the situation worse, in that we have reduced our sample size but not corrected for group imbalance in the unknown variable. It would have been better to retain all the participants and correct for the gender imbalance using some form of regression analysis.

Attrition can change the results of a trial. For example, consider a trial of education vouchers for children of poor parents. The use of vouchers to enable parents of poor children to access private education is controversial. In the state of New York, USA, a certain amount of vouchers is provided to enable children from poor backgrounds to attend private schools. The budget for these vouchers is constrained and applications exceed availability. Consequently, vouchers are given to households randomly, which forms the basis, therefore, of a randomised experiment. To assess the effect of vouchers on educational outcomes researchers measured students who received vouchers and those who did not before they started private school and at a point some time later. However, these tests had missing data: some children did not complete the pre-test and some did not complete the post-test. Consequently, a significant proportion (40 per cent) had missing data. A complete case analysis including only children who had measurements at both time points seemed to indicate that black children from poor backgrounds benefited from the vouchers in terms of academic achievement (Krueger and Zhu, 2002). However, when the data were re-analysed including students who had state standardised tests, which substantially reduced the number of children missing due to attrition, this apparent benefit was no longer statistically significant. In this instance attrition may have produced misleading results.

5.5   Recruitment or consent bias

Usually refusal of participant consent does not introduce bias, as this occurs before randomisation and non-consenting people are not included in the trial. In some trial designs, however, consent is obtained *after* randomisation and this can introduce bias. In an individually randomised trial using Zelen's method (Zelen, 1979) randomisation occurs *before* consent to participate is obtained. This is similar to cluster randomised trials where, like Zelen's method, consent can occur *after* randomisation (Torgerson, 2001a). As an example of selection bias occurring in the latter situation, consider a trial of hip protectors (padded underwear) for hip fracture prevention. In this cluster trial 9 per cent of the control patients refused consent, whereas over 30 per cent of the intervention participants refused to take part in the study (Kannus et al., 2000). This led to a significant imbalance between important prognostic variables (i.e., age and weight), which may have confounded the results. Indeed, there was evidence of bias within the trial as the intervention of padded pants apparently reduced wrist fractures by 30 per cent. In Figure 5.1 we show the problem schematically. In the trial, 22 clusters of patients were randomised to receive or not receive the offer of hip protectors. In the control group there were 15 clusters containing 1075 participants, whilst in the intervention group there were 8 clusters containing 650 participants.

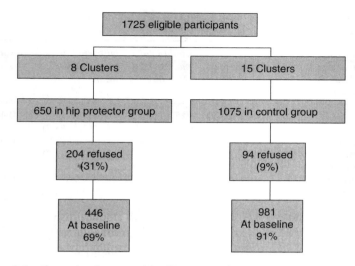

Figure 5.1:   Example of consent bias (Kannus et al., 2000)

After randomisation the participants were approached in the intervention group and were asked to wear the hip protectors and provide
outcome data. In this group 31 per cent of the participants refused. In
the control group, however, the participants were asked to provide outcome data only: only 9 per cent refused. This differential refusal rate is
likely to have introduced bias into the study, making the results less reliable. In this instance the trialists should have asked those participants in
the hip protector group who refused to use hip protectors to provide the
researchers with data on their fracture rate. It is likely that, of the 31 per
cent who initially refused, 22 per cent would have agreed to do this and
the refusal bias would have been potentially reduced or eliminated.

Recruitment bias can occur quite often in cluster trials (Torgerson, 2001a;
Puffer et al., 2003). This occurs when clusters are randomised *before* participants are identified. For example, one might undertake a cluster trial
of training GPs to identify and treat people with depression. If the participants have not been identified in advance it is likely that the GPs
who have been trained will identify different sorts of participants compared with untrained GPs. This form of bias was noted in a pilot trial of
the MRC's UK BEAM study (Farrin et al., 2005). In this study some of the
GP practices were allocated to a training arm whereby the GPs and the
practice staff were taught techniques of active back pain management. It
was found, however, that the active management practices recruited more,

Table 5.5:   Characteristics of participants at recruitment by allocated group for managing back pain in the UK BEAM pilot study

Patient characteristics recruited in pilot for UK BEAM Mean (SE)	Active Management (N = 165)	Traditional management (N = 66)	Difference in mean practice means (95% CI)[a]	p value[a]
Age	44.3 (0.82)	45.5 (1.29)	− 1.19 (− 4.35, 1.97)	0.44
Roland Disability Questionnaire (0–24, 0 = good)	8.9 (0.31)	10.3 (0.54)	− 1.37 (− 2.80, 0.07)	0.06
Aberdeen Back Pain Scale (0–100, 0 = good)	28.6 (0.79)	34.2 (1.76)	− 5.85 (− 10.15,− 1.56)	0.01
Binary characteristics			Difference in mean practice percentage (95% CI)	
Number (%)				
Female	97 (59%)	46 (70%)	− 10.9 (− 23.9, 2.05)	0.09
Further education after school	81 (50%)	21 (32%)	18.3 (4.4, 32.1)	0.01
Currently in full-time employment	93 (57%)	20 (31%)	26.8 (8.3, 45.3)	0.007

[a] p values adjusted for clustered data. (*Source*: Farrin et al., 2005).

less severe, back pain participants than the control practices. As this was leading to bias, this aspect of the design was dropped and all practices consequently received active management.

Table 5.5 shows how differential recruitment within cluster trials can lead to bias. The main outcomes in this trial were measures of back pain. The two measures that were being considered for use in the main trial were the Roland Disability Questionnaire (RDQ) and the Aberdeen Back Pain Scale. As Table 5.5 shows, both these measures of back pain favoured the intervention group. Therefore, even before the patient could have benefited from any intervention their scores in the intervention group were greater. Notice also that the numbers in the intervention group are more than double those in the control group. This means that in this trial the GPs in the intervention group were tending to include patients with milder back pain symptoms than those in the control group, thus biasing the trial. This trial does show one important finding: if primary care staff have received training in a medical condition, they will recruit more patients to a randomised trial. This finding is very useful to those who have difficulty in recruiting trial participants.

'Recruitment bias' can lead to a form of selection bias, which means the groups are not comparable in important prognostic factors. This form of bias can be avoided if all members of the cluster are identified *in advance* of randomisation. Even when non-consent is similar, bias can still occur as different people from each arm might refuse consent. For example, in a randomised trial of an intervention to reduce bullying in schools, about 30 per cent of parents did not give consent for their children to fill in the questionnaires, which formed the basis of the outcome measurement (Grossman et al., 1997). It is possible that this high refusal rate could have introduced bias. Consent bias can be eliminated, however, by acquiring consent before randomisation. For instance, in the UK BEAM study, identifying all recent back pain patients from the GP registers could have avoided the problem. These patients could have been invited to participate in repeated questionnaire surveys of their back pain. Once consent to this had taken place then the practices could have been randomised to receive the training or not receive it. The effect of training then would have been evaluated on patients who had a history of back pain. The question being addressed is slightly different from the original one. We would not be evaluating the effect of training on patients presenting to their GP with back pain, but rather evaluating the effect on those with a previous history of back pain. Because back pain recurs, many of these patients will be the same. If the training were effective we would have to assume it was also effective on new incident cases of back pain. Importantly, however, this approach would prevent any possibility of recruitment bias.

If it is not possible, or practical, to identify participants before randomisation, differential consent can be avoided by offering standard therapy to non-consenting participants in the active arm and obtaining consent for follow-up.

5.6 Ascertainment, reporting or detection bias

Ascertainment, reporting or detection bias occurs when investigators consciously or unconsciously bias a trial by reporting events more conscientiously in one treatment arm compared with the other arm. For example, teachers may be, understandably, more sensitive to any potential problems, or benefits, of a new teaching method. In this instance, the new method could appear to carry an increased risk of problems merely due to increased surveillance of the intervention group. Alternatively, the teacher may be convinced of the efficacy of the new approach and be more assiduous in reporting problems in the control arm than in the intervention group. Reporting of the trial blind to treatment allocation can minimise detection bias.

For example, in a trial evaluating the effectiveness of volunteer tutoring on reading among first grade children, Rimm-Kaufman et al. (1999) used blinded assessment of outcome in both pre- and post-tests.

> Examiners were blind as to whether or not the child was in the tutored or control group. (Rimm-Kaufman et al., 1999)

Alternatively, event reporting can be ascertained from differential sources (e.g., participant and participant's teacher or doctor), which should minimise the risk of detection bias. A good example of the bias that can be introduced by unblinded assessors is in the area of multiple sclerosis (Noseworthy et al., 1994). In this study physicians were asked to ascertain whether or not a patient's condition had improved. Two sets of physicians were asked to make the judgement. Physicians in one group were blinded to whether the patient was taking the placebo or the active therapy, whilst the physicians in the other group were not blinded. For the blinded physicians no apparent difference between the groups of patients was observed. In contrast, the unblinded clinicians rated patients taking the active treatment as having fewer symptoms, and this difference was statistically significant. Consequently, failure to blind assessment, as distinct from failure to blind participants, can introduce significant bias.

5.7   Performance or dilution bias

Dilution bias occurs when participants in any of the alternative interventions after randomisation receive one of the comparator interventions. For example, in a trial evaluating the effectiveness of social worker visits on levels of domestic violence (Davis and Taylor, 1997) a proportion of the control group participants received the visits, whilst a larger number of the intervention group participants failed to receive the treatment, thus tending to 'dilute' any observable treatment effects. Alternatively, or in addition, participants in the control group may seek out alternatives, which can produce a biased underestimate of effect. For example, if in an RCT evaluating early morning classes, parents of children allocated to the control group differentially sought private evening tuition to make up for the perceived disadvantage of being allocated to the control group, this would have the effect of producing a biased underestimate of the effect of early morning classes and increase the possibility of a Type II error (i.e., erroneously concluding there was no difference when, in fact, there was). This problem can be reduced by, if possible, blinding the participant to the nature of the experiment. Alternatively, one could use some form of balanced or crossover design. In the example of early morning classes, one could either inform the parents of the control children that their children would receive the intervention the following term, which should reduce the likelihood of parents seeking out extra tuition. However, this approach would limit the length of follow-up and prevent an assessment of any longer-term effects of booster classes. Alternatively, or in addition, we could allocate half of the children to early morning classes in maths whilst the other half could be allocated to additional literacy lessons, and each group could act as the control for the other in the two different subjects. Another approach to dealing with dilution problems is to address this statistically. If it is possible to measure which participants did not get the intervention, then a latent or instrumental variable analysis could be undertaken, which in principle would control for the effect of non-compliance (Hewitt et al., 2006).

5.8　Delay bias

Often there is a delay between treatment allocation and intervention. In between allocation and intervention, study events can and do occur. This may lead to a dilution in the effect of the treatment due to the delay. For example, the MRC's GRIT trial may have been affected by delay bias (GRIT Study Group, 2004). This trial was an evaluation of two treatment policies for pregnant women whose babies were failing to thrive. One policy for women who were more than 24 weeks pregnant was to deliver the baby as soon as possible. This approach, however, had risks for the baby, in that prematurity is an important risk factor for a number of disabilities (e.g., blindness, learning disabilities). Therefore, the alternative policy was to wait and see, which had the disadvantage that it might endanger the babies' lives. Because of the uncertainty about which was the best approach, the GRIT study randomised pregnant women into two groups: immediate or delayed delivery. Clearly, to observe an effect of the two policies there must have been as wide a gap as possible in the average delivery times between the two groups. However, 'immediate' was supposed to be within 24 hours, but often tended to be much longer due to various issues, such as scheduling women for theatre;

more than 25 per cent of the women were delayed more than one day before delivery. Therefore, the time gap between the treatment groups was relatively small (four days), which may have biased the results away from the beneficial or harmful effects of delayed delivery. In this instance, however, the trial did show a benefit for delay among relatively early pregnancies. Because of the dilution effects of delay ideally, therefore, allocation must take place as close as possible to treatment.

5.9   Hawthorne effects

The 'Hawthorne effect' refers to a non-randomised experiment undertaken in a factory. The researchers were looking at methods for increasing production among workers and they measured changes in productivity after manipulating certain variables, such as lighting and heating. They found, to their surprise, that productivity increased even when working conditions worsened. This effect was put down to workers responding to being in an experiment rather than because of any of the changes to their working conditions (Silverman, 1998). Extrapolating this effect to a trial, it is possible that an intervention group may improve, not through any intrinsic effect of the intervention but due to merely taking part in the experiment. This will produce a Type I error: that is erroneously concluding there is a difference when, in truth, there is not.

Hawthorne effects can be avoided or minimised if the control group is either given an alternative or 'sham' intervention that would induce similar Hawthorne effects as those affecting the intervention group, thereby cancelling out its effects. Some form of balanced design would address the Hawthorne problem.

5.10   Resentful demoralisation

Where participants have a strong preference for one of the interventions and are allocated to the perceived 'wrong' treatment, this can lead to the phenomenon of 'resentful demoralisation' (Brewin and Bradley, 1989), which can in turn lead to performance or dilution bias. This might, for instance, mean that the control participants seek out some form of alternative intervention, which, if effective, will dilute the effects of the intervention. Alternatively, the controls may comply less well than usual with their 'standard' intervention, and reduce the effectiveness of the control intervention. This will tend to exaggerate any beneficial effects. In theory it is possible for such an effect within a trial to lead to an apparent overall benefit of the novel intervention when, in truth, no such treatment effect exists. Even if resentful demoralisation does not lead to other forms of bias, it may create a bias in its own right by altering the psychological outcomes of participants in the control group to such an extent that they will 'under-perform' on the various outcome measures. Resentful demoralisation can be addressed in a number of ways. First, the potential participants can be asked their preferences at baseline. These preferences can then be used in an adjusted analysis. Second, the standard intervention can be made to look more attractive in order to reduce any disappointment effects.

5.11 Chance imbalances

Even when randomisation is properly undertaken there is always the possibility that the groups will be different in an important covariate, by chance: this is sometimes known as chance bias, although strictly speaking it is not a bias (Altman and Doré, 1991). Randomisation *will* ensure that, in the long run, the 'average' randomised trial will be completely balanced in the important covariates. Nevertheless, some trials will be unbalanced by chance, which will affect outcome. It is of little consolation to the trialist to find that, despite using randomisation in the design, the trial has had the misfortune to be the one in twenty that, by chance, is unbalanced in an important covariate. This problem can never completely be resolved; however, the possibility of it occurring can be reduced. When planning a trial, trialists can identify one or two important predictors of outcome, and then a stratified form of randomisation can be undertaken which will ensure that these important covariates *will* be balanced between the groups. Alternatively, as noted previously, post-randomisation stratification may be best, by identifying and measuring important covariates before the trial starts and ensuring that these are included in the analysis at the end.

5.12 Intention to treat

If a rigorous trial has been undertaken which avoids all the design biases that can affect the results of the study, using an inappropriate analytical approach can introduce bias. The most robust analytical method that should be used when analysing the results of randomised trials is through the use of intention to treat analysis (ITT) (Hollis and Campbell, 1999). Once a participant has been randomised they should remain within their allocated group for analytical purposes even if they 'cross over' into the other intervention arm or stop their intervention.

For example, consider a trial of extra classes for children. Some children allocated to receive extra tuition will either not go to any classes or stop going after one or two classes. In other words, they have crossed over to the no-treatment group. If we exclude these children from the analysis we will undermine the random allocation as such children will be very different from the children who continue with the classes. Importantly, the children with similar characteristics will remain in the no treatment arm. Comparison with the exclusion of the drop-outs will seriously bias the study. Therefore, if possible, all children should be analysed in the groups to which they were originally assigned: that is, using intention to teach (or treat) analysis (Torgerson and Torgerson, 2003). Exploratory analyses of those who attended classes to generate more research hypotheses are acceptable as long as the results are not used to inform educational policy.

As an example of how ITT analysis should be used, consider two similar trials in the area of criminal justice. Both trials examined the effectiveness of interventions to reduce domestic violence. In the first trial by Davis and Taylor (1997) seven participants allocated to the control condition (1.6 per cent) received the intervention, whilst 65 allocated to the intervention failed to receive treatment (15 per cent). It would have been tempting, but incorrect, to analyse the seven participants in the control group as being in the active group and vice versa for the 65 who did not receive the intervention. Fortunately, the authors were aware of the dangers of bias that this could have produced and the resulting analysis included all participants in their originally assigned group. Feder and Dugan (2002) were faced with a similar problem. Fourteen participants who had been allocated to the control group received the intervention because the judge over-rode the random assignment and insisted that these individuals should receive the intervention. The authors yielded to the temptation of putting these fourteen participants into the intervention group for the analysis. The problem with including them in the experimental group is that these fourteen men were very likely to have been different from the 'average' offender; indeed, it is likely that they were more violent than average. This could have significantly weakened the effect of the intervention by allowing them to cross over in the analysis. Including these men in the 'wrong' group could have biased the trial in a number of ways. First, they could have been more likely to 'regress to the mean' and increase the average effect of the intervention, making it appear effective when it was not. Second, these men may have been more resistant to the intervention and pulled down the average treatment effect, resulting in a no-effect observation.

In an educational example Carlton and colleagues, evaluating the role of peer tutoring, failed to use intention to teach analysis (Carlton et al., 1985). In an attempt to avoid any dilution bias the authors excluded non-adherent participants:

> While the experimental group consisted of 74 students, 14 were excluded from statistical analysis because of absences in excess of five (5) days during the experimental program. (Carlton et al., 1985)

Similarly Martinussen and Kirby (1998), evaluating the effect of instruction on phonological awareness for kindergarten children, removed two participants:

> Two children in the successive-phonological condition missed 25% of the lessons due to school absences and therefore were removed from the study, reducing the group size to 13. (Martinussen and Kirby, 1998)

For another example where intention to treat has not been used, consider the report by Feldman and Fish (1991) on the use of computer technology to support reading instruction. They stated the following:

> It was found in each sample that approximately 86% of the students with access to reading supports used them. Therefore, one-way ANOVAs were computed for each school sample, comparing this sub-sample with subjects who did not have access to reading supports. (Feldman and Fish, 1991)

In this example the authors violated the randomisation procedure by comparing only those who actually used the intervention after randomisation. Therefore, they excluded the 14 per cent of students who, for whatever reason, chose not to use the computer technology. However, by doing this they were not comparing like with like, as the 14 per cent of students who would have not used the technology had they been offered it, remained in the control group. These students were likely to have had different learning characteristics from those who used the technology. Consequently it is likely that their presence in the control group and absence in the intervention group biased the trial's results.

Let us consider a hypothetical example of how this might work. In Table 5.6 we show the composition of a trial after random allocation. We can see that the average score for each group is 18. Because of randomisation, we assume that the average score for each group is the same.

Table 5.6:   Baseline characteristics of a trial with two distinct subgroups

Subgroups	Intervention (N = 100)	Control (N = 100)
Group low	10 (n = 20)	10 (n = 20)
Group high	20 (n = 80)	20 (n = 80)
Total average score	18	18

Table 5.7:   Follow-up scores after excluding those who did not get the intervention

Subgroups	Intervention (N = 80)	Control (N = 100)
Group low	0 (n = 0)	10 (n = 20)
Group high	20 (n = 80)	20 (n = 80)
Total average score	20	18

Note, however, that within both the intervention and the control groups we have two distinct subgroups. One group, which is the smaller group, has a very low mean score of 10, whilst the higher scoring subgroup, the larger group, has a mean score of 20. This composition would be typical within most randomised trials. In a trial of blood pressure, for example, we could easily form subgroups of older and younger participants and the older participants would have a higher blood pressure compared with the younger patients. In an educational trial the older children may have higher pre-test scores than the younger children. But because this is a trial we are not worried about these subgroup differences within each of the randomised groups as random allocation ensures that they exist in equal proportions. Consequently the group means are the same: 18 points each. However, this benefit of randomisation only exists if we can keep all the randomised participants within the study analysis. In Table 5.7 we show what could happen if we do not use ITT analysis.

In this example participants within the low subgroup were not included in the analysis. This might be because they did not receive the intervention and the analysts mistakenly thought they should not include them in the analysis or it might be because they had dropped out. Whatever the reason, the consequences are the same: bias has been introduced. Consequently we can see that in the follow-up data analysis the intervention group appears to be better than the control group with an average score of 20. However, in this example, the intervention was

Table 5.8: Follow-up scores after using 'on-treatment' analysis

Subgroups	Intervention (N = 80)	Control (N = 120)
Group low	0 (n = 0)	10 (n = 40)
Group high	20 (n = 80)	20 (n = 80)
Total average score	20	16.7

ineffective and the difference in scores was purely a result of not using ITT analysis because we differentially excluded the low-scoring group.

If we decide to use on-treatment analysis this makes the bias worse. In on-treatment analysis we put those who received the intervention into a treatment-received group even if they had not been randomised to that group. In Table 5.8 we show those in the intervention group who did not receive the intervention placed in the control group.

As we can see, using this strategy increases the bias even more than using a strategy of not including them. We cannot deal with the above problem by excluding similar participants from the control group because we do not know who they are. One of the main reasons we randomise is to control for the *unknown* variables. In this example the characteristic of participants who are 'low' may be unmeasurable. Therefore we cannot identify the participants with the same characteristic from the control group. We cannot attempt to do this by removing participants who have similar baseline scores. Whilst this might seem to be a solution, it is not. This is because, even if they were matched on pre-test scores, the ones who refused the intervention may have some other characteristic that means that they are better or worse at improving on their baseline score. As we do not know what this characteristic is, we cannot adjust for it by either removing similar people from the control group or by using statistical approaches such as regression analysis. Because of the potential problem of selection bias, on-treatment analysis should always be treated very cautiously, as it has the potential to produce misleading results.

Let us examine another example of failure to use ITT. In a trial of an intervention to improve attainment, a number of students did not use the intervention (Tucker et al., 1998). The response by the trialists was as follows:

The Default Control Group consisted of students initially assigned to the Experimental Group, but who did not follow through in participating as they had agreed. (Tucker et al., 1998)

From reading the paper it would appear that most of the 'default control group' were actually from the experimental group as there were 17 participants in this group, 42 in the control group and 24 in the experimental group: thus assuming an equal allocation ratio we would expect about 42 in each group as 17 + 24 is 41 then it seems likely that virtually all were from the experimental arm.

In Table 5.9 we show how failure to use intention to treat can exaggerate treatment effects. In the table we have taken data from Tucker et al. (1998). If we examine the baseline maths score we can see that the experimental group has the highest score, the control group has a lower score and the default control has the lowest score. Given that this is a randomised trial then we would expect the baseline values to be fairly similar. However, the control group's mean score is 10 per cent lower. On the other hand if we calculate what the score of all the controls is likely to have been we can see the baseline difference is halved (i.e., 5 per cent).

At follow-up we can see that the difference between the experimental group and the control group is about half a standard deviation (i.e., half an effect size). If we then put all the default control participants in with the experimental group we can see that the difference is only 0.19 of a standard deviation: a much smaller effect. The failure of the authors in this case to analyse by randomisation status is likely to have exaggerated any effect of their intervention.

Intention to treat analysis can actually be quite difficult to achieve. In theory ITT analysis only occurs when 100 per cent of participants are included in the analysis. This is rarely achieved. There will nearly always be some form of attrition. Participants who are completely lost to follow-up after randomisation and do not provide any data for the analysis will have to be excluded from the analysis. Such an analysis is unlikely to be biased if the attrition rate is low and is equally distributed between the study arms. If some data are provided then these can be used in the

Table 5.9:   Comparison of on-treatment versus intention to treat analysis

Group	Baseline maths	Year 1 maths
Experimental group	2.20 (0.84)	2.51 (0.94)
Control	1.98 (1.08)	2.05 (1.18)
Default control	1.91 (1.11)	1.86 (1.24)
[a]Experimental group + Default control	2.08 (0.96)	2.24 (1.07)

[a] Estimated values.

analysis. Although 'pure' intention to treat analysis will be impossible to achieve in many trials, the analytical philosophy for every trial should be ITT.

5.13 Application of inclusion/exclusion criteria

Exclusion bias occurs after randomisation when participants are excluded from the study. Sometimes it is legitimate to exclude participants after they have been randomised as some will have been randomised in error. Quite often those recruiting a participant may misinterpret the inclusion criteria and recruit a participant that should not be included in a trial. As an extreme example, in a study of hip protectors for the prevention of hip fractures among women, a man was accidentally recruited (Birks et al., 2004). This is because the woman to whom the invitation was extended to take part was uninterested in the trial; however, her husband *was* interested in the trial. Consequently he completed the consent and eligibility forms and posted them back to the trial centre and received padded underwear suitable for women! Because this was all done by post the researchers did not realise until some time after the randomisation that he breached one of the eligibility criteria, namely being a woman. Consequently he was excluded from the study. In this instance, the exclusion criterion was obvious and this exclusion would not have led to bias. However, there may be grey areas with respect to applying the inclusion/exclusion criteria. If the person who is reviewing these criteria post-randomisation is not masked to the group allocation then they may consciously or unconsciously exclude participants selectively and bias the trial. If it is suspected that there are people in the trial who violate the inclusion/exclusion criteria the question is what should be done with these participants within the analysis? If knowledge of their group allocation is known when the decision is being made as to whether they should be included or excluded, this can lead to bias. Similarly, some of the reported outcomes may or may not be the *a priori* study outcomes. Again the decision whether to classify such outcomes may be biased if the allocation schedule is known. This form of bias can be avoided if all the crucial analytical decisions are made with the analyst 'blind' to treatment allocation, or if, alternatively, once randomised the participant remains within the analysis even if they do not strictly fulfil the relevant criteria. An example of potentially biased exclusion occurred in a large randomised controlled trial of breast cancer screening in the USA (Gøtzsche and Olsen, 2000). In this study the women were randomised using a matched pairs design, which appears not to have been done properly as there were unequal numbers in the groups. After randomisation women who had had a diagnosis of breast cancer in the past were excluded. However, because the women were randomised the numbers of exclusions should have been the same: this was not the case. In the group that received screening there were 30 131 women, whilst for the control group there were 30 565 (Gøtzsche and Olsen, 2000). Note, the exclusions were higher for the intervention group than for the control group. In a methodological critique of the trial Gøtzsche and Olsen calculated that there were significant imbalances in age of menopause and previous history of a lump in the breast (both $p < 0.0001$), both of which are significantly associated with future development of breast cancer. Consequently the results of this trial should be treated with caution.

Sometimes participants are dropped from an analysis for reasons that are not quite clear. For example, Castle and colleagues (1994) evaluated a phonemic awareness programme and dropped a pair of participants because one of the control students had personal difficulties:

> However, we dropped one pair of data from the study after posttesting was completed because of personal problems, outside the control of the school, experienced by one child in the control group. (Castle et al., 1994)

Note that in this instance all of the data had been collected on the control child. It is not good practice to drop data on this basis as the results may be known and this could have driven the decision to remove the participants and introduced bias. As a minimum the authors should report an analysis with *all* of the participants as well as the one without.

Another relatively common mistake is to exclude 'outliers' from the analysis. Some participants have a huge change in test scores and many analysts remove these values to ensure a better statistical distribution of the data. Such an approach may introduce bias, as this violates intention to treat analysis.

5.14   Subgroup analysis

Another form of analytical bias is that of unplanned subgroup analysis. Often there is a temptation to see whether the intervention has worked more effectively among some types of participants than others. This is especially true if the overall effect observed in a trial is of 'no difference' between the groups. If sufficient subgroup analyses are undertaken then a statistically significant difference *will* be found. Thus, in twenty subgroup analyses there is a high chance of one being statistically significant when, in truth, there is no difference. Indeed, far fewer subgroup analyses are required to substantially increase the risk of a chance finding. As a demonstration of the problem of subgroup analyses in a health care trial, statisticians analysing a large trial of the effects of aspirin noted that for people who had the star signs Gemini and Libra aspirin was ineffective, but very effective for people born under other star signs (ISIS-2, 1988). This analysis was done as an entertaining protest as the *Lancet* referees had required a large number of subgroup analyses, which were done, but a nonsensical subgroup analysis was also included to make the point that this was an unscientific practice. An example of how subgroup analyses can mislead is with respect to the use of antimicrobial agents for the prevention of pre-term birth. On the basis of a subgroup analysis, which appeared to show a benefit of antimicrobial agents for pregnant women at high risk of preterm delivery, a trial to test this was undertaken (Shennan et al., 2006). This trial was stopped early because the use of such agents *increased* the risk of preterm birth rather than prevented it (Shennan et al., 2006).

For another example of how subgroup analyses can be misleading let us consider a large RCT of raloxifene. This trial was designed to assess the effects of raloxifene on osteoporotic fractures (Barrett-Connor et al., 2002). The authors also looked at the effect of this treatment on cardiovascular events. They found that overall there was no difference between women taking placebo or those taking raloxifene in terms of cardiovascular outcomes. However, they then looked at a subgroup of women who were at high risk of sustaining a cardiovascular event. Among this subgroup they found a statistically significant reduction in cardiovascular events among the women taking raloxifene. Note, however, if this effect is real it also must mean that raloxifene increases cardiovascular events among lower risk women. The authors did counsel caution about accepting these results at face value and recommended a second trial to confirm their findings. A follow-up trial would be required by the regulatory bodies before the manufacturers could make claims about their product's effectiveness with respect to cardiovascular disease. Such a follow-up trial was undertaken and this study recruited women at higher risk of cardiovascular disease (i.e., similar characteristics to the subgroup in the earlier trial). No effect of raloxifene was found on cardiovascular outcomes (Barrett-Connor et al., 2006). This example illustrates the possible dangers of accepting the findings of subgroup analyses.

To avoid this problem subgroup analyses must be pre-specified before data are analysed. In addition, there needs to be a good scientific justification for each subgroup analysis. Finally, any subgroup analysis undertaken after the results of the main trial comparison are known should be described as a *post hoc* analysis, and the results should be treated with caution. Indeed, the results should be interpreted as an indication for further research rather than evidence to drive policy or practice.

5.15 Conclusions

This chapter has described a number of potential biases that can affect a randomised controlled trial. Unfortunately many RCTs are susceptible to the biases described previously because the researchers have not planned or executed the study with sufficient care to avoid them. It must be emphasised, however, that these biases can equally affect non-randomised designs. Consequently the potential of them occurring must not be used as an excuse to adopt a less rigorous approach to evaluation. As Berk (2005) argued in the context of criminal justice trials: 'If the alternative to a randomized experiment is an observational study, the difficulties are likely to be even worse.'

What is required is careful thought and planning to ensure that such biases are prevented from occurring.

5.16 Key points

- Trial allocation can be subverted unless undertaken independently and concealed.
- Careful attention needs to be paid to computer software when using computer randomisation to avoid technical errors.
- Recruitment bias can occur if randomisation precedes consent.
- Exclusion bias can occur if an unblinded researcher excludes participants after allocation.
- Attrition bias can occur if drop-out is substantial and/or different between groups.
- Resentful demoralisation can occur if participants are not allocated to their desired treatment.
- Performance bias can occur if participants access a trial intervention or similar treatment during the study.
- Ascertainment bias can occur if the researcher is not blinded to group allocations when assessing outcomes.
- Multiple subgroup analyses can mislead.

6
Placebo and Sham Trials

6.1 Background

The traditional view of a randomised trial is the double- or triple-blind placebo drug trial in health care research. The basic outline of this study design is as follows. Participants are randomly allocated to receive an active or placebo drug. A placebo looks and tastes the same as an active drug. The use of placebo achieves several important theoretical goals. First, it 'blinds' or masks the participant, researchers and the clinicians to the group allocation. This reduces the chance of a Hawthorne effect differentially affecting one of the trial arms, which would bias the results. It avoids the resentful demoralisation of the control group, as they will not be aware they are taking an inactive treatment. Differential attrition bias may be less likely, as any attrition will be evenly spread across both groups (unless one treatment has side-effects). It also addresses performance bias, as participants are less likely to differentially seek alternative treatments to compensate for their allocation to the control arm. Finally, subversion bias is less likely, as concealment of allocation is more easily attainable than in a non-placebo trial.

In surgical trials placebo controlled trials are possible, although rare, for obvious ethical reasons. Control participants can be given a 'sham' operation, which usually consists of making a minimal incision in the skin. This sham operation 'blinds' the patient, but does not, however, blind the surgeon or the surgical team. Doctors and other health care professionals who are not part of the direct surgical team *can* be 'blinded'. Indeed, in one surgical trial, blood-colour liquid was used to stain the dressings used with the control group participants to mask the patient and the nursing staff to the patient's relatively minimal surgery (Majeed et al., 1996). By blinding in this fashion this trial demonstrated that minimally invasive surgery did not lead to a shorter length of hospital stay for laparoscopic surgery compared with open surgery (contrary to previous unblinded trials).

Whilst the placebo trial has many undoubted scientific advantages, it is not without its critics. One major criticism is that the use of placebos abolishes the placebo effect, which may be an important component of the overall treatment (if it exists). When a doctor prescribes a medicine to a patient in 'real life', then both the doctor and the patient know that the patient is receiving an active treatment. The expectations of receiving an active treatment may enhance its effect, which should be counted as part of the overall benefit of treatment. The use of placebos eliminates this effect and thereby may reduce the estimate of the overall benefit of the drug when used outside the context of a clinical trial. A similar criticism of the placebo trial is that the novel treatment is not evaluated against routine clinical practice, because this does not involve the use of placebos. It is possible that the response profile of patients may be entirely different if they know they are receiving an active treatment.

It is sometimes assumed that patients and their physicians need to remain blind to the treatment allocation for a placebo controlled trial to be effective (Fergusson et al., 2004). However, this is only true if the treatment is ineffective (Senn, 2004). If the treatment is effective then patients in the intervention group are more likely to guess their treatment allocation, compared with patients in the control group. Patients receiving effective treatments who feel better are more likely to guess they are on the active rather than the placebo therapy, and therefore patient blinding appears to fail in this instance. If the quality of a trial is judged on the success or not of blinding then we might rapidly conclude, incorrectly, that the only good placebo trials are those of ineffective therapies! The main purpose of the placebo, from the perspective of the trialists, is to blind the patient, the treatment assessors and the patient's physicians to the treatment groups at the start of the trial. Maintaining patient blinding is most important when there is no treatment effect; if the treatment has no benefit or harm and no side-effects patients should remain blind at the end of the intervention. Thus the placebo guards against a Type I error: that is, erroneously concluding an intervention is effective when it is not.

With an ineffective therapy blinding prevents bias occurring because participants believe that they feel better merely because they think they are taking an active or novel treatment. With an effective or harmful treatment the blinding is less important as the effects of the treatment will tend to break the blinding differentially between groups.

The placebo control design is perceived as a rigorous method of evaluating the efficacy of a treatment, but it may not be the best design when estimating the effectiveness of treatments in routine clinical practice. Placebo control is ideal for estimating any intrinsic biological effect of a therapy but is less helpful when we want to decide how routine practice should be changed.

6.2 Evidence for placebo trials

As far as we are aware there are two randomised studies comparing the use of a placebo with an 'open' trial design. Avenell and colleagues randomised patients participating in a calcium and vitamin D trial to be informed about either a placebo trial or an open trial. The aim of the study was to examine recruitment rates between the two arms (Avenell et al., 2004). The results showed a statistically significant increase of about 10 per cent in recruitment into the open study compared with the placebo trial. The authors also found a lower drop-out rate among participants in the open study; however, this lower drop-out was mainly confined to patients in the open control group – there was a significant drop-out among patients taking the calcium treatment compared with patients in the no treatment group. Therefore, in this instance the use of placebo prevented differential drop-out but did not reduce drop-out overall. It appears that patients were confused between taking the intervention and staying in the trial. Trial participants assumed that if they no longer wanted to take the tablets they were no longer needed for the trial and therefore they withdrew. This trial reinforces the importance of emphasising to participants that treatment withdrawal and trial withdrawal are two distinct issues. Treatment withdrawal does not automatically mean trial withdrawal and participants should be encouraged to remain in the study to provide follow-up data to allow an intention to treat analysis.

Hemminki et al. (2004) conducted another RCT of the placebo design among women being recruited to a study of hormone replacement therapy. Women were randomised to be asked to take part in an open design or a placebo control design. Recruitment was significantly enhanced in the open arm: there was a similar 10 per cent absolute increase in recruitment rates. Therefore, not using a placebo appears to lead to recruitment of a more representative sample of the population into a trial, which increases its external validity.

6.3 The placebo effect

It is important to know whether the placebo effect is due simply to a combination of regression to the mean effects and temporal change or to a 'true' placebo effect, as it is an intrinsic component of therapies that include this phenomenon. In a randomised controlled trial of different types of placebo treatment (sham acupuncture versus oral placebo for persistent arm pain) Kaptchuk et al. (2006) attempted to shed light on this question. Their trial demonstrated that placebo acupuncture produced statistically significantly greater effects on self-reported arm pain compared with the placebo pill. This suggests, therefore, that the 'placebo effect' is enhanced by a more credible placebo treatment.

6.4 Is it a placebo?

It is not unknown for mistakes to occur during placebo manufacture resulting in identical placebo and active treatment. For example, in a randomised controlled trial of magnetic bracelets for arthritis of the knee, three groups were formed: true magnets group, placebo magnets group and dummy magnets group (Harlow et al., 2004). The placebo magnets were intended to contain a weak, non-therapeutic, magnetic field to blind the patient. The dummy magnet was ordinary steel, which could easily be unblinded. At the trial's conclusion, however, it was discovered that, due to a manufacturing error, some of the placebo magnets contained a full strength magnetic field.

Another problem with placebo control is that sometimes this may contain an active treatment in its own right. For instance, a placebo cream for wound dressings could potentially irritate the wound and retard healing and in this instance we could then observe an effect of the active cream.

6.5 Conclusions

Placebo controlled trials are the main work horses of trials in clinical medicine. Their use has been invaluable in the search for effective and safe pharmacological therapies. They are a valuable means of implementing blinding, which helps avoid associated biases. Their use will often enhance the validity of a trial design. Placebos reduce the risk of an ineffective therapy appearing to be effective due to post-randomisation biases, such as the Hawthorne effect or patient preference. For many proponents of evidence-based medicine they represent the gold-standard in terms of trial based research and some will assign less credibility to 'open', that is non-placebo, trials. This is a pity because whilst placebo trials do have a place in the pantheon of trial research they are only one of a number of different trial designs and may not be appropriate to address some questions. They can be used for some therapies; however, for the broadest range of potential interventions across the social sciences their potential is rather more limited. Indeed, for some types of trial their use, even if possible, may not be appropriate. In particular, in a pragmatic randomised controlled trial, placebos may not be necessary. The use of placebos may also hinder recruitment and make the trial less generalisable. In the next chapter we examine the use of pragmatic trials.

6.6   Key points

- Placebo trials are often considered the 'gold-standard' in RCT design in health care research.
- Placebo control facilitates blinding and can prevent some post-randomisation biases.
- Placebo trials may not be appropriate or possible in many instances.
- The evidence base for placebo trials is in the form of two RCTs of placebos which suggest that they have a lower recruitment and higher drop-out rate than 'open' trials.

7
Pragmatic and Explanatory Trials

7.1 Background

> It cannot be overemphasized that unless an experiment can be generalized at least a bit, time and resources have been wasted. One does not really care about the results of a study unless its conclusions can be used to guide future decisions. (Berk, 2005)

The randomised controlled trial is the 'gold-standard' method for estimating effectiveness because it eliminates selection bias. Random allocation provides a powerful means of establishing causation (Torgerson and Torgerson, 2001) and ensures that any differences in post-test results are causally related to the intervention. However, the results of the trial may not be generalisable to a wider population beyond the participants in the trial, unless those participants were randomly sampled from an underlying population. A trial may not have a wider application if the intervention, context and sample are unusual. For example, an educational intervention might have been undertaken in 'laboratory' conditions unrelated to the real-life context of a school. Even if the sample of students participating in such a trial represents the wider population of students, the lack of a pragmatic setting would limit its wider application. Similarly, a health care trial that used placebo or sham treatments and was delivered by specialist physicians may not be applicable to patients seen in routine care.

The randomised controlled trial has excellent internal validity as it controls for both the known and unknown confounders. Many critics of the RCT method have criticised the design, arguing that the issue of generalising from an RCT to the whole population that may benefit from the intervention is problematic. There are several reasons why many, if not most, trials have some problems with external validity.

7.2   Consent issues

In many trials potential participants who could be included in a study sometimes refuse consent. Ethically there is nothing that can be done about this issue. Some researchers are harsh in their condemnation of 'trial dodgers' especially if they demand the untested treatment outside of the trial (Silverman, 1997). In this latter case an untested treatment should always be refused outside of a trial; this is ethical as, if we do not know that a treatment is effective, we could be exposing someone to unknown risks. Whilst a proportion of participants will be exposed to the more hazardous treatment within a trial setting they will also have the chance of being given the safety of the superior treatment, which may mean no intervention at all. If they are given an unproven active treatment then there is no chance that they would get the safest treatment, in the event that the active therapy is hazardous.

People who volunteer to take part in trials are different from those who do not (Silverman, 1997). This does threaten the external validity of a study as, once the trial is finished, one has to assume that the results will apply to all potential patients who fit the biomedical inclusion criteria even if they belong to a group that refuses to participate in a trial.

Many trials exclude those who cannot give informed consent (e.g., patients suffering from some form of dementia) or will not take part. Often such people are at very high risk of a given illness and would benefit from an effective treatment. Excluding such participants will mean that we can never be completely sure that the treatment is effective in that group. Some groups are deliberately excluded from trials because of medico-legal problems. For example, children are often excluded from clinical trials because they require 'proxy' consent from a parent or guardian. Whether proxy consent is legally valid is unclear and could potentially leave the sponsors of the trial open to future legal action from children who may have been damaged as a consequence of taking part in the trial. This issue is particularly disturbing as, for example, drugs often have differential effects among children compared with adults, not least in terms of dosage. Therefore, many doctors are compelled to use treatments for children out of the strict terms of the drug's licence because they have not properly been evaluated in children. More children end up being exposed to unproven doses than would have been the case if a trial had included them, because of this potential legal problem.

7.3   Statistical issues

As well as consent barriers to participation, there are often statistical reasons for excluding certain groups. For instance, many of the trials evaluating cardiac drugs only include male participants, whilst many trials evaluating anti-fracture treatments only include female participants. This is because for some diseases the incidence is so much greater for one gender than the other. Therefore, whilst osteoporosis is a problem for men the fracture rate is much greater among women. If a trial included men it would need to be larger and longer to observe a statistically significant benefit compared with a study with female participants only. This, unfortunately, leads to the problem that the results of an effectiveness trial for a therapy that has mainly been evaluated in one gender cannot be directly extrapolated to the other gender. Clearly, the solution to this problem is to undertake trials in both genders. However, to do this of course requires more funds to support such studies.

7.4   Inclusion/exclusion criteria

Another barrier to external generalisability is the use of strict inclusion/exclusion criteria. To avoid this problem such criteria must be kept as loose as possible and also closely reflect the 'real world' patient. In practice this means making the trial as pragmatic as possible. On the other hand, some criteria have been chosen to minimise loss to follow-up. For instance, excluding the very old is sometimes done on the basis that the mortality rate is high and many participants may not live to reach the end of the trial. Further, some participants are excluded in that they have an 'unorthodox' lifestyle which means they are at high risk of loss to follow-up. In terms of loss due to mortality, this should not be an issue as it will be recorded and should not be a source of bias, although losing participants through mortality will reduce the power of the trial as the effective sample size decreases.

Loss to follow-up can result in bias if the participant is completely unaccounted for. There is a trade-off between trying to recruit as many participants from as wide a sample as possible and attempting to include only participants who will follow the trial protocol and not drop out, thereby maximising the internal validity of the trial. Loss to follow-up can be an important source of bias. Consequently many researchers will tend not to recruit participants who are deemed to be at high risk of dropping out of the trial completely.

7.5 Internal versus external validity

The critics of the generalisability of RCT methods need to ask themselves: is it better to have the 'right' answer among a relatively narrow group of participants or the 'wrong' answer amongst everyone? For a study to have external validity it must, first, have internal validity. Hormone replacement therapy observational studies have high external validity, in the sense that the women are more representative of the likely users of HRT than those participating in trials, but they give completely the wrong result. Because of biased observational studies it was believed for many years that HRT prevented cardiovascular outcomes. These large non-randomised studies had 'good' external validity in that they observed the effects of HRT as it was being used by clinicians (Grady et al., 1992). Nevertheless, because of uncontrolled biases the very precise answers these studies gave were wrong. In contrast, the Women's Health Initiative (WHI) trial, whilst placebo controlled and possessing a wide range of exclusion criteria (such as excluding women who had menopausal symptoms), showed that the actual effect of HRT was to significantly increase stokes and cardiac events (Writing Group, 2002).

7.6 Explanatory trials

Many, if not most, health care trials are explanatory or mechanistic studies. These are characterised by having tightly defined entry criteria, the use of placebos, and the intervention delivered in a specialist centre. These studies tend to be tightly controlled in order to reduce the statistical variation within the sample and to make sure that if there is an effect within a given sample size the researcher is best placed to observe the effect. Such studies are useful in the early stages of developing an intervention, where they may be dubbed 'phase II' trials, in the sense that they help researchers to witness the effectiveness of an intervention under ideal circumstances. They are of less help, however, when informing routine policy and practice where trials are needed that have been designed with this in mind. We need to design trials that maximise external validity whilst retaining the high internal validity that randomisation affords. It is not the act of randomisation that gives a trial poor external validity; other design aspects cause this.

7.7 Pragmatic trials

A trial needs to be generalisable. A trial that cannot be extrapolated to other populations is not worth doing (Berk, 2005) because the purpose of the trial is to help the wider population improve their health, education or offending status.

Poor ecological validity or generalisability has been long debated in health care trials. In the 1960s Schwartz and Lellouch (1967) argued strongly that randomised controlled trials should be 'pragmatic' when undertaken in health care to improve generalisability of the health care treatments. Researchers in other fields, such as educational research, were using pragmatic trial designs at around the same time:

> The 'Field Experiment' approach which has been followed in our first main experiment requires the maintenance of everyday-life conditions as far as is possible within limits imposed by the need for control of variables. (Downing and Jones, 1966)

To make policy and practice more effective requires evidence from large, rigorous, pragmatic experiments, not mechanistic or explanatory trials with selected populations within unusual settings, which are difficult to generalise to the usual population. Tunis and colleagues (2003), writing in the context of health care trials, argued that the lack of pragmatic trials is an important problem for clinicians and other health care decision-makers.

We can design trials that maximise external or ecological validity. Indeed, we need to consider this issue for all trials we design unless we do not expect or want the results to be applied widely.

7.8   Participant selection

One of the first design issues we need to consider when designing a pragmatic trial is what kind of participants we will include. We want to avoid the situation, as far as possible, of excluding any participant who has the potential to benefit from the intervention. For example, recruiting patients and delivering an experimental treatment within primary care will make the trial results far more generalisable to the bulk of patients with a given condition, compared with a trial based in secondary care and delivered by specialist physicians. In many situations, particularly in health care, we will never be able to recruit a random sample of people into the trial. This is because of a mixture of ethical and practical reasons. If we wanted to undertake a trial among patients with heart failure, ideally we would identify all such patients and take a random sample. However, this is simply not possible as patients have to give informed consent and since some refuse this will result in a selected sample. Further, even if we were to ignore the issue of consent then simply identifying the relevant population may not be possible.

It has been suggested that patients should not be allowed to refuse consent to take part in a trial (Evans, 2004). The argument falls along the lines of social responsibility: we should contribute to the fight against disease by taking part in clinical trials because we all benefit from treatments that some participants have made possible by taking part in such trials. Just as people are not allowed to 'free ride' on tax funded services, people should not be allowed to have medical treatments that others have volunteered to evaluate (Evans, 2004). Even if one agrees with this point of view and considers it appropriate to force people to participate in trials, scientifically it may produce other problems. It is likely that those being made to take part would comply badly with treatment, fill in outcome measures badly, and in short behave in such a manner as to bias the trial.

Within the context of other areas, such as education, the same philosophy applies. If we have developed a novel literacy intervention then we need to test it among a sample of children that represents as closely as possible the population of children to which the intervention will be applied if found to be effective.

7.9   Outcomes in pragmatic trials

A key aspect of generalisability is the type of outcome assessed. Many health care trials assess surrogate outcomes such as blood pressure, cholesterol levels or bone density. Whilst these outcomes are of biological interest to the physicians, they are of less importance to the patient and the policy-maker. Most people with high blood pressure will not go on to have a stroke. An estimate of treatment effectiveness in terms of strokes prevented is more important to the patient and the doctor than the measured reduction in blood pressure. Similarly, increases in bone density do not directly benefit or disadvantage a patient – the impact of treatment on fracture occurrence is the important outcome. In other settings, such as education and crime and justice, the same principle applies. For example, for those managing offenders, the important outcome is reduction in reoffending rate, rather than changes in perceived potential to offend.

Pragmatic trials should measure the true or final outcome of interest, whereas explanatory trials are often not large enough to do this. Consequently a defining feature of a pragmatic trial is that its main outcome is as close as possible to the outcome that is most important to the participant, practitioner and policy-maker.

7.10   Explanatory or pragmatic interventions

One issue with respect to designing more pragmatic trials is the type of intervention we wish to evaluate. A pragmatic approach to the definition of an intervention might differ considerably from that of an 'explanatory' approach. For example, in a trial by Little and colleagues, patients with a sore throat were randomised to receive antibiotics or no antibiotics (Little et al., 1997). In this instance placebos were not used, although they could have been. This trial was pragmatic in that it was designed to be as close as possible to routine care. In routine care of patients with a sore throat GPs generally do not use placebos. They generally explain to the patient that they either would be getting an antibiotic or they would not. In this instance the only difference was that the GP randomised patients to receive an antibiotic or no antibiotic. The patient and the GP were aware of their treatment allocation, just as they would be in normal practice. In this instance, the trial failed to show any benefit of antibiotics on the resolution of the sore throat. Importantly, however, in further follow-ups the trialists noted the patients allocated to receive antibiotics were *more* likely to visit their doctor with another sore throat than patients who were allocated to the control group. This is because all patients with sore throats eventually improved anyway. The patients who received the antibiotics mistakenly ascribed their recovery to the drug. However, if placebos had been used then patients in both trial arms would have ascribed their recovery to the antibiotic. The results of the trial were actually *more* policy relevant because it was not placebo controlled and was of a pragmatic design. GPs now know that if they give patients antibiotics for sore throats not only will this have no effect, but the patient will be more likely to return in subsequent months for further prescriptions when they next contract a sore throat.

7.11   Dealing with post-randomisation bias in pragmatic trials

Because pragmatic trials in general should not use placebos or sham controls, this makes them more susceptible to post-randomisation biases. Potential biases might be the Hawthorne effect or resentful demoralisation. For example, participants might be interested in taking part in a trial of counselling or physiotherapy and will feel demoralised if they are allocated to 'usual' care. As noted in Chapter 5, this demoralisation process could introduce bias and we need to avoid this if possible. There are several design solutions we might consider to reduce this possibility.

We discuss in future chapters the role that patient preference or cluster designs might play in ameliorating such problems. One relatively straight-forward approach might be to use a balanced incomplete block design. In this design two, mutually exclusive, interventions are evaluated. Instead of the control group being offered an unattractive intervention, such as usual care, we might test two attractive interventions and these are used to control for problems such as the Hawthorne effect. We might evaluate two different curricula, such as geography and maths. One group is given a new geography curriculum whilst the other a new maths curriculum. This is attractive to schools and students as both groups are in receipt of a new intervention. This not only controls for the Hawthorne effect and resentful demoralisation but might also make the trial more attractive in terms of recruitment to teachers and children.

A health care example might include the evaluation of clinical guidelines. If we wanted to assess whether guidelines for angina were effective we might balance this by giving the control group guidelines for diabetes treatments.

Alternatively we might allocate participants to a waiting list control, which may avoid any bias through demoralisation, although this may not avoid Hawthorne effects.

The suggestions made above control for biases arising from the participant. We need also to be careful about controlling for ascertainment bias. However, this is probably easier to deal with than participant biases by masking the assessors to group allocation when they perform the post-tests.

Box 7.1:   Evidence for the use of a balanced design

Verstappen and colleagues (2003, 2004) used a balanced design in the evaluation of guidelines for ordering tests. Twenty-six physicians were allocated to an intervention providing feedback on their requests for diagnostic tests. Half were allocated to receive feedback on the clinical problems of cardiovascular complaints, upper and lower abdominal problems, whilst the other half got feedback on asthma and degenerative joint complaints. The trial showed a reduction in the designated clinical conditions. Interestingly the same group included a third arm that did not have any control conditions. When an intervention group was compared with the 'untreated' control group it was found the difference was much greater compared with the control group that had had an intervention, which suggests that the Hawthorne effect in this instance could exaggerate the treatment effects (Verstappen et al., 2003, 2004).

Table 7.1:   Summary of different trial characteristics of pragmatic versus explanatory trials

Trial characteristic	Explanatory	Pragmatic
Primary aim	Inform understanding of interventions effects and mechanisms.	Inform policy and practice
Sample size	Small	Large to cope with heterogeneous population
Outcome measures	Surrogates (e.g., blood pressure)	Participant relevant outcomes (e.g., stroke, literacy, offending)
Use of placebos/sham	Yes	No
Setting	Specialist centres	Usual practice
Entry criteria	Restricted	Broad

In Table 7.1 we summarise the general differential characteristics of pragmatic and explanatory trial design.

7.12   Discussion

The pragmatic randomised controlled trial is a powerful tool for informing practice and policy. The pragmatic design might be actually more cost effective than the explanatory approach and given that the control condition is usual practice we should not need much in the way of extra resources for half the study population. We may also use standard assessments and tests and therefore may not require too much extra work for the practitioners we expect to deliver the experimental interventions. As we are less interested in the mechanisms of how an intervention works rather than in whether it works or not, costs can often be saved by not requiring intensive investigations of patients (e.g., blood tests).

Some referees and funding bodies are not amenable to the concept of a pragmatic trial. In a recent randomised trial of computer software to aid the teaching of spelling the trial results were rejected by a number of journals (Brooks et al., 2006), partly because of the pragmatic nature of the study:

It purports to be a randomized controlled trial, but it demonstrates none of the attributes of one. Educational research should begin with a theory, a causal argument, based on a careful examination of the literature. We need to understand in an experiment why such an approach would be examined, the historical linkages of past research to present investigations. What conditions would lead one to believe that this technology could make a difference in spelling? Is it something in the software, on the computer screen, on children's interaction with the particular curriculum. This is often the most important part of a study, the question, and the rationale for why the investigation is critically important. (anonymous referee)

This trial was an evaluation of the use of computer technology to improve the literacy abilities of children aged 11–12 years. Children were randomly allocated to receive the intervention via a laptop computer in addition to their normal literacy classes at the beginning of the autumn term. The control children received the intervention at the end of the term. Both groups were followed up just before the control group received the intervention. The trial was pragmatic in design as it was based in a usual school setting. The only difference in implementation was that arbitrary assignment to the intervention was replaced by random allocation. The intervention is widely used in schools on the basis of little or no randomised evidence. For the trialists evaluating the program, the educational, psychological theory behind the program was of relatively little importance as the software program was already being implemented. The key question to the trialists was whether, when the implementation was evaluated using the RCT, it worked. Interestingly the trial produced no evidence to show that it was effective (Brooks et al., 2006). Similarly, for many medical treatments, the theory underpinning their mode of action is either not yet understood, is misunderstood or is plain wrong, yet this is not important if a treatment is effective or ineffective. However, because explanatory trials have traditionally fitted into the basic science research paradigm this may have resulted in funding problems for pragmatic trials (Tunis et al., 2003).

In conclusion, pragmatic trials are more likely to be policy and practitioner relevant than explanatory or mechanistic studies. The latter are important to inform the development of effective interventions; however, the pragmatic study is crucial to evaluate an intervention in a 'real world' setting. Clearly some pragmatic trials share attributes of explanatory trials. If we were evaluating a new treatment in a pragmatic setting then taking blood samples or other biological measurements would usefully add value to the study by enabling us to understand better some of the mechanisms underpinning the intervention. By doing this we may be able to inform future research on how to improve an intervention so that it works even better or, conversely, we may be able to explain why an intervention has failed to work.

Trials can have poor external validity. The challenge for trialists is to minimise this whilst retaining the scientific rigour of their study design. Alternatives to trials, whilst purporting to have addressed the problem of poor external validity, run the risk of obtaining the wrong answer. It is better to be right about some people than wrong about everyone.

7.13   Key points

- Pragmatic trials are essential for addressing practice and policy questions.
- They can address some of the external validity problems of mechanistic trials.
- They need some careful design to avoid post-randomisation bias.

8
Designs to Deal with Participant Preference

8.1   Background

Randomisation equalises characteristics of participants between the two or more randomised groups, but it does not deal with people's hopes and treatment expectations. In open trials the participant is informed of treatment assignment, which can lead to psychological expectations and introduce bias. A key source of this potential bias within a trial is the role of participants' preferences. When presented with different interventions many participants will 'prefer' one of the alternatives. These preferences can introduce bias if one of the treatment options is only available within the context of randomised trial. If, for example, 50 per cent of those being recruited to a trial of A versus B prefer intervention A, and this is only available within the trial, then they are likely to consent to participate. However, half of those 50 per cent of participants preferring A will be disappointed as they will be allocated to treatment B. If participants are randomised to an intervention that they do not want they may consciously or unconsciously perform less well in the outcome measures, in the knowledge that there was a preferable alternative.

8.2   Theoretical effect of preferences

In theory, preferences can affect outcome. In Table 8.1 we show how this may occur. Let us assume 200 participants are randomised in a trial: 100 participants prefer treatment A and the remainder have no preference. Let us also assume that the intervention has no intrinsic effect and that both groups should score 10 on their pre-test scores, but their preferences affect their post-test scores. Those who prefer and receive intervention A score 20 per cent greater at post-test than those who are 'indifferent' and

Table 8.1:   Theoretical impact of preferences

	Intervention A N = 100	Intervention B N = 100
Number with preference for A (mean score)	50 (12)	50 (8)
Indifferent	50 (10)	50 (10)
Average score	11	9

receive treatment A. In contrast, those who prefer intervention A but are allocated to intervention B feel demoralised and do not perform as well on their post-test, and only score 8 points. The table illustrates this possibility. Despite the intervention having no intrinsic effects, in this theoretical example we could conclude that intervention A is more effective than intervention B.

8.3   Accounting for preferences

One approach to dealing with preferences is to *ask* for the participants' preferences. We can randomise the 'indifferent' participants and exclude from the randomisation participants with strong preferences who could bias the trial (Brewin and Bradley, 1989). This method, called the 'patient preference design', comprehensive cohort or Brewin–Bradley approach, requires that the non-randomised groups are also followed up to inform policy and practice with respect to what happens to people who receive the intervention that they desire.

One problem with this approach is that it may reduce the external validity of the study. Another problem with the approach concerns the statistical analysis of the 'preference' arms. These groups have been selected by the patients themselves and bias can result. For example, an RCT of an RCT by Luellen and colleagues showed that there were biases between the non-randomised and the randomised groups (Luellen et al., 2005).

Advocates of preference designs argue that, by following up the choices of preference participants, we can gain valuable information about the effects of the intervention on those who exercise their preference, albeit in an observational or non-randomised fashion. For example, a preference design used by Henshaw and colleagues compared the effectiveness of surgical versus medical termination of unwanted pregnancies (Henshaw et al., 1993). In the randomised arms of the study no difference in effectiveness between the two approaches was observed; however, in the preference arms it was noted that women who preferred the surgical approach lived much greater distances from the hospital than

> ### *Box 8.1*:   Evidence for preference effects in education
>
> In an RCT of 454 undergraduate psychology students Luellen et al. (2005) tested the notion that participants choosing their intervention would have different effect size scores from those randomised to their intervention. The design was as follows: students were randomised into two groups. In one group they were then re-randomised to either maths training or vocabulary training. In the other group they chose maths or vocabulary training. In the randomised comparison those getting maths training scored 3.92 points better than those receiving vocabulary training, but in the choice group the students scored 4.65 points greater. The exercise of choice biased the effectiveness of training upwards.

women who opted for the medical termination. In health policy terms the results indicated that both treatments should be made available to women, but in a rural community there should be greater provision of surgical facilities as this was the preferred option for women having to travel distances because it involved fewer visits to the hospital than medical termination.

Another variation of the preference design is to use the preferences of the practitioner (for example, doctor or teacher). In a trial evaluating the effects of an orthopaedic physician, where a patient's referring GP had no preference regarding whether the patient was seen by an orthopaedic surgeon or physician the patient was allocated by alternation (Leigh-Brown et al., 2001); where a patient's GP had a preference the patient was seen by the preferred clinician.

Whilst accepting that only randomising indifferent participants will eliminate preference biases, critics of the preference approach doubt that the effort of following up people who exercise a preference is worthwhile (Cooper et al., 1997). This is because observed treatment effects in the non-randomised groups will be confounded due to selection bias, which will render the results uninterpretable.

A randomised trial of a preference design tested the effects on participant recruitment to a trial (Cooper et al., 1997). In this trial of treatments for menorrhagia, women were randomised to take part in either a preference trial or in an ordinary trial. The results of this study showed that the preference trial had more participants due to the inclusion of women in the preference arms but, importantly, recruitment to the randomised arms was neither enhanced nor reduced. The authors concluded

Treatment A	Treatment B
Prefer A	Prefer B
No preference	No preference
Sum of effects	Sum of effects

Figure 8.1:   Composition of participants for two alternative interventions

that, in this instance, an ordinary non-preference design might have been better, with the extra resources devoted to following up the preference participants used to recruit more to the randomised arms.

In Figure 8.1 we illustrate the composition of patients who in real life are offered two alternatives: intervention A or intervention B. Those that do not have a treatment preference are the indifferent participants and are arbitrarily assigned to one treatment or the other, whilst those with a preference are allocated to the treatment they prefer. In a pragmatic trial we would like to know the sum of the effectiveness of treatment of those who do not have a treatment allocation preference and those that would prefer a given treatment. The Brewin–Bradley design attempts to provide some of this information. However, it fails to do this in an unbiased manner due to the selection effects of the participants who choose their treatment.

8.4   Fully randomised preference design

An alternative to the preference approach is to adopt a fully randomised preference design (Torgerson et al., 1996). Usually some participants have a preference but because they cannot have the new treatment without taking part in the trial they are willing to consent to randomisation. If these preferences are recorded before randomisation, then one can estimate the effect of the intervention among participants without a preference but also among those with a preference.

Figure 8.2 shows the composition of the randomised population in a normal randomised trial. We can potentially have six subgroups in a two-armed trial. Normally the largest preference group contains those who prefer the novel intervention as those who prefer the usual intervention do not usually consent to go into the trial; they can get what they prefer by not going into the trial. However, some people, despite having a preference for the usual intervention, will still allow themselves to be randomised.

Treatment A
Prefer A
Prefer B
No preference
Sum of effects

Treatment B
Prefer B
Prefer A
No preference
Sum of effects

Figure 8.2:   Composition of participants in a fully randomised preference design

For example, in a randomised trial of a physiotherapy intervention the following groups of participants were produced:

(a) indifferent participants allocated to physiotherapy;
(b) indifferent participants allocated to standard care;
(c) participants preferring physiotherapy who were allocated to receive it;
(d) participants preferring physiotherapy who were allocated to standard care (Klaber-Moffett et al., 1999).

Note, in this instance there were no patients who preferred standard care who consented to randomisation. Using this *fully randomised preference design* the trialists demonstrated that the treatment was effective across the different preference groups and appeared to have been unaffected by patient preference. Indeed, the study showed the treatment was equally effective among those who preferred the treatment and were allocated to receive it as it was among the indifferent participants. In contrast, a similar approach was used in a trial of health visitors and this trial showed a marked effect on treatment satisfaction by initial treatment preference (Clement et al., 1998), although in this study preference was asked after randomisation (Clement, personal communication).

In contrast to the back pain study, where there appeared to be no interaction between preference and outcome, let us consider another musculoskeletal trial, this time looking at the effects of preference within an intervention aimed at alleviating neck pain (Klaber-Moffett et al., 2005). In this study participants were presented with two treatment options: usual care consisting of between five and ten physiotherapy treatments or brief intervention which was conducted as a one-off treatment session to teach the patient to 'self-treat' using principles of cognitive behavioural therapy. In contrast with the back pain study participants exhibited preferences for both treatment groups. Consequently there were six treatment groups:

(a) indifferent randomised to standard care;
(b) indifferent randomised to brief intervention;
(c) preferred standard care and randomised to standard care;
(d) preferred standard care and randomised to brief intervention;
(e) preferred brief intervention and randomised to brief intervention;
(f) preferred brief intervention and randomised to standard care.

Figure 8.3 shows the main results: among the indifferent participants standard care resulted in better outcomes relative to the brief intervention. Remember in the indifferent group, patient preferences are eliminated so any difference between the groups should be the 'true' treatment effect unaffected by preference. The results among the subgroup of patients who had a preference for standard care were similar, but note that those who were randomised to brief intervention actually got slightly worse. The final group, those who preferred brief intervention, produced the most interesting result. In this group we can see the direction of effect was reversed. Patients who preferred brief intervention but were allocated to standard care actually did worse than those who received brief intervention. This was despite us knowing that, in the absence of preferences, standard care was the superior treatment. This trial, therefore, shows that preferences can reverse treatment effects. If participants' preferences had

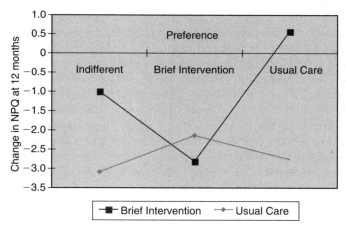

Figure 8.3:   Preference results of neck pain trial
Source: Klaber-Moffet et al.

not been ascertained then we would have concluded that standard care was most effective and all patients should be offered it. However, we now can advise clinicians that patients who have no preference or who want standard care should be offered this treatment; however, those who express a desire for the brief intervention should get this.

The fully randomised preference approach has not been widely used. However, a number of trials have started to use this approach and Table 8.2 describes some of the studies that have elicited preference from participants before they are randomised.

The table shows eliciting patients' preferences before randomisation has been used in a number of studies, primarily musculoskeletal interventions. Asking preferences prior to randomisation is probably the most robust solution to controlling for the impact of patient preferences; however, it is not the complete answer. Participants who have a very strong preference for standard or usual care will probably still refuse randomisation. It is likely, therefore, that those who have a preference for the intervention they would receive *outside* the trial represent a subset of that preference group and will tend to represent the milder end of the preference spectrum. Consequently if the novel intervention is found to be effective and is adopted, thereby completely displacing the older treatment, we will never be completely confident that the intervention will be effective among those who preferred the former usual care.

8.5   Pre-randomised consent or Zelen's method

Another approach to dealing with the potential biases due to patient preference is to use the randomised consent or Zelen's design (Zelen, 1979).

Table 8.2:   Published examples of trials using the fully randomised preference design

Reference	Trial description	Effect of preference
Adamson et al., 2005	Treatment for alcohol dependence	No
Carr et al., 2006	Exercise for low back pain	No
Johnson et al., 2007	Exercise for low back pain	Yes
Kitchener et al., 2006	Surgery for urinary incontinence	Not stated
Klaber-Moffett et al., 1999	Exercise for low back pain	No
Klaber-Moffett et al., 2005	Treatments for neck pain	Yes
Salter et al., 2006	Acupuncture for neck pain	No
Sherman et al., 2005	Yoga for low back pain	Not stated
Thomas et al., 2004	Treatment for shoulder pain	No

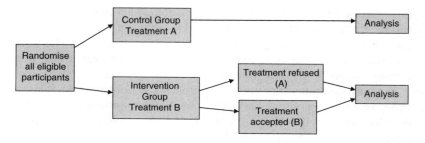

Figure 8.4:   Zelen's single consent method

Zelen's method often provokes strong reactions among researchers because participants are not asked their consent to be randomised. Potential participants for a trial are identified and then randomised without their knowledge. Participants are only asked for their consent to treatment *after* randomisation (Torgerson and Roland, 1998). There are two versions of Zelen's method: the single consent design and the double consent method.

In the single consent method (Figure 8.4) participants are randomised and consent sought from those allocated to the novel treatment. Those refusing consent are then given the standard treatment. This is considered ethical because access to the new treatment is only allowed through participation in the trial. Importantly, however, in this trial design ITT analysis is used: thus, participants are included for analytical purposes in their originally assigned groups.

It is important, however, that intention to treat (ITT) analysis should be used in Zelen's method. All people who refuse treatment should be retained in their original group for analytical purposes. Failure to do so will result in selection bias. In a review of Zelen's method as used in health care, out of 51 trials included in the review, fifteen (29 per cent) trials failed to use ITT analysis (Adamson et al., 2006).

In the double consent method participants allocated to either treatment can refuse the allocated treatment and obtain unhindered access to the other intervention. An example of this is a study by Sinclair and colleagues (2005). In this education trial, students were

> randomly assigned to the treatment or control group prior to the process of obtaining permission using a stratified sampling procedure. (Sinclair et al., 2005)

Zelen first proposed the single consent method for ethical reasons in that it avoids the disappointment of patients who are allocated to the control treatment and makes the process of obtaining consent for the novel treatment easier. For example, one trial that attempted to use Zelen's method for ethical reasons was an evaluation of Extracoporeal Membrane Oxygenation (ECMO) for premature infants or babies with pulmonary hypertension (O'Rourke et al., 1989). The reason the trialists, in this instance, felt Zelen's method was appropriate was because in such circumstances those consenting, the parents, would be suffering acute anxiety because of their child's condition. Clearly, because of randomisation, half of all parents would be disappointed as their child would receive standard care, which was known to have very high mortality and morbidity rates. The trialists, therefore, felt that it was more ethical *not* to ask for consent to randomise and *only* seek consent from those randomised to the ECMO group. This trial of ECMO did not actually recruit sufficient participants to test the hypothesis that it would improve survival. Interestingly, the trial that eventually did prove the benefit of ECMO used conventional randomisation (i.e., asking parents before randomisation for their consent) (Field et al., 1996). Indeed, a qualitative study of ECMO parents of the possibility of using Zelen's method for ethical reasons found that most parents would have preferred to have been told and given their consent although many in the intervention group did not realise that they could have been allocated to the control treatment (Snowden et al., 1997).

Because participants in the control group do not know about the trial (for the single consent version) this allows Zelen's method to form an alternative to the patient preference design. Some screening trials use Zelen's method as this produces a pragmatic estimate of the effectiveness of a screening programme. For example, in a randomised controlled trial of bone density screening, women were randomised to be invited to attend screening or to act as controls. One year later both groups were followed up to ascertain whether screening had had an adverse effect on quality of life and whether those in the screened group were more likely to be using HRT (Torgerson et al., 1997). Similarly, several trials of colorectal cancer screening have used Zelen's method. Hardcastle and colleagues, for example, identified a section of the male population within a UK city and randomised them into two groups (Hardcastle et al., 1996). One group was screened for colorectal cancer whilst the other was not. Both groups were then followed up via cancer registries to assess whether screening reduced the incidence of colorectal cancer. The trial showed that screening reduced bowel cancer by 30 per cent. In screening evaluations participants who are allocated to screening can, and do, refuse consent to being screened (typically between 30–40 per cent of participants). This might be seen as a disadvantage of the design as it introduces dilution bias. As approximately a third of the population do not receive the intervention this will weaken or dilute any apparent benefit of screening. However, the estimate of effect will be pragmatic and more useful to policy-makers than if we had designed a trial whereby 100 per cent of the participants in the intervention group were screened. Such a trial, with a 100 per cent uptake, will not reflect the costs and benefits of introducing screening to the general population, as no routine screening programme (e.g., breast screening) obtains a screening uptake exceeding 80 per cent.

Zelen's method can be controversial, ethically, when it is associated with individually randomised trials. In group, cluster or class randomised trials Zelen's method is routinely used with little controversy, despite members of the group not giving individual consent to be randomised.

Zelen's method is not without its scientific drawbacks (Torgerson, 2001b). If sufficient numbers of participants refuse their treatment allocation then unacceptable treatment dilution can occur. This is made worse if participants swap treatment arms (i.e., in the double consent design). If they refuse the novel treatment and receive the standard treatment then the dilution is greater. In a review of cancer trials that used Zelen's method, Altman and colleagues found the refusal rate among patients randomised to the novel treatment ranged between 10–36 per cent with an average of 18 per cent (Altman et al., 1995). Therefore, not asking consent can introduce substantial dilution bias, which can undermine any treatment effect and increase the probability of a Type II error. On the other hand, a more recent review of Zelen's method, mainly in non-cancer trials, found that cross-over rates were not too onerous, with a median of about 9 per cent (Adamson et al., 2006). In the only example we are aware of in a non-health care setting (education) non-acceptance after randomisation was 15 per cent (Sinclair et al., 2005). This weakens the power of the study. Also with Zelen's method differential attrition is more likely, which can introduce bias.

8.6 Regression discontinuity and randomisation

Sometimes it is not possible to randomise individuals that have some measurable characteristic. It might be considered unethical, for instance, to randomise patients with hypertension to a placebo. Or we might be unable to randomise children who have achieved a test score below a certain threshold not to attend a summer school (Jacob and Lefgren, 2004). As noted previously, we could evaluate these interventions

Box 8.2: **Evidence for Zelen's method**

Adamson and colleagues (2006) undertook a methodological review and searched for all health care trials that had used Zelen's method between 1990 and April 2005. They found only 58 trials that had used the method. The majority (45) used the single consent design. Most used the method to avoid biases associated with patients knowing about the alternative treatment (e.g., Hawthorne effects, resentful demoralisation, avoidance of contamination), rather than as an aid to participant recruitment. Cross-over rates were modest (9 per cent). The areas where they were used included: screening; surgery; drugs; service configuration; and education (in a health context). Few trials (4) explicitly included a cross-over factor in their sample size calculation. Intention to treat, as recommended by Zelen, was used in the majority of trials although in a significant minority (26 per cent) it was not.

using a regression discontinuity design, whereby we follow up a cohort of participants including those who are ineligible for the intervention and then look to see if there is a break in the slope of the regression line of pre-treatment scores against post-treatment scores. We could strengthen this design, however, by including a randomised trial for those for whom it is still possible to randomise. Such an approach could be done as follows. Those participants that are above (or below) a threshold in an identified cohort of participants receive the intervention. Those who fall below (or above) the threshold are randomised into two groups – the novel or usual intervention. This design has the advantage that we can note whether or not the intervention is effective among a lower risk population. We can also estimate the effectiveness of the intervention in the high risk group, where we cannot randomise. Finally, it also controls for the possible problem in the regression discontinuity design of a natural break or change coinciding with the choice of threshold.

8.7 Discussion

Participant preference can lead to bias in trials. Ignoring the role of preference on outcome can lead to concluding something is effective, when it is not, or the reverse. The simplest and, in our view, most robust method of dealing with this is to measure preference as a covariate at baseline: that is, to ask the participants if they have a preference. By doing this the potential bias of the preference can be quantified and incorporated into the analysis. Failure to ask about and measure preferences does not mean that they will disappear – the result will be a potentially biased analysis if preference *does* have an effect. This approach is a partial solution to the problem of preferences because, as noted previously, it will not deal with strong preferences for usual care or cope with ethical barriers to allocation. Consequently we do need to consider the use of other designs.

There are alternative methods for dealing with preference effects. One is to use Zelen's approach, another may be to use a trial design in combination with the regression discontinuity method. The choice of the different approaches will depend upon a combination of the research question, outcomes and the practicalities or ethical impact of the choice of design. An alternative to these approaches that may also deal with participants' preferences is the use of cluster or group randomisation. In the next chapter we describe and discuss this type of trial design.

8.8   Key points

- Trials can produce biased results because of the operation of participants' preferences through such effects as resentful demoralisation.
- One way to examine the impact of preferences is to ascertain pre-treatment preferences and use these as a factor when interpreting or analysing the results (fully randomised preference design).
- In some circumstances prior randomisation before consent is appropriate and this may eliminate the bias due to preference effects.

9
Cluster Randomised Controlled Trials

9.1 Background

The unit of random allocation usually takes one of two forms: individual or cluster. In previous chapters we have considered randomised trials where *individuals* are randomised to one of the comparator groups. A *cluster* trial, sometimes known as a group or place randomised trial, randomises groups of individuals to the relevant trial arms. Thus, for example, classes or schools become the unit of allocation rather than individual students, or hospital wards or GPs form the unit of allocation rather than individual patients. Geographical areas might form a cluster: some parts of a country, for example, might be allocated to a preventative strategy for malaria or the implementation of a new teaching curriculum. If, for practical reasons, we want to use an intervention at certain times, then *time* can form the cluster unit of allocation. For instance, we might want to evaluate a new piece of equipment or a new service, and make this available during some time periods and remove it during others. A study to look at the use of advocates to advise women at risk of partner abuse could take the form of a cluster trial using week of antenatal appointment as the unit of allocation. The weeks in a year would be randomised; the advocate would be present for half of the weeks and not available for the other half. The use of cluster randomised trials to evaluate non-drug treatments means that in health care research the use of the method is increasing in popularity (Bland, 2004).

9.2 Advantages and disadvantages of cluster allocation

Cluster trials have a number of advantages over individually randomised studies. Sometimes cluster randomisation is the only feasible method of doing a trial. For example, it may only be feasible to implement a new curriculum at the school level. Therefore, a randomised trial evaluating the curriculum would need to randomise some schools to adopt the new curriculum while others would be allocated to continue with the existing curriculum. Cluster randomisation also avoids, or reduces, the risk of 'contamination' between the intervention group and the control group. Contamination occurs when those who are exposed to the intervention transfer some of the knowledge to the control group (Torgerson, 2001a). This will 'dilute' any intervention effects and make it more difficult to show a difference between the groups. For example, in order to evaluate a 'problem solving' method of learning, children could be individually randomised to intervention or control group, but those allocated to the control group could be 'contaminated' by their friends or peers in the intervention group. If this is thought to be a genuine possibility children could be randomised by school, which will greatly reduce the risk of such contamination. Guideline evaluation or medical education trials typically use cluster allocation. If we want to evaluate two methods of educating doctors to manage patients with depression we would randomise doctors and evaluate the impact of the education at the level of the patient. It is inconceivable that we could evaluate a medical education approach by asking the clinicians to apply their new knowledge to a random half of their patients. On the other hand, patients can be individually randomised to see a clinician, randomised to receive or not receive additional training. That said, this approach is likely to be impractical for a number of reasons, not least in terms of patient consent.

Potential contamination of the control group is an important reason for using cluster allocation. For instance a study by Steptoe and colleagues (1999) used a cluster design to evaluate the effect of behavioural counselling among adults with an increased risk of coronary heart disease. Although not stated, they presumably used cluster allocation to prevent contamination between the control and intervention groups. They may also have used the design to avoid resentful demoralisation among those participants allocated to the control group.

Cluster trials have a number of drawbacks. First, they require larger sample sizes of participants than individually randomised trials; typically, between 50 per cent and 200 per cent more participants are required because the standard statistical methods used for analysis and power calculation assume that outcomes for individuals within a trial have no relationship with the outcomes of others within the trial. In a cluster trial this is usually not the case. If we randomise classes of children the outcomes of children within any given class are going to be more similar to each other than to those of children in another class. This is because children of similar characteristics are often selected into a class, and they are all taught by the same teacher in the same environment. This correlation between individuals within a cluster is known as the intracluster correlation coefficient (ICC). When we undertake a power calculation to determine how large our trial needs to be (see later) we take this ICC into account in our calculation. When the ICC is 0 then the sample size is equivalent to that of an individually randomised trial; however, the ICC is typically larger than this, which will affect the sample size estimate. The reasons for this are discussed later. Cluster trials also require more sophisticated statistical techniques to deal with the multilevel characteristics of the data. The analytical and sample size issues of cluster trials are widely discussed elsewhere. Most methodological texts on cluster randomisation discuss these issues at length (e.g., Donner and Klar, 2000; Murray, 1998).

A more important issue, not covered at all in the main methodological texts on cluster trials, concerns design biases which can introduce selection bias after randomisation. As noted earlier, sophisticated statistical analyses cannot rescue a poorly designed and executed trial, and this applies particularly to cluster randomised trials.

The first bias that cluster trials are prone to is biased recruitment (Puffer et al., 2003; Farrin et al., 2005). Many cluster trials first recruit the clusters, then randomise and *finally* recruit the participants: such an approach invites bias. The allocation is usually known to those recruiting the participants, so it can be selective, which introduces post-randomisation selection bias. To avoid the possibility of recruitment bias, potential participants within a cluster must ideally be identified in advance of randomisation.

Another potential problem, not peculiar to cluster trials, is the practice of post-randomisation exclusion. Like consent bias, this relates to lack of blinding by the person applying the inclusion and exclusion criteria. For example, Jellema and colleagues (2005) undertook a cluster randomised trial of an intervention to train family doctors to treat back pain. The intervention group recruited 17 per cent more patients than the control group – suggesting recruitment bias – but they also excluded 14 per cent of patients in the intervention group after allocation compared with only 3 per cent of the control group. This differential recruitment and exclusion *may not* have introduced selection bias; however, we cannot be sure, and this uncertainty undermines the credibility of the study.

The next problem with cluster trials relates to dilution bias. Because participants are often allocated without their consent all the problems of Zelen's method can be visited upon the cluster design. Dilution effects can be likely, as some participants may refuse consent to the allocated treatment. For example, in a trial testing the effectiveness of childhood accident prevention through a process of education and offer of safety measures such as stair gates, 25 per cent of the treatment group refused the intervention (Kendrick et al., 1999). Consequently, in that trial any intervention effects were diluted by 25 per cent.

In order to improve the quality of cluster trials participants should be identified before the cluster randomisation which can avoid both recruitment bias and dilution effects. If, in the study by Kendrick et al. (1999) the families had been identified, and consent obtained *before* randomisation, most of the 25 per cent of participants who would go on to refuse the intervention would be identified at this stage and excluded, thereby reducing dilution effects. Prior identification also avoids recruitment bias and differential application of inclusion/exclusion criteria.

Cluster trials are more difficult to undertake rigorously than individually randomised trials, although many of their problems can be avoided with a little care. In a methodological review of cluster trials published in three leading medical journals Puffer and colleagues found evidence for bias in nearly 40 per cent of the studies identified (Puffer et al., 2003). Many of these biases were due to unconcealed allocation, which caused differential recruitment to trial arms. Even among trials that recruited participants before randomisation there was some evidence of differential exclusion.

Finally, a two-cluster trial is not a trial at all. Several clusters, at least, per arm are needed to allow balance of cluster level covariates: the more clusters the better. However, as a general rule there should be at least four clusters per arm (i.e., eight for a two arm trial) to allow any chance of cluster level covariation to be balanced out (Murray, 1998) and some authors recommend at least seven per arm (Donner and Klar, 2000).

9.3   Assessment of outcomes

The methods for collecting outcomes can differ in a cluster randomised controlled trial compared with an individually randomised trial. Participants can be identified at pre-test, measured, and then re-tested at some future date, as is the case for an individually randomised trial. A cluster trial may pre- and post-test on different individuals. We might, for example, measure outcomes on a random sample of cluster members before we randomise clusters and then at a future date take another random sample of cluster members on which to measure post-test outcomes. It is quite possible that completely different participants are measured at pre- and post-test. In some cases it is not possible to follow up pre-test participants; consequently, we can only measure the success of our programme at post-test. For example, we might want to look at the impact of an education programme for breast-feeding among women giving birth in various labour wards. We might measure the breast-feeding prevalence at baseline among women leaving the various hospitals to enable us to use these data to either stratify the randomisation and/or to use the data as a covariate in the statistical analysis (this would give us more power – see later). A year later we would then measure the breast-feeding prevalence among another group of women admitted to the labour wards and then compare the twelve-month differences between the labour wards which were allocated to the educational intervention and those which were not, adjusting for baseline breast-feeding prevalence.

Another reason we might do this is if the pre-test has a potential training effect on the post-test, which might occur in an educational trial. Although this would affect both groups equally as it is a randomised trial, if we only have one validated form of the test this might increase the chances of the test having a ceiling problem. Consequently we might take a random sample of children and give them the baseline test and use the other children to take the post-test. In some circumstances this may also increase the statistical power.

If this approach is adopted it must be emphasised that one should obtain a random sample of participants at both pre- and post-test – if participants are chosen on some characteristic, such as ease of contact, then this will introduce selection bias. Like randomisation, random selection should be done by someone masked to the study hypothesis, the participants' characteristics and the initial group allocation.

9.4   Evidence for bias in cluster trials from a systematic review

In certain substantive areas both cluster and individual randomisation have been used. One area is in the use of hip protectors (Hahn et al., 2005). Figure 9.1 shows a plot of effect sizes from a systematic review of randomised trials of hip protectors. In the figure the trials divide into cluster randomised studies or individually randomised trials. With the exception of one study all the cluster trials have severe methodological flaws and all show an impressive benefit of using hip protectors. This contrasts with the individually randomised trials, which collectively show no benefit of hip protectors. One explanation for the differences in outcomes between the trials is that the individually randomised studies

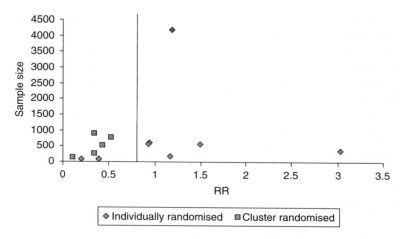

Figure 9.1:   Cluster and individually randomised trials of hip protectors
Source: Hahn et al., 2005.

are largely of better quality than the cluster trials. Cluster trials require larger sample sizes, more sophisticated statistical analysis and they are more prone to post-randomisation biases.

9.5   Alternative to cluster randomisation

An alternative to using a cluster design in many instances is to remain with the individually randomised method and compensate for the dilution effects of contamination by inflating the sample size (Torgerson, 2001a). Let us suppose, for example, that there is some contamination of the control group which will potentially dilute the treatment effect. Steptoe and colleagues undertook a cluster randomised trial of counselling for cardiovascular risk factors (Steptoe et al., 1999). To detect a difference of 9 per cent in smoking prevalence using individual allocation would have required 1282 participants for 90 per cent power. However, because cluster allocation was used 2000 participants were needed due to loss in power through randomising by cluster. Individually randomising 2000 participants would have given 90 per cent power to show a 7 per cent difference in smoking prevalence, which would have allowed 20 per cent of the control group to have been 'contaminated' by the intervention. The question arises: is it really the case that the intervention patients will be able to deliver the treatment to control participants as effectively as health care professionals and contaminate 20 per cent of their fellow patients? However, contamination of control participants would have to exceed 30 per cent in order for a cluster trial to be more efficient for a given sample size than the individually randomised design (Torgerson, 2001a). In the Steptoe study a difference in smoking prevalence was observed, but this was not statistically significant: had they used individual randomisation, and had the same difference been observed, then this would have been statistically significant.

An example of an individually randomised trial that was originally intended to be a cluster design was a study by Spencer and colleagues (2005). In this trial students were randomised to receive a financial incentive to improve their academic performance. The trialists initially wanted to randomise by school to avoid contamination; however, the funder and schools did not like this approach, as no students in schools allocated to the control group would receive an incentive. Consequently the trialists allocated by individual but put into place conditions to lessen the threat of contamination. Thus, teachers were not informed of group allocation to avoid possible differential teacher effects on the students. In addition, siblings were randomised to the same group. Interestingly, despite the hypothesised threat of contamination there were statistically significant improvements in the intervention group compared with the control group (Spencer et al., 2005). The authors randomised 534 participants. Now let us suppose that they had retained their original design and randomised by school. If we assume 25 participants per school and an ICC of 0.01, then the authors would have needed 662 participants for the same power (i.e., a 24 per cent increase), or conversely the power of their achieved sample size would have been reduced.

Trialists should always think very carefully about whether to use a cluster design or not and, if possible, they should select individual randomisation or possibly a mixture of both designs.

9.6 Partial split-plot design

It is possible to test for possible contamination by combining cluster randomisation with individual randomisation in a so-called split-plot design. In this design, we randomise at the cluster level, and then randomise at the individual level in half of the clusters. We can then undertake a within-cluster analysis and a between-cluster analysis. The power consequences of losing some participants in the intervention cluster to the control group are relatively modest, as the main driver of statistical power in a cluster trial is the number of clusters rather than the number of individuals. It can be a useful approach to test for contamination effects.

A health care trial that used a split-plot approach found no 'contamination' effects. In this trial of a lifestyle intervention among people at high risk of cardiovascular disease by Wood and colleagues (1994), practices were randomised as clusters, but within the active treatment group, half of the participants were randomised to act as 'internal' controls. Despite fairly intensive lifestyle interventions, 'contamination' of control participants registered within the same practices does not appear to have occurred.

In a trial to evaluate the role of praise to enhance students' performance Craven and colleagues randomised in clusters, and within the intervention clusters they also randomised at the student level. In the intervention group the teachers were asked to increase the amount of praise given when a student answered questions correctly or produced good work. Within the intervention class, however, it was difficult for the teacher to withhold praise from the control students. Consequently, significant effects of contamination that diluted the effectiveness of the intervention were observed within the individually randomised participants (Craven et al., 2001). Therefore, the sensible analysis was to compare individuals in the intervention group who were praised with those in the cluster controls who were not, rather than with the individual controls.

Nevertheless, unless the threat of contamination is overwhelming, such as in the previous example, it is best to avoid using a cluster design. Indeed, if contamination is a perceived threat it is best to test this in a pilot trial before finally settling on a cluster design.

A variation on the split-plot design has been proposed whereby within each cluster some participants are randomised to the opposite treatment (Borm et al., 2005). In a cluster trial comparing interventions A and B, most of the participants in clusters randomised to intervention A would receive treatment A (e.g., 80 per cent) whilst most of those allocated to intervention B would receive treatment B. Some participants, however, would be allocated to the opposite group. The reasoning behind this is that, because some participants are receiving the opposite treatment, then those who are recruiting individuals to the trial will retain some blinding as to which group their cluster belongs. This should encourage them to recruit similar numbers of participants and avoid recruitment bias, as described earlier. By keeping the numbers of participants within each cluster receiving the opposite treatment it is hoped that the contamination effects will be minimised.

9.7 Conclusions

Cluster randomised trials are essential to evaluate some interventions. There are a number of methodological challenges inherent within the cluster design and consequently these trials can be prone to bias unless careful consideration is given to their drawbacks, and methods are put into place to deal with the biases described previously.

Cluster trials, however, can be undertaken robustly. We need to be aware that all the lessons learned from individually randomised trials are equally applicable to cluster randomised trials. Lack of allocation concealment is widely seen as being a major flaw for individually randomised trials, with many methodological studies supporting this view. The same threat is present for cluster randomised trials. We need to design our studies to avoid this. As noted previously, we should, if possible, identify individual participants before we randomise the clusters. If this is not possible then the person recruiting should be masked to the allocation of the cluster and, if possible, to the research question(s).

Another threat to the cluster design is post-randomisation exclusions which must be undertaken by someone masked to the group allocation. Sample size issues are also a problem. Cluster trials are almost always invariably much larger than individually randomised trials, and sample size calculations need to be used to identify the correct numbers of participants required in the study.

The threat of contamination is widely used as a justification for the use of cluster randomisation. It might be best to test this assumption using a pilot study or accepting some form of contamination and consequently a diluted estimate of effect. Generally it is best, if possible, to use an individual design.

9.8 Key points

- In cluster trials groups of individuals are randomised.
- Cluster trials were first used in education when classes or schools were the unit of allocation.
- They are more prone to post-randomisation biases (such as consent bias) than individually randomised studies.
- They are challenging to do and require specialist skills.

10
Unequal Randomisation

10.1   Background

In RCTs participants are usually allocated in equal numbers to either the control or active arms. There are many instances, however, when it is preferable to allocate more participants to one trial arm compared with the other, i.e. to use unequal allocation. The ratio of group size can be as large as is desired; however, generally it does not exceed 3:1 and more commonly it is 2:1 or 3:2.

Most trials are designed by statisticians to obtain the maximum amount of statistical power. Given a fixed sample size, it is nearly always true that the largest chance of detecting, as statistically significant, a difference between the two groups will occur with groups of the same size. Placing more participants in one group relative to the other reduces the chance of observing a difference, although the power of the statistical test does not greatly decline unless the ratio exceeds 3:1. For instance, if we have a trial of 300 participants with approximately equal numbers, then this might give us 80 per cent power to detect a certain difference. However, if we allocate 200 to one group and 100 to the other group we will have 75 per cent power to detect the same difference.

Some researchers believe that unequal allocation is 'unscientific' and may lead to bias. This is untrue. Randomisation of participants assumes that there is a probability that the participant will be entered into one of the groups and this probability has no relationship to the participant characteristics. The probability is usually 50 per cent; however, it can be any other probability we choose (although obviously not 1).

10.2   Different costs of interventions

One of the main reasons for allocating more participants to one group than to another is resource constraints or costs (Torgerson and Campbell,

1997, 2000). For example, Hundley and colleagues allocated more participants to an evaluation of a labour ward run by midwives for resource reasons (Hundley et al., 1994). The ward was only established for the purposes of the trial, and needed to run as closely to full capacity as possible. If equal allocation had been used the ward would have been under-utilised.

One treatment may be more expensive than another treatment. The total cost of the trial can either be reduced, or more participants can be recruited within the same budget by using unequal allocation. For example, the MRC sponsored a trial of paclitaxel for the treatment of ovarian cancer (ICON Group, 2002). The drug was extremely expensive, running into many thousands of pounds per woman for the active therapy. The cost of this trial was reduced by allocating more women to receive the control treatment than to receive the active therapy. Similarly, a trial of colonoscopy for the screening of colorectal cancer used unequal randomisation (along with Zelen's method) in favour of the control group (Atkin et al., 2001; UK Flexible Sigmoidoscopy Screening Trial Investigators, 2002). Indeed, an earlier trial of colorectal cancer screening could have been undertaken with substantially lower costs if unequal allocation in favour of the cheaper, control condition had been used (Hardcastle et al., 1996). Similarly, an RCT of increased police patrolling could have obtained greater statistical power had unequal allocation been used (Sherman and Wiesburd, 1995). In this RCT 150 crime areas were identified as eligible for the study; however, constraints on police resources limited the experimental treatment (increased patrols) to 55 crime spots. The authors randomised 110 areas to allow for an equal allocation ratio, thereby decreasing statistical power. If they had instead allocated on an approximate 1.73:1 ratio (with 55 areas in the intervention group and 95 areas in the control group) the experiment would have obtained a useful increase in both statistical power (from 80 per cent to approximately 88 per cent) and the chances of any observed difference being statistically significant.

In an educational example where statistical power was lost consider the study by Carlton and colleagues (1985) who evaluated a peer tutoring programme. They used a subsample of control students to achieve equal group size:

> Of the 62 students in the control condition, 30 were selected at random to achieve equal group sizes (i.e., n = 30 for all groups). (Carlton et al., 1985)

Unequal randomisation reduces statistical power when the sample size is fixed, but this is simply not the case when the barrier to increased power is the available resource. If an intervention resource is limited we might *increase* the power of the study to detect a smaller difference by increasing the sample size of the alternative group (Table 10.1). Consequently the view that equal allocation is best for statistical power only applies *if the total sample size of the trial is fixed.* If resources are limited then this no longer holds. However, there is a limit to the numbers we can allocate to the larger group and still gain statistical power. From Table 10.1 we can see useful gains are made for ratios of up to 3:1.

A trial that used unequal allocation ratios due to cost pressures was a large randomised trial of hip protectors (Birks et al., 2004). In this trial the study budget had to pay for the cost of hip protectors. To reduce this cost a 2:1 allocation ratio was used. Although the total sample size had to be increased to offset the reduction in power, this enabled the trial to stay within the budget. Another study that encountered a similar issue was a trial of calcium and vitamin D supplementation (Porthouse et al., 2005). Supplements were provided by a pharmaceutical company (at no cost). However, it was necessary for practice nurses to check that the patients had no contraindications to the treatment before giving them the therapy, and this had cost implications. By allocating more participants to the control group, resources to fund the nurses' time were saved. Another example relates to a pilot study of acupuncture (Salter et al., 2006), which was constrained by the fact that the budget was only sufficient for ten acupuncture treatments. By using unequal allocation (2:1) the authors increased their sample size from 20 to 30, which in turn increased the overall power of the study.

A simple and precise method of calculating the allocation ratio for unequal randomisation based on cost is simply the square root of the cost ratio. For example, if the cost of the intervention is four times the cost of the control condition, twice as many participants need to be

Table 10.1:   Effect on detectable difference by increasing size of control group

Size of resource limited group	Size of unlimited group	Total	Detectable difference (%)	Increase in sample size (%)
100	100	200	19	–
100	150	250	18	25
100	200	300	17	50
100	300	400	16	100
100	500	600	15	300

Note: Calculations assume an event rate of 50 per cent in the control group with 80 per cent power and 5 per cent significance.

allocated to the cheaper treatment. Similarly, if the cost of the intervention is nine times the cost of the control condition we will need to allocate using a 3:1 ratio to make the most efficient use of our study budget.

10.3   Learning curve

Another reason for using unequal allocation is to allow more experience of the new technique (Pocock, 1983), which will enable more subgroup analyses to be undertaken. For example, a trial of a surgical intervention will have more power if the effectiveness of surgery is compared when surgeons are deemed to be at the 'top of their learning curve'. A new surgical procedure is generally 'tried out' on a number of patients in a non-randomised evaluation. Such studies do not have to be peer reviewed and are not seen by ethics committees. The surgeons gain experience and patients are randomised only when the surgeons are confident with the technique. By using this approach we do not know how long it takes to train a surgeon in a new technique. If we had randomised from the first patient we could then gauge the length of the learning curve and allow the technique to be exposed to the scrutiny of an ethics committee.

10.4   Review evidence

In their review Dumville et al. (2006a) found very few trials that used unequal randomisation, and resource constraints were not often cited for its use. The most frequently cited reason for its use was for clinicians to gain experience of the novel intervention. Other reasons cited were to

---

Box 10.1:   **Review of unequal allocation**

Dumville and colleagues (2006a) identified a sample of 65 trials that used unequal allocation. Most trials (57 per cent) did not describe the reasons for using unequal allocation. The majority of trials (84 per cent) used an allocation ratio of 2:1 or less. Only 10 per cent of the trials reported cost as the main reason for using unequal allocation. Experience of the new treatment was the most commonly stated reason. It was not clear in some trials whether or not the sample size calculations had taken into account the loss of power due to unequal allocation, with only 22 per cent of the studies giving enough information to ascertain this.

maximise recruitment (some trialists thought recruitment would be easier if participants felt they had a greater than 50:50 chance of receiving one of the treatments), anticipated high drop-out rates from one arm (although unequal allocation would help with the loss of power in this situation, it would not deal with the potential of attrition bias) and ethical reasons (fewer participants will be allocated to the group where there is the greatest anticipated hazard).

In a trial of monetary incentives to improve educational outcomes Spencer et al. (2005) decided to place more participants in the intervention group because the trial funders were reluctant to accept equal allocation:

> The third adjustment involved changing the sampling fracture from a 50/50 split (i.e., equal proportions in the Stipend and Delayed Stipend groups) to a 60/40 split to address the Foundation's concerns to serve as many eligible students as possible. (Spencer et al., 2005)

Allocation ratios favouring the intervention group may enhance recruitment, as participants may be more likely to take part in the trial if they think they have a greater than 50:50 chance of receiving the novel intervention.

10.5   Some possible problems with unequal allocation

It is sometimes necessary to change the allocation ratio part way through the trial. For instance, Porthouse et al. (2005) changed their allocation ratio towards the end of their trial because the predicted cost difference between the two groups was not as great as the actual cost difference found in the trial. Consequently a smaller allocation ratio favouring the control group was more efficient than the ratio adopted at the outset of the trial. If the allocation ratio changes in a trial it is necessary to take this into account in the analysis, otherwise a simple arithmetical phenomenon can introduce bias.

Consider a trial of two treatments that are equivalent in effectiveness (see Table 10.2). In year one, 1000 participants are allocated to treatment A and 2000 participants are allocated to treatment B. In year one 10 per cent of participants in both groups experience an 'event'. In year two of the trial, the allocation ratio is changed so that 1000 are now randomised to each group. If we add the total events and divide by the numbers of participants in the trial, this gives 300 events among 2000 participants in treatment A and 500 events among 3000 participants in treatment B, a higher event rate in treatment B than in treatment A despite no difference in effectiveness between the two treatments.

Table 10.2: Changing allocation ratios part way through the trial

	Year 1 (events)	Year (events)	2 Total
Treatment A	1000 (100)	1000 (100)	300 events (15%)
		1000 (100)	2000 participants
Treatment B	2000 (200)	2000 (200)	500 events (16.7%)
		1000 (100)	3000 participants

Consequently, if the allocation ratio is changed part way through the trial a variable must be included in a regression analysis to control for this. Sometimes authors forget to do this. For example, Bech and colleagues (2007) undertook a randomised trial looking at the effects of caffeine on birth weight. The randomisation ratio appeared to change from 1:1 to an unequal ratio; however, the authors did not describe any adjustment for the change in the ratio in the analysis.

Another problem with unequal allocation is that, as noted above, it may be seen as being 'unscientific'. One of us (DJT) has received referees' comments on a number of grant applications criticising the use of unequal allocation, despite the fact that in all cases this would have saved resources. Indeed, one of the statistical referees for the Porthouse et al. study (2005) stated that they found the allocation ratio (2:1) 'extreme'.

10.6 Conclusions

Equal allocation is the best method of ensuring maximum statistical power, given a fixed total sample size. Sample sizes, however, are rarely fixed, and budgets are rarely open-ended. Consequently, in order to obtain the greatest power from a randomised trial, it is better to use unequal randomisation. For example, in the Hardcastle et al. trial (1996) of bowel cancer screening, the authors would have achieved greater power if more participants had been recruited and allocated in a ratio that favoured the control group. There are other, non-cost, reasons for using unequal allocation, such as monitoring a learning curve, and statistical reasons, such as anticipated unequal variances. Unequal allocation ratios are, however, generally under-used and should be more widely applied.

10.7 Key points

- Unequal allocation is under-used and should be more widely applied because it can deliver a more powerful trial within resource constraints.
- It is sometimes seen, erroneously, as being unscientific.
- Changing the allocation ratio part way through the trial should be accounted for in the analysis.

11
Factorial Randomised Controlled Trials

11.1 Background

The cost effectiveness of a trial can be improved through the use of a factorial design, where we can evaluate two interventions for the 'price' (in terms of sample size) of evaluating a single intervention. A factorial design can also reveal whether or not there is an interaction between two interventions. We can test if intervention A is better than no intervention and whether intervention B is better than no intervention. We can also test if interventions A + B work together in synergy, or are additive, or do not work as well in the presence of each other. However, if we are intent on observing an intervention-by-intervention interaction we need to boost our sample size by a factor of about 4, and consequently reduce the appeal of evaluating 'two interventions for the price of one'. Few factorial trials are powered *a priori* to detect interactions, and whilst interactions are commonly held as an important reason for using a factorial design, they are not usually justified in sample size calculations.

11.2   2 × 2 factorial

The simplest factorial design is a 2 × 2 factorial where we have four groups rather than two. By way of illustration, consider a trial that tested whether individual learning of the highway code was more or less effective than group learning (Gray et al., 1998). The researchers wanted to compare a game based on the highway code with the highway code book, and they did so by undertaking a 2 × 2 factorial. In Table 11.1 we show the four cells in the resulting 2 × 2 table.

In this trial, three distinct hypotheses were tested: (1) Is group learning more effective than individual learning? This is tested by comparing

Table 11.1: Factorial trial of learning the highway code

Individual Highway Code	A
Individual Game	B
Group Highway Code	C
Group Game	D

the groups A + B vs C + D; (2) Is learning by a game more effective than individual learning? This is tested by comparing A + C vs B + D; (3) Is there an interaction between the two styles of learning? First, group learning was found to be no more or less effective than individual learning; second, game-based learning was found to be more effective than the book learning; third, no interaction was found between the two forms of learning, that is, game-based learning did not interact with group learning such that it *only* worked or worked much better when used in groups rather than when used alone. Note, however, this last question was imprecisely addressed due to lack of statistical power to rule out an important interaction term.

Factorial designs are commonly used in educational psychological experiments in particular. They can be particularly valuable in 'unpacking' a complex intervention by allowing us to test the interventions singly or in combination. In the example above, had the researchers randomised children to learn the highway code individually or to play the game in a group, we would have observed a significant effect, but we could not have known whether it was the game or the group learning that was responsible for the increased knowledge of the highway code.

A 2 × 2 factorial is the simplest factorial design. If we want to examine a 'dose response' relationship we can increase the numbers of factors. For example, we might wish to test whether early morning classes in numeracy are effective in improving numeracy abilities with students with learning difficulties and also whether the use of computers is effective in this context, but we are not sure whether one or two extra morning classes a week is the most appropriate. In this instance we could design a 3 × 2 factorial trial (Table 11.2).

There are a number of drawbacks to factorial designs. One problem is their increased complexity, particularly if evaluating drug and non-drug treatments. The process of recruiting participants may be confusing for both researchers and participants, as some participants receive a combination of treatments and some do not.

An advantage of factorial trials is their ability to detect an interaction effect. However, unwanted interactions can be also be a drawback.

Table 11.2:   3 × 2 factorial design

No early morning class and no computer learning	1 hour early morning class with no computer learning	2 × 1 hour early morning classes with no computer learning
No early morning class but access to computer learning in 'normal' maths lessons	1 hour early morning class with computer learning	2 × 1 hour early morning classes with computer learning

Interactions are when a treatment works more effectively in the presence of another intervention or conversely is less effective. For example, in a trial of two drugs for the treatment of low bone mass there appeared to be a negative interaction, that is, the sum of the two treatments was not as great as their individual components (Finkelstein et al., 2003). This is an important finding; however, if the interaction is unexpected and unwanted it will lead to a reduction in the power to detect the main effects of an intervention as we have to analyse the study as two separate trials, which reduces the overall sample size. But, as noted previously, to reliably detect an interaction requires an enormous increase in sample size: consequently few factorial trials are sufficiently powered to detect interaction effects and it is unlikely that even if there are interactions we will have sufficient power to detect these.

11.3   Example of different factorial trials

One area where factorial trials tend to be used is in evaluating different approaches to increasing questionnaire response rates. For example, in a questionnaire survey about the use of HRT and the menopause it was decided to test the relative effectiveness of a lottery or a payment to increase response rates (Roberts et al., 2000). A factorial design was used to test whether a £5 incentive or an entry into a prize draw for £50 had an impact on response rates (Table 11.3).

Note, in this instance the factorial design was also combined with unequal allocation to reduce the cost of the payments. The trial showed that direct payment increased the response rate by 11 per cent, which was statistically significant, whilst the lottery only increased response rates by 5 per cent, which was not.

Another variation on the factorial design is to design a three-armed study where one of the arms does not contain all of the interventions (Table 11.4). In this study design we can evaluate whether A is better

Table 11:3:   Factorial design of incentives trial

	No lottery	Lottery	
£5 payment	£5	£5 plus lottery	N = 125
No payment	Nothing	Lottery	N = 374
	N = 374	N = 374	

Table 11.4:   2 × 2 factorial with untreated control group

	A	B	Control
C	A + C	B + C	Control
D	A + D	B + D	Control

than B and whether C is better than D but also whether these interventions are better than no treatment or usual care.

11.4   Review evidence

In a systematic review McAlister and colleagues (2003) found that the majority of factorial trials (82 per cent) (in cardiac care) were designed for reasons of efficiency, that is, the trial authors wanted to test two or more treatments within the same sample. The review authors noted that interaction tests are notoriously underpowered, and suggested that an interaction ratio greater than 1.25 or less than 0.80 should be considered significant. In a hand search of all health care trials published in December 2000 they found that only 1 per cent were factorial studies (McAlister et al., 2003). Few trials (6 per cent) found statistically significant interactions between the treatments, and in only one of the 44 trials included in the review would this have led to an erroneous conclusion. The authors therefore concluded that the factorial design was safe to use and was an important method of increasing the number of treatments that could be evaluated.

11.5   Analysing factorial trials

Ideally we should treat the data from factorial trials as two separate studies in order to obtain the most power from our sample size. However, if there is an interaction between the two interventions then it may be appropriate to analyse the groups separately. Consequently, the first analysis should use an interaction test, which, if not statistically significant, will give an indication that the assumption of treating the data as two separate trials holds. Factorial trial designs are sometimes used, but not reported as such. For example, a large RCT looking at a health and workplace intervention to improve return to work after illness appeared to use a factorial design with four groups: health intervention; work place intervention; combined interventions; no intervention (Purdon et al., 2006); however, the authors analysed the study as four separate groups.

11.6 Conclusions

A factorial design is a useful and cost-effective method of evaluating different interventions within the same study population. In essence it gives two opportunities of finding an effective intervention. Unfortunately, like unequal allocation, the factorial design is under-used.

11.7 Key points

- Factorial trials enable investigators to evaluate two more treatments within the same sample.
- They are under-used and should be undertaken more widely.

12
Pilot Randomised Controlled Trials

12.1 Background

Pilot studies are usually very helpful precursors to definitive RCTs. Possibly the first educational RCT (Walters, 1931), which looked at the role of counselling among undergraduate students, was later described as an 'introductory experiment' (Walters, 1932). We would now describe this trial as a pilot study. As discussed in a later chapter on recruitment issues, pilots play an invaluable role in helping this aspect of an RCT. However, they also play an important role in other design issues. In this chapter we discuss some of the characteristics of pilot studies and describe how they can be helpful when designing a definitive RCT.

There are two types of pilot study: external pilots and internal pilots. An external pilot study is completed independently of the definitive study, whilst the internal pilot is part of the main study and is treated as a 'run-in' phase of the definitive study (Lancaster et al., 2004).

12.2 How do we define a pilot study?

As noted elsewhere, many trials across the social sciences are tiny and some of these should probably only be considered as pilots for major trials that have yet to be undertaken. A methodological review of health care trials, specifically searching for pilot studies, found no formal definition or description of what constitutes a pilot trial (Lancaster et al., 2004).

Therefore, we propose to define a pilot as a study that is either too small to have a reasonable chance of detecting a minimally important effect size (size of the difference between the groups at post-test), and/or a study that is evaluating an incompletely developed intervention. In terms of effect size we might consider that (as discussed in Chapter 13

Box 12.1:   Review of pilot trials

Lancaster et al. (2004) searched major medical journals in the years 2000–1 for pilot studies. They found 90 studies (2 per cent of all studies) which appeared to be pilot trials. Half of the pilots indicated further studies were needed but only four stated that they were specifically undertaken in preparation for a larger RCT; most of the others were piloting new treatment techniques.

---

on sample size and analysis) the smallest minimal difference that is important is at least half an effect size, and at least a halving or doubling of a dichotomous outcome. Note, however, these differences are on the large side of what we can expect from an effective intervention. Generally, effective interventions, especially if being compared against an active control group, will tend to produce smaller differential effect sizes. Consequently, a descriptive definition of a pilot study might be one that has fewer than about 128 participants when the outcome is a continuous variable. This definition will, however, classify many social science trials as being pilot studies.

The pilot setting may differ from the setting of the definitive trial, and may often be an explanatory type of study. We might undertake a pilot under the best possible circumstances in order to test out the feasibility of the study with the knowledge that if we cannot execute a study under optimum conditions we are unlikely to successfully undertake the definitive trial in less than ideal circumstances. The disadvantage, however, of such an explanatory type of pilot as a precursor to a pragmatic trial, is that its results may be less helpful for planning purposes and we may over-estimate our ability to do the main trial.

12.3   Functions of a pilot study

Obtaining regulatory approval, for example, is a key barrier to the successful start and completion of a trial. A pilot will identify any ethical issues and other potential problems, such as possible breaches of health and safety legislation, which need addressing before either the pilot or the main trial can commence. For example, a pilot study of yoga for low back pain identified an issue with liability insurance, which took a few months to address. Had this issue arisen in the main trial it could have jeopardised participant recruitment.

A pilot is often undertaken with a view to estimating the mean or the standard deviation of a parameter in order to inform the power calculation for the main trial (Browne, 1995; Lancaster et al., 2004; Salter et al., 2006). Sometimes an internal pilot is used to adjust the final sample size of the definitive trial, although it can become problematic if the pilot suggests a sample size smaller than the one originally intended for the main trial. Because any effect size observed in an internal pilot is imprecise due to the relatively small sample size, we may mislead ourselves into contracting the total sample size and increasing the risk of a Type II error. Also, using an internal pilot can increase our Type I error rate, as looking at the results of a pilot trial is tantamount to a preliminary sight of the data, whereas our sample size for our definitive trial is for a single data analysis only. Consequently, it has been recommended that the effect of internal pilots on the sample size should be restricted in the sense that the results could be used to increase the sample size of the definitive trial but not to decrease it (Wittes et al., 1999). Note, if the sample size of the main trial is driven by an estimate from a pilot one should err on the side of caution. This is because any estimate of a parameter from a pilot trial will have a high error value (Browne, 1995), simply because of the relatively small sample size. In contrast, an estimate derived from elsewhere will either be a fixed value, such as that deemed to be of clinical, educational or economic importance and therefore will not have a sampling error component. Even estimates derived from other stochastic data (e.g., estimate from a systematic review) are likely to have smaller error components than an estimate derived from a single small pilot.

A pilot can be used to look at the best ways of collecting outcome information. For example, the UK BEAM pilot (Farrin et al., 2005) experimented with two different methods of collecting cost data: a prospective diary or a retrospective questionnaire, and found that the latter produced better information. Similarly, the pilot also examined the role of two different measures of back pain before settling on one for the main trial.

A pilot is also crucial at identifying the likely recruitment rates that can be expected in the main trial (e.g., Farrin et al., 2005; Salter et al., 2006). This allows the trialists to adjust inclusion/exclusion criteria in order to maximise recruitment for the main trial. The pilot also allows us to identify the likely retention and adherence rates for the study (both of which may lead to an amendment to the sample size for the main trial), and refine our cost estimates of the trial (which will affect any grant costings and help to determine the most efficient allocation).

Refining the intervention, especially a complex intervention, is also a vital component of the pilot. We might, for example, refine the duration and dose of the intervention.

Our choice of randomised design may be influenced by the pilot, and we may decide to radically change our design or our intervention in response to the pilot. The UK BEAM trial design, which was initially a complex multifactorial split-plot design was extensively piloted (Farrin et al., 2005), and as a consequence the cluster level randomisation was dropped; education of primary care clinicians was adopted to boost recruitment; outcome questionnaires were changed; and extra sites were recruited.

12.4   How big should a pilot be?

Sample size calculation for any study is an uncertain science. For a pilot study it is more difficult, especially as part of the function of a pilot is to gather information to inform the sample size. Before commencing a definitive trial we should have identified the difference that either is important to the practitioner, policy-maker, economist or consumer or we should have noted differences from a meta-analysis or an epidemiological study, which can then be used to determine the size of a trial. With respect to a pilot study, we do not intend to power the trial to detect this important difference, as the study will then no longer be a pilot trial. It could be argued that we do not need to undertake a formal sample size calculation; however, this feels somehow 'unscientific'. It may be best to set an indicative sample size, perhaps based on a surrogate measure of outcome, to determine the difference in primary outcome. We might, for example, run a pilot to look at differences in adherence levels between groups. Outcomes for a pilot for the calcium and vitamin D trial (Porthouse et al., 2005) were the proportion of contamination of the control group and differences in falls between the two groups. Contamination (i.e., participants in the control group going out to buy calcium supplements) was important because the main trial's sample size might have needed adjusting for the potential for this. If the contamination was deemed to be excessive then the main trial would not be considered to be feasible. Because the level of contamination was completely unknown, the initial sample size calculations for the calcium and vitamin D pilot were based on differences in falls incidence. Interestingly, the pilot of that trial did not achieve its intended recruitment target. Nevertheless, because of the problems identified in the pilot the main trial actually exceeded its recruitment target (Porthouse et al., 2005).

A minimum sample size that we would recommend for a pilot study is 32. This sample size is the size a study needs to be to enable us to observe a difference of one standard deviation (i.e., one effect size) difference between the two randomised groups with 80 per cent power. This gives it some mathematical justification and if, unexpectedly, the intervention is extremely effective we would have a reasonable chance of observing this. It is important, however, to note that even if we observe such a difference and this is statistically significant, we should still continue with the definitive trial. This is because with such a tiny sample size the estimate will be imprecise, with large confidence intervals, and therefore we will be unsure as to the true effectiveness of the intervention. An exception to this might be if the pilot demonstrates a significant harm of the novel intervention.

An alternative minimum sample size has been suggested as being 30 as this allows a reasonable estimate of a particular parameter, such as the mean or the standard deviation (Browne, 1995). However, one should not use the point estimate of the standard deviation; rather it is better to use the upper 80 per cent confidence interval. This is because, as noted previously, that point estimate, due the small sample size, has a high chance of over-estimating the size of the standard deviation.

12.5   Should a pilot be randomised?

Often pilot studies use before and after pre- and post-test designs without randomisation. For example, a study of hydrotherapy for people with arthritis undertook an external non-randomised controlled trial pilot (Cochrane et al., 2005). For the pilot phase of the study people were recruited by advertisement, the intervention was tested out among these participants, and their symptoms were compared with a similarly recruited control group. Similarly, a pilot study looking at the herbal treatment, black cohosh, for menopausal symptoms also used a before and after design (Pockaj et al., 2004). The justification for using this design in a pilot might be that, given that the pilot will not recruit a sufficient number of participants to observe an important difference between the groups anyway, we might as well put all the pilot participants in the intervention to gain more experience in delivering the treatment. We can obtain some idea of the likely effect size by looking at change scores. Ironically, it is often more difficult to get ethical approval for a pilot RCT than a non-randomised pilot. Consequently many researchers may be tempted to go for the easier and quicker option of getting approval for the scientifically, and arguably ethically, inferior study type. The problem with this is that we lose a lot of very important information by not randomising. For instance, the recruitment rate, which is a vital function of a pilot study, is likely to be incorrectly estimated through a before and after study. Participants have no incentive to refuse recruitment if they know that they will inevitably receive the new intervention if they consent to the study. Consequently the pilot could grossly over-estimate the recruitment rate. We also would have no idea of the retention rate in a non-randomised pilot. Because we are including people who may not consent to be randomised then it is likely they may comply with the intervention differently from those who would consent to participate in an RCT.

In addition, if the pilot study is being used to inform the sample size for the main trial then the estimate from the pilot may be exaggerated. For instance, the pilot by Cochrane and colleagues (2005) observed an effect size of 0.44. They based their sample size for their main study on this estimate. However, the estimate was much larger than the one observed in the definitive RCT, which may have led to their main trial being under-powered. Similarly, the pilot study of black cohosh, which used a before and after design, noted a 50 per cent reduction in menopausal symptoms (Pockaj et al., 2004). A later definitive trial noted an approximate 30 per cent reduction in menopausal symptoms among women taking black cohosh; however, there was no difference compared with the placebo group (Newton et al., 2006). Indeed, the participants in the definitive trial tended to have less severe symptoms than those in the pilot. The reason for this could be that women with the most severe symptoms may have refused possible allocation to placebo and therefore the pilot included women with worse self-reported symptoms. Consequently, any effect was likely to have been exaggerated by regression to the mean effects and change over time. Had a randomised pilot study design been chosen instead it is less likely that these problems would have occurred. Therefore, whilst a non-randomised pilot will provide important information to plan the main study, a randomised pilot provides even more. Furthermore, a randomised pilot, assuming it is published, can usefully add to any meta-analysis of RCTs or its data can be added to the main study.

12.6   Study designs for pilots

Generally the study design for a pilot should be as similar as possible to the anticipated design for the main study, as this allows for all the characteristics of the definitive study to be tested before the main trial is begun. Importantly, if the pilot is very similar to the main trial then it may be possible to incorporate some of the data from the pilot study into the main trial. Consider the UK BEAM pilot as an example (Farrin et al., 2005). In this pilot, the main aims were to test the feasibility of the cluster level randomisation as well as collection of secondary outcome measures.

Within the cluster randomisation, participants were randomised individually to receive manipulation for their back pain, exercise or usual care. The main outcome for the pilot was a back pain disability scale, which remained the main outcome in the definitive study. Consequently, it was possible to include pilot participants in the main study's analysis for the main outcome, and the information on the pilot patients added value to the main trial. In a similar fashion participants taking part in two pilot trials for fracture prevention (hip protectors and calcium supplements) were also included in the main trial (Birks et al., 2004; Porthouse et al., 2005).

On the other hand, some researchers counsel against including external pilot data within the main trial's analysis. Lancaster and colleagues (2004) argue that including an external pilot increases the Type I error rate and can also introduce selection bias. The Type I error rate may be inflated if we undertake two statistical tests: analysing the pilot and again analysing the main trial. This slightly inflated rate would need to be set against the benefits of an increased sample size. In terms of selection bias, inclusion of the pilot data is not likely to bias between trial arms as the groups have been formed by random allocation. Pilot participants, however, may be different from main trial participants in that the inclusion criteria may have been changed. If this is the case then there could be an interaction between the type of participant and the intervention, which may dilute the treatment effect in the main trial. Or the intervention in the pilot may have been incompletely developed so as to appear relatively ineffective, which again may dilute the effectiveness of treatment. The decision about whether or not the pilot participants should be included will depend on the features of the pilot study. For instance we may never formally test differences between the groups in terms of the main outcomes, so the Type I error rate will not apply. For example, the pilots for trials of fracture prevention (i.e., Birks et al., 2004; Porthouse et al., 2005) did not attempt to look at differences in fracture rates as fewer than 200 participants were followed up for less than twelve months, when the definitive trials required several thousand participants followed up for years. Similarly, the UK BEAM trialists did not undertake any between-group analyses of the pilot data in advance of the main data analysis. The decision, therefore, to include or exclude pilot data will depend upon the pilot and the main trial.

12.7   Discussion

A pilot study is immensely useful in planning the main trial. External pilots are the most useful as they allow lessons learned from the pilot to be fully absorbed into the design of the definitive trial. However, external pilots are likely to delay the start of the definitive trial, which is one reason internal pilots tend to be attractive. Also it can be difficult to get external pilot studies funded. An internal pilot is very useful, particularly if it is possible to get some centres started early (in a multi-centred study) and then lessons learned can be incorporated into the later centres. A problem with internal pilots is that it may be difficult to fully absorb the lessons learned from them and apply them to the main trial. For example, if the pilot indicates an alternative recruitment strategy then we would need to gain ethical clearance for this change, which will delay the start of the main trial. We may also not be able to include some pilot data in the main trial if the internal pilot demonstrates that different outcomes need to be collected.

Although we have distinguished between internal and external pilots, sometimes the two concepts merge. For example, in the UK BEAM pilot (Farrin et al., 2005), the calcium and vitamin D pilot and the hip protector pilots were all originally external pilots; however, because their designs did not differ radically from the main study designs their data were included in the main results.

Pilots are sometimes difficult to fund and pass through ethics committees. Their sample sizes are generally too small to demonstrate an important difference between the groups. Consequently some ethics committee members may view them as unethical, believing that the research cannot inform policy or practice decisions. This is untrue, as the pilot will inform these decisions through its impact on the definitive study.

12.8   Key points

- Pilots are extremely useful for informing the definitive study design.
- They are not large enough to identify important differences in outcomes; therefore any differences in outcomes should be treated cautiously.
- They can be used to inform sample size calculations, study design, recruitment rates, and the feasibility of the intervention.

13
Sample Size and Analytical Issues

13.1 Background

In this chapter we consider some basic statistical issues around trial design and analysis. Most trials, particularly large and well conducted trials with little or no attrition, require only the simplest statistical methods, which usually give similar, if not the same, results as more complicated approaches. We do not look here in detail at methods of analysing trial data. Rather, the reader is directed to other books that focus specifically on statistical methods (e.g., Bland, 2000; Altman, 1991). We focus instead on a few important statistical design issues that are important to trial design, and give an overview of the main statistical issues of trial design and analysis.

13.2 Sample size

We want to be confident that any difference we find in a trial between the interventions has not occurred by chance. The probability of a chance finding, for any given effect size, declines with increasing sample size. Nevertheless, there is always a possibility that any difference we observe will have occurred by chance, no matter how large the difference or how big the sample size. This possibility is commonly reflected in the statistical significance level or p value. By convention the p value usually chosen is 5 per cent (p = 0.05). This value is arbitrary, and in some non-medical areas of research the 10 per cent value is used more commonly (e.g., economics). For instance, in a crime and justice trial, Sherman and Weisburd (1995) used a p value of 0.10 to denote statistical significance. Indeed, there is controversy over the obsession with a single point estimate of statistical significance (Sterne and Davey-Smith,

2001). An effect size that is significant with a p = 0.04 compared with a p = 0.06 is not materially different but can lead to widely different interpretations. Some researchers and practitioners enslave themselves to particular p values, when a p value should be only used as a guide to the interpretation of the study's results.

A common problem that occurs when interpreting the results of a trial is a Type II error. This error occurs when we conclude there is no difference between the groups when in reality there is a difference. This can occur when a trial is too small. A trial must have sufficient participants to demonstrate that any observed difference between the outcomes did not occur by chance. The smaller any potential difference, the larger the trial must be for such a difference to be 'statistically significant'. Unless a trial is large enough to show any observed difference as being statistically significant we cannot be sure whether that difference is a 'true' difference or just a chance effect.

A common misperception is that a small p value (e.g. $p < 0.001$) is an indication of a strong effect. The p value is driven by the sample size of the study and the frequency of events. Therefore, even a very small, trivial, difference can be highly statistically significant as long as the sample size is of sufficient size. Therefore, to ascertain whether an intervention has a large or a small effect we should look at the size of differences between the groups rather than the p value.

Sample sizes needed are inversely related to the differences we wish to detect. The smaller the difference, the larger the sample size required to demonstrate such a difference. However, determination of the correct sample size is less related to statistical considerations than to whether or not any difference is of educational, clinical, policy or economic significance, which may depend upon the context, cost and nature of the intervention. It is often difficult to specify in advance of the trial the estimate of effect that is of clinical or educational significance. A review in the field of health care research by Burnand et al. (1990) attempted to ascertain what authors of studies define as being a worthwhile difference. The reviewers found that authors considered a ratio of two means greater than 1.20 to be important, with ratios of 1.35 and 2.00 being perceived as substantially significant and highly significant respectively (Burnand et al., 1990). In other words, if a control intervention obtained an effect size of 0.50 and the novel intervention achieved an effect size of 0.60, this would be classed as significant. For differences in rates these are 0.28, 0.35 and 0.65 for significant, substantially significant and highly significant respectively, whilst for the odds ratios of two rates the corresponding values are 2.2, 2.5 and 4.0. The authors, however, caution against accepting these differences without question as they are based on an average of papers that were published in an unrepresentative sample of journals.

Systematic reviews of randomised controlled trials in education and health care have shown that these are usually too small to be able to detect a worthwhile difference between the groups. In other words there is a high chance of experiencing a Type II error. For example, a systematic review of seven randomised controlled trials evaluating the effectiveness of ICT on spelling instruction found that the trials ranged in size from only 14 participants to 79 participants (Torgerson and Elbourne, 2002). Similarly, a review of seven randomised trials evaluating the effectiveness of volunteers in literacy learning ranged from 16 participants to 99 participants (Torgerson et al., 2002). Such trials are too small to observe important educational differences that an effective intervention might produce. Indeed, we might only really consider these trials to be exploratory studies.

In health care research there is a long history of trials that are too small (Freiman et al., 1978). In a review of 96 placebo-controlled trials published in major general medical journals (i.e., *BMJ*, *Lancet*, *JAMA*, *New England Journal of Medicine*) since 1990, it was found that 58 per cent published before 1997 were under-powered, whilst 33 per cent of trials published since 1996 were still under-powered (Torgerson et al., 2002). However, a trend towards improvement was noted particularly among studies published in major medical journals (Torgerson et al., 2002).

The same problem also affects some crime and justice trials (Sherman and Weisburd, 1995). An experiment that concluded that extra policing did not reduce crime levels was widely criticised as being too small and susceptible to a Type II error (Sherman and Weisburd, 1995). It took a larger, adequately powered trial to detect a modest intervention effect.

Sample size estimates are usually based on a range of factors. The point estimate of a systematic review of previous evidence can be used. If, for example, a review of a group of smaller trials showed a 30 per cent, not statistically significant, reduction in events, then this might be taken to be the difference on which to power a trial. A less rigorous approach, which is very often used, is to estimate how many participants can realistically be recruited into a study and then calculate backwards to work out what likely difference in outcome these numbers of participants would detect (Goodman and Berlin, 1994). This difference is then judged as being 'clinically' significant. Unfortunately, this approach too often leads to sample sizes that are simply too small to detect plausible differences. In education psychology research the 'black box' of sample size calculation seems to be based around the 'magic' number of 30, which appears to have developed from 'custom and practice' or is possibly driven by the fact that most class sizes are around 30.

An alternative approach to sample size estimation is to use economic criteria. For example, it was argued in a trial for treatment of menorrhagia that the study should be planned to show an 8 per cent reduction in re-treatment rates between a laser treatment versus other forms of resection (Torgerson and Campbell, 2000). This difference was based on the cost differences between the two treatments. If laser therapy, which was initially more expensive, reduced re-treatments by 8 percentage points this would be 'cost-neutral'.

As a general rule, however, a trial should be sufficiently large to detect at least a half a standardised difference between groups when the outcome measured is a continuous variable (e.g., blood pressure, spelling test scores) or a halving or doubling of a dichotomous variable (e.g., deaths or exam pass rates). A standardised difference is a change measured in standard deviation units. An improvement in the effect size of 1.0 describes an improvement of an average 1 standard deviation in the intervention group compared with the control. One can show that, for a trial to detect a difference of 1.0 in effect size, requires 32 participants (i.e., 16 in each group) to have an 80 per cent power to show the difference with a significance level of 5 per cent, or 42 participants for 90 per cent power. As the effect size halves, the numbers in the trial quadruple. To detect an effect size of a half requires 128 participants; a quarter requires 512.

Many trials use some form of test with a continuous measure as the outcome (e.g., changes in blood pressure, changes in a spelling test). We can describe an effect in terms of differences in standard deviations or standardised effect sizes. A standardised effect is calculated by taking the differences in post-test means and dividing these by a 'pooled' standard deviation of the post-test scores, or the standard deviation of the control group. A standardised effect of 1 or more is considered a very large difference. Such an effect might only occur when an intervention is compared against no intervention.

More commonly, and realistically, we would want to investigate the effectiveness of a new intervention versus the traditional method. If the control group is also receiving an effective intervention, differences can be expected to be much lower. Therefore, an effect size as low as 0.20 is much more likely.

We can convert effect sizes into numbers needed to treat or teach (NNT): the number of people required to receive the new intervention in order to get one extra person through an educationally important threshold. For example, we might consider an intervention worthwhile if it means that one extra person in a class of 25 will pass an important exam. If we look at Table 13.1 an NNT of 25 is equivalent to a very small effect size of only 0.1.

One problem with NNTs is that, although they can usefully describe the likely effectiveness of an intervention, they can be misleading. An NNT of 100 for an intervention that is inexpensive (e.g., aspirin or seating children in rows) is worth having but an NNT for an expensive intervention (e.g., personal laptop computers, beta interferon) or something with significant unwanted side-effects, may be too high.

As well as the difference we wish to detect and the statistical probability of that difference, another issue regarding sample size is power. Statistical power relates to the chance of finding that a pre-specified difference is statistically significant. Again, the larger the sample size the greater the reliability to detect a difference, if one actually exists. Statistical power is commonly set at 80 per cent or 90 per cent, that is, given a sample size we would have an 80 per cent chance of detecting a specified difference, with a p value of 0.05. For example, let us assume we want to detect a half a standardised difference in an intervention comparing two methods of instruction. Assuming we have individually randomised the children we would need approximately 128 individuals (i.e., 64 in each group) to give us 80 per cent power to detect such a difference with a p value of 5 per cent.

Table 13.1: Effect size and numbers needed to treat or teach (NNT)

Mean effect size	Number of extra students passing a 50% test threshold	Numbers needed to treat or teach
0	0%	–
0.1	4%	25
0.2	8%	13
0.3	12%	8
0.4	16%	6
0.5	19%	5
0.6	23%	4*
0.7	26%	4
0.8	29%	3*
0.9	32%	3
1.0	34%	3*

*Rounded to the nearest whole number.

13.3 Calculating sample sizes

> Most hand calculations diabolically strain human limits, even for the
> easiest formula. (Schulz and Grimes, 2005)

There are numerous statistical packages that will compute relatively complex formulae to estimate sample size calculations. Rather than discuss these
we show a simple approach that gives a very close estimate of the 'true'
sample size which can be easily undertaken using a handheld calculator.

Lehr described a relatively simple approach to estimating sample size
(Lehr, 1992). The method generates samples that are very similar in size
to the more usual complex methods. However, it over-estimates the
sample slightly for small samples – a good thing. For a sample size of 80
per cent power at a 5 per cent significance level we divide 32 by the
square of the effect size (42 for 90 per cent power). For example, let us
assume we want to detect an improvement of an effect size of 0.30 in a
quality of life measure, such as the SF36. This measure has a mean of 50
with a SD of 10 (i.e., 3 points). If we square 0.30 we get 0.09; dividing
this into 32 gives us a total sample size of 356 (i.e., 178 in each group).
The formula for the total sample size, which can be memorised, is:

$$\text{Approximate } N = \frac{32}{d^2}$$

For dichotomous outcomes the calculation becomes a little more complex. First, we need to estimate a standardised effect size, which is calculated as follows. Let us suppose we want to detect a difference of 10
percentage points between 35 per cent and 45 per cent in a dichotomous
outcome. First we need to estimate the variance. We do this by taking an
average of the two proportions (i.e., $(0.35 + 0.45)/2 = 0.40$). Next we
multiply this by 1 – the average (i.e., 0.60), which gives us 0.24. We then
take the square root of this, which is about 0.49. We can now work out
a standardised effect size by dividing the difference, in this instance 0.1
by the measure of the variance (0.49), which gives us 0.204. We now
divide 32 by the square of this, which gives us a sample size of 768.

Again, the formula can be memorised relatively easily. We use a (in
our example 0.45) to mean the mean (average) proportion, and d to
mean the difference between proportions (in our example, 0.1).

$$\text{Approximate } N = 32 / \left(\frac{d}{\sqrt{a(1-a)}} \right)^2$$

Algebraic manipulation gives a formula, which may be easier to remember.

$$\text{Approximate N} = 32 / \left(\frac{d^2}{a - a^2} \right)$$

13.4 Worked examples

In a study of various interventions among men who assaulted their female partners (Dunford, 2000) the re-assault rate was 20 per cent within twelve months. In order to design a trial of an intervention to reduce this, the sample size calculation would be as follows. An effective intervention should show a halving of the assault rate from 20 per cent to 10 per cent. The effect size, therefore, is 0.2 − 0.1 = 0.1 (i.e., 10 per cent). The average proportion is 0.15 (i.e., (0.1 + 0.2)/2). Using the formulae above, we can do the following calculation:

d^2 = x 0.1 = 0.01; a = 0.15 and a^2 = 0.0225; a−a^2 = 0.1275;
d^2/a − a^2 = 0.078

The sample size therefore is 32 divided by 0.078, which equals 408. Using a more accurate sample size formula from a computer program gives us a sample size of 398, slightly lower, but the simpler method gives a reasonably good estimate.

If, on the other hand, we want to observe differences in means rather than proportions and we are interested in observing an effect size of 0.2 we simply divide the square of this (0.04) into 32, which results in a sample size of 800. Again using a computer package the sample size is slightly lower at 784.

13.5 Sample sizes and cluster trials

The preceding discussion on sample sizes relates to individually randomised trials. Many educational trials randomise groups of individuals in clusters. In this case the usual statistical assumption of each person in the trial being independent no longer holds true. Consider a class of children randomised as a group. Their outcomes will not be independent of each other, as they all have the same teacher. It is also unlikely that the children within the class will be a random sample. These factors mean the outcomes of children within a group will be correlated. Statisticians refer to this correlation as an intra-class correlation coefficient (ICC). This has an effect on the sample size: the bigger the ICC the larger the sample size required to overcome this natural clustering. The same applies to patients of a given doctor, or offenders with the same probation officer; all share some characteristics with other members of their 'group' or cluster.

To adjust for this clustering in the sample size calculation an estimate of the ICC is required. This can be difficult as these are often not available until after the study has been completed. Therefore, one needs to look to other, similar, studies to estimate an ICC. Unfortunately, these are not routinely reported and the ICC needs to be estimated through informed guesswork. Once an estimate of the ICC is available we can then calculate an 'inflation factor' by which to increase our individually randomised calculations for a cluster trial. The process of calculating a relevant sample size for a cluster trial is as follows. First, we estimate an important difference such as 0.5 of an effect size. Second, we calculate a sample size for an individually randomised trial (i.e., 128). Third, we take an estimate of the ICC (let us assume this to be 0.01). Fourth, we assume classes of 25 children are randomised. Fifth, we apply the following formula: $1 + ((\text{cluster size} - 1) \times \text{ICC})$.

> $25 - 1 = 24$ (where 25 is the size of cluster) multiplied by ICC (0.01) = 0.24 plus 1 (inflation factor) = 1.24 times 128 = a total sample size of 158 (i.e., a 24 per cent increase).

Note, although this implies that we would 'only' need to randomise six schools, it is generally recommended that we should allocate at least eight clusters in order to achieve some balance at the cluster level (Murray, 1998). Some researchers suggest that ideally at least fourteen clusters should be included (Donner and Klar, 2000).

It is important to note the following issues regarding the sample size for cluster trials. The first is related to the cluster size. The larger the cluster size the greater the inflation factor. Assume for example we randomise by school rather than class and the average school contains 500 children. This will give an inflation factor of nearly six times (i.e., $0.01 \times (500 - 1) = 4.99 + 1 = 5.99$). In other words, our sample increases from 128 for individual randomisation to 158 for class as the unit of allocation to 766 if school is the unit of randomisation. If the ICC is greater than 0.01, say 0.05, which is not uncommon, our sample size will rapidly increase (i.e., 128 to 282 for class allocation to 3322 for school randomisation).

The numbers of clusters in a cluster randomised trial can be reduced if we include powerful predictors, such as baseline scores, in our calculations. Indeed, the same applies for individually randomised trials. For instance, if the baseline test has a correlation of 0.5 with the post-test, then we may be able to reduce our sample size by 25 per cent (Donner and Klar, 2000). Cook argues that the usual 'rule of thumb' of 40 to 50 schools needed to demonstrate an educationally important difference can be reduced to as few as 22 schools when the pre- and post-test correlation is as high as 0.85 (Cook, 2005).

13.6   Use of confidence intervals

Even the largest trial showing a very strong effect will still have some uncertainty around the estimate of effectiveness: the smaller the trial, the bigger the uncertainty. Statistically, a relatively simple method of expressing this uncertainty is through the use of confidence intervals. If a trial is undertaken 100 times then 95 of the 100 confidence intervals will include the true value. If an intervention has an effect size of 0.25 we can put a confidence interval around this. For example, this might be a confidence interval between 0.20 and 0.30. From this we can be fairly confident that the intervention has an effect size of between 0.20 and 0.30. Therefore, the reporting of confidence intervals that surround a trial's results is absolutely essential to express the range of uncertainty surrounding the result of even the largest trial.

For example, in his experimental study of preventing violence towards women partners Dunford (2000) noted that 83 per cent of men in the intervention group did not re-assault their partners compared with 79 per cent of the men in the control group. Whilst this difference was not statistically significant, the confidence intervals around the 4 per cent difference were − 3 per cent to 12 per cent. In other words, the experiment could not have ruled out a benefit as large as 12 per cent in favour of the intervention or a harmful effect of 3 per cent. On the other hand, Bourduin and colleagues (1995) found a 45 per cent statistically significant reduction in arrests of juvenile offenders when using a multi-systemic treatment compared with a control intervention. The 95 per cent confidence intervals around this estimate ranged from 31 per cent to 58 per cent. Therefore, we can be reasonably confident that the intervention reduced further arrests by at least 31 per cent and possibly by as great as 58 per cent. Interestingly, neither of these studies actually reported confidence intervals in their papers.

Confidence intervals are a function of sample size and outcome frequency: the smaller the sample size, the wider the confidence intervals. In Table 13.2 we show the effect sizes of four randomised trials from educational research. Three of the four trials note similar, positive, effect sizes

Table 13.2:   Effect sizes and confidence intervals

Study (Study context)	Sample size	Effect size	95% Confidence intervals
Rimm-Kaufman et al., 1999 (Use of volunteers)	42	0.43	−0.18 to 1.04
Baker et al. 2000 (Volunteers for literacy instruction)	84	0.45	0.01 to 0.88
Berninger et al., 1998 (Spelling instruction)	24	0.59	−0.23 to 1.41
Martinson and Friedlander, 1994 (Adult education)	1115	0.021	−0.096 to 0.138

Note: If the confidence intervals pass through 0 then the difference is not statistically significant.

for the intervention. However, only one of these studies shows a statistically significant benefit of the intervention (Baker et al., 2000). The other two studies, despite showing a similar effect, have inconclusive results. Thus, Berninger et al. (1998) show a fairly large effect size but this is not statistically significant. One of two conclusions can be drawn from this study: (1) there is truly no effect of the intervention; or, (2) there is a benefit but it is not statistically significant because of the small sample size.

By looking at the confidence intervals we can see that the intervention used by Berninger et al. (1998) has a potentially large effect on spelling abilities. Therefore we should try to replicate this study and see whether we can confirm these results in a much larger trial. In contrast, the fourth trial in the table, a large study of an adult education programme by Martinson and Friedlander (1994), showed only a small effect with relatively tight confidence intervals. Whilst there remains a possibility of a larger effect size, the upper 95 per cent confidence interval indicates that the possibility of a very large effect size is small and therefore it would not be worthwhile to undertake another trial of this particular intervention, or indeed to implement it.

Confidence intervals are useful to represent uncertainty but it is important to note that the point estimate from a study is the *most* likely single estimate of the true value of the intervention. The likelihood of the true estimate being another value declines as we move towards the extremes of the confidence interval. An erroneous belief is that the true estimate has an equal probability of falling anywhere along the confidence interval. It does not.

13.7   Analysis of trials with a clustering effect

Many trials contain data with a clustering effect. This means that the individuals who contribute the data are not independent of each other. This is most frequently the case with cluster randomised trials. If a trial is randomised by cluster then the effect of the cluster needs to be taken into account in the analysis. If we use analytical methods appropriate for non-clustered data, these will tend to yield optimistic statistical significance levels. Even trials that are individually randomised can be problematic, as so often the intervention is dependent upon the teacher or therapist. Therefore, the outcomes of the participants will correlate with fellow participants who have the same teacher, doctor, therapist or social worker etc. This correlation between participants needs to be taken into account in any analysis.

Some trials include both individual randomisation and cluster allocation. For example, some studies randomise as individuals but family members are randomised together (e.g., Sinclair et al., 2005). We cannot treat the family members as independent units and, therefore, we need to take this into account. Sinclair and colleagues (2005) allocated individual students, but siblings were put into the same group. However, in their analysis the authors treated siblings as individuals. The simplest approach here would have been to choose an 'index' sibling (e.g., the oldest) and only include this participant in the analysis. Although this wastes information, it is more conservative than treating the participants as individuals and will not yield too small a p value. However, there are other statistical approaches to dealing with this problem that do not waste information. It is beyond the scope of this book to discuss the statistical analysis of trials with clustering effects; suffice to say that some form of multi-level modelling is usually required to adequately deal with these data.

If we randomise clusters with relatively similar sample sizes with continuous outcomes, then the simplest method of adjusting for the clustering effects is to simply take the mean value of each group and do a t-test on the group means. Or, if there are differences in cluster size, a regression based approach, using cluster mean as the dependent variable with group assignment and cluster size as explanatory variables, is likely to be a simple method yet generates estimates similar to more complex approaches. We can adjust for other covariates using the same approach and calculate the cluster means of the covariates. However, when planning any trial it is important to involve a statistician in the design as well as the analysis of the trial.

13.8   Sample size calculation: what is current practice?

Many trials do not report the underlying justification for their sample sizes and do not report any *a priori* sample size calculation at all. Many trials are under-powered, that is, the studies are not large enough to detect, as statistically significant, differences that are worth knowing about even if they exist. In a review of the quality of trials in health care and education, many trials were found to be under-powered (Torgerson et al., 2005). An examination of a sample of trials published since 1990 found that only about 50 per cent of trials published in major medical journals were of an adequate size. Education trials were worse, with only 16 per cent being of an adequate size. No educational trial out of 84 included in the sample gave a rationale for its sample size. Since the review was published we have become aware of a few trials in educational research that have reported an *a priori* sample size calculation (see for example, Brooks et al., 2006; Spencer et al., 2005). Most educational trials are simply too small to detect modest but important effects on outcomes.

13.9   Baseline or pre-test analysis

The first analysis many trialists perform is a statistical comparison of the baseline or pre-test characteristics of the randomised groups. Many statisticians do not recommend this approach (e.g., Altman and Doré, 1991). Indeed, the major UK medical journals (*Lancet* and *British Medical Journal*) do not allow the p values of these baseline comparisons to be included within the table showing the comparability of the randomised groups. There are a number of reasons why it is thought generally not helpful to undertake baseline comparisons.

Assuming we have undertaken our randomisation properly then any baseline differences between the two groups will be, by definition, attributable simply to chance. Confirming this is not particularly helpful. In fact by doing the tests we can mislead ourselves. This is because, inevitably, there will be some statistically significant differences between the two groups if we undertake sufficient numbers of tests. If we do twenty statistical tests of baseline variables (not uncommon), we will on average find at least one that is statistically significant by chance. If we find a variable that is in imbalance we might be tempted to 'correct' for this imbalance using regression analysis. However, unless the variable is strongly predictive of outcome this will not help us, and may result in a loss of power, and in some instances may actually bias the results. Indeed, a p value is not a good guide to whether or not we should adjust for a variable in an analysis. A variable that strongly predicts outcome, but is in imbalance by a non-statistically significant amount, can still produce a biased post-test analysis. Consequently, what we should do is specify in advance the key variables that we think are important to the outcome of the study. These variables should then be included in an adjusted analysis irrespective of whether or not they are in balance through the randomisation process. Including strongly predictive variables will improve the precision of our treatment estimate and therefore this should be done.

There is a dissenting view to the legitimacy of baseline testing, however. Berger (2005), for example, views baseline testing as a legitimate method of identifying trials that may have been subverted. If key variables (e.g., age, pre-test scores) are in imbalance and there is a trend for several predictor variables to favour one of the treatment groups, then one might regard this as evidence for subversion and consequently treat the trial with a degree of scepticism. On the other hand, for subversion to be noticeable on baseline tests, it would have to be quite gross (Berger, 2005). In a systematic review of trials of calcium supplements nearly all of the trials had baseline imbalance but none of these was individually significant (Trowman et al., 2006). It has been suggested that trials using blocked allocation should undertake a statistical test based on the outcome variable and relate this to the position of the participant on the block. Such a test may be more sensitive to subversion (Berger, 2005).

Another problem with looking at comparability of randomised groups is how this relates to analysed groups. If we use 100 per cent intention to treat and have no loss to follow-up, then at baseline the groups will reflect the prognostic characteristics of the groups at follow-up. However, in many health care trials, there is often 10–20 per cent attrition and therefore in these cases we do not have data on a substantial minority of participants. Baseline tests will tell us nothing about the comparability of the analysed groups when we have participants who are lost after randomisation.

Some trialists realise that attrition is a problem which may bias their results. One approach widely used to look at this potential problem, is to compare the baseline characteristics of those who drop out with those who remain in the trial. For example, in a trial of parenting classes Hutchings and colleagues (2007) noted that 17 per cent of the intervention group were lost to follow-up. To assess whether this introduced bias in observable variables, they compared the baseline characteristics of those who were lost to follow-up with those who remained in the trial and noted that there were no statistically significant differences (Hutchings et al., 2007). However, this is not of great interest because it is unclear how we would interpret any statistically significant or non-significant findings when we do this. If the differences are not significant this does not mean that participants have not selectively removed themselves differently from the randomised groups. For example, in a trial of interventions A and B, where 50 per cent of the participants are women we might find that 25 per cent of women leave Group A and 75 per cent of women leave Group B giving an average of 50 per cent of females in the attrition group, which would be the same as the total sample in the analysed group (Table 13.3). Even if we only compare the participants from Group A who were lost to follow-up with those remaining, as Hutchings et al. (2007) did, whether or not this is significant is still unhelpful. Even if the attrition group is significantly different from those who remain in the trial, we cannot conclude that the two groups that are analysed are not in balance. Therefore, it is of more interest to look at the comparability of groups that are actually analysed (Dumville et al., 2006b). Therefore, in the hypothetical example described above we would examine differences in gender between the groups after we have excluded those who have been lost to follow-up. If we do this we see that the groups are in imbalance with respect to gender, whereas we would not see this if we had either analysed all randomised patients or compared those who were lost with those who were not. Therefore, there may be a case for statistically testing the comparability of analysed groups as opposed to the randomised groups if these groups differ due to attrition. In Table 13.3 we show the different strategies for testing baseline values. In our view, unless we suspect subversion, only the last comparison should inform our analysis and interpretation of the trial; however, this is very rarely done.

Table 13.3:   Different strategies for comparing pre-test characteristics of randomised groups

	Intervention group N = 100	Control group N = 100
Number of women randomised	50 (a)	50 (b)
Number of men randomised	50 (c)	50 (d)
Loss to follow-up women	12 (e)	38 (f)
Loss to follow-up men	10 (g)	10 (h)

Baseline comparison of all randomised participants: = a + c vs b + d.
Loss to follow-up comparison with treatment follow-up: = e + f + g + h vs (a − e) + (b − f) + (c − g) + (d − h).
As analysed comparison: = (a + c) − (e + g) vs (b + d) − (f + h).

13.10   Post-test analysis

It is important to pre-specify the principal analytical strategy, ideally in a published trial protocol. This is to prevent accusations of 'data dredging'. We should also always use an ITT analysis as the main analytical strategy for the trial. We can use other techniques for secondary analyses; however, the ITT is the most robust approach and remains faithful to the randomised groups.

Within an ITT analysis there are two broad analytical strategies: unadjusted and adjusted analyses. For large sample sizes both approaches usually give similar results, although the unadjusted analysis tends to have larger confidence intervals. Often both adjusted and unadjusted results are presented. The difference between the two approaches is that the unadjusted approach simply compares either the means or the proportions of the groups. The differences in the proportions or means are calculated and a statistical test, such as the Student's t-test or Chi squared test is applied and confidence intervals are calculated. An adjusted analysis is more complex and usually involves some form of regression-type approach, but given modern software and computers is relatively easy to do. If we use an important predictor of outcome, an adjusted analysis will substantially reduce the standard error, and consequently reduce the width of the confidence intervals. This occasionally makes a non-statistically significant result into a significant one. Also for small trials there is a greater risk of a chance imbalance among a powerful predictor variable and this may change the estimate of the intervention effect.

In Table 13.4 we illustrate the effect that adjusted analyses can have on the results of a trial. In the first trial we have used data from an RCT of physiotherapy for neck pain (Klaber-Moffett et al., 2005) where the outcome was a measure of neck pain. The correlation between pre- and post-test was a modest 0.40, and the randomisation ensured that both groups were very well balanced in terms of their pre-test scores. The adjusted and unadjusted estimates of the treatment differences at twelve months were very similar: nearly a two-point difference favouring the control group. However, the baseline value does predict the follow-up measure. Consequently we would expect a more precise estimate of effect if we were to use this information in our analysis. Adjusting for the effect of baseline test reduces the standard error of the estimate from about 0.86 to 0.79, and this reduces the width of the confidence intervals. Note, however, the estimate of the treatment effect is very similar to the unadjusted analysis. In this instance the adjusted analysis does

Table 13.4:   Effect of adjusted and unadjusted analyses on trial results

Trial	Correlation coefficient*	Estimate (standard error)	p value and confidence interval
SPRINTER (Klaber-Moffett et al., 2005)	0.40		
Unadjusted analysis		1.91 (0.86)	P = 0.026, 0.23 to 3.58
Adjusted analysis		1.94 (0.79)	P = 0.014, 0.39 to 3.49
ICT trial (Brooks et al., 2006)	0.78		
Unadjusted analysis		1.41 (1.09)	P = 0.20, − 0.74 to 3.56
Adjusted analysis		1.66 (0.71)	P = 0.02, 0.26 to 3.07

*Correlation between pre-test values and post-test.

not change our interpretation of the trial's findings. It merely increases, slightly, our confidence in the results.

In the second example we use data from a recent trial in education (Brooks et al., 2006). This trial evaluated the use of ICT to improve children's literacy skills. The adjusted estimate is a bit larger than the unadjusted estimate. This is because in this instance, by chance, the groups were more unbalanced at baseline, so adjusting for the pre-test scores gives us an estimate of the effect, had the groups been better balanced at baseline. Note, the correlation coefficient between pre- and post-test in this instance is much greater than for the health care trial, which tends to be more typical of educational trials compared with health care studies. Because pre-test is a more powerful predictor of post-test in this field, then the standard error is more reduced with a greater effect on the width of the confidence intervals. In this instance the result changes from being not statistically significant in the unadjusted analysis to statistical significance in the adjusted results.

By using important covariates we can increase the power of our trial, which is usually easier to do than the alternative approach to increasing study power, that is, by recruiting more participants. In education trials the correlation between pre and post- test is usually somewhat greater than in health care trials. Consequently, collection of accurate pre-test data in educational trials is usually worthwhile and can add significant study power. Nevertheless even in health care trials pre-test data are usually helpful in an analysis.

Adjusted analyses are more precise than unadjusted analyses yet some researchers present unadjusted results. There are a number of reasons for this. First the unadjusted analysis is simpler and easier to understand and prevents the possibility that the findings were due to statistical trickery, rather than to the effect of an intervention. Second, sometimes we do not know which variables predict outcomes. Third, sometimes the design of the trial precludes us from collecting important predictors of outcome. Generally we would recommend using adjusted analyses as the main analysis if strong pre-test data are available.

13.11   Separate group paired analysis

One quite widespread, and bizarre, method of analysing trial data is to analyse the trial data as two before and after studies and use paired tests and then compare the two p values. What commonly happens is that one paired test is statistically significant and this is reported whilst the other is not. The intervention is deemed to be effective on the basis of the paired statistical test. Given that we are interested in the between-group differences not within-group differences this is the wrong method of analysing the data. Such an analysis is prone to regression to the mean effects and it is quite possible that, possibly due to chance imbalances, one may see that one p value is significant and the other is not, yet when the correct analysis is undertaken there is no significant difference between the groups.

13.12   Dealing with non-adherence

In many trials, some participants allocated to the intervention do not receive it, because they receive the 'control' treatment. We need to include them within the group they were randomised to in order to avoid bias. This will dilute any observed treatment effect. When Fisher designed trials in the 1920s and 1930s in agricultural research non-adherence was not an issue. Plants do not need to consent, they do not move, and generally they do what the experimenter wishes them to do. Furthermore, in crop research we are not interested in the fate of an individual plant. If a new fertiliser triples crop yields but kills half the plants then overall this is a good thing for the farmer: this is not true in human experiments. In the social sciences we are interested in the effect on individuals and their outcomes. In human trials of any description, whether they are medical, educational or in the field of crime and justice, participants change their minds or move houses or schools. Consequently, in many social science trials significant proportions of participants are allocated to, but do not receive, the intended intervention. We use ITT analysis to avoid bias, and therefore dilute our estimates of treatment effects.

As noted before, many trialists try to correct for non-adherence by undertaking an on-treatment or per protocol analysis. Unfortunately this approach can produce a biased estimate of effect. An alternative method, which, in principle, is unbiased, is to use an 'instrumental' variable approach to the analysis (Hewitt et al., 2006). As a worked example of this, let us consider a randomised trial of hip protectors (Birks et al., 2004). In this trial, women at risk of hip fracture were offered hip protectors to protect their hips if they fell. In the intention to treat analysis 2.8 per cent of the intervention group had a hip fracture compared with 2.4 per cent of the control group. However, only about 38 per cent of the intervention population reported using the hip protectors on a regular basis. Therefore, the lack of any effect may have been due to non-compliance rather than to any intrinsic ineffectiveness. A key question that ITT cannot answer is: what is the effect of hip protectors on a woman's risk of hip fracture if she wears them regularly?

Instrumental variables can potentially answer this question in an unbiased manner. The approach is based on two assumptions: (1) if the control group had been offered hip protectors then the same proportion would have used them as the proportion observed in the intervention group; (2) merely being offered hip protectors will not have any effect on hip fracture risk. Assumption 1 must be true as this is a randomised trial, whilst we can assume the second assumption to be true in this instance, as there is no reason why simply being offered hip protectors will reduce the risk of fracture. In Table 13.5 we can see that 38 per cent of the intervention group complied with the intervention. Consequently, we can assume that there will be a similar proportion of compliers and non-compliers in the control group *had they been offered hip protectors.*

In the 'non-compliant' control group we can assume that the hip fracture incidence (i.e., 2.9 per cent) will be the same as the non-compliant intervention group because merely being offered hip protectors should not reduce fracture risk. As we know the total numbers of hip fractures in the control group, we can then estimate the likely fracture rate in the remaining cell of the table, which in this instance is 1.5 per cent. We can see that the relative risk of hip fracture (relative risk = 1.73) is actually

Table 13.5: Risk of hip fracture by compliance status

	Hip protector (N = 1387)	*Control (N = 2781)*
Compliers (38%)	14/529 = 2.6%	16/1061 = 1.5%*
Non-compliers (62%)	25/858 = 2.9%	50/1720 = 2.9%*
Total hip fractures	39/1387 = 2.8%	66/2781 = 2.4%
ITT RR = approx 1.17		
(i.e., 2.8/2.4)		

*Estimated proportions.

higher in this example than the ITT analysis suggests (i.e., relative risk = 1.17). This analysis suggests, therefore, that hip protectors are unlikely to be an effective intervention even if people use them on a regular basis.

Instrumental variable analysis or complier average causal effect (CACE) analysis tends to be widely used by economists when analysing trials with non-adherence. Health care trialists are less familiar with the technique and tend to use the flawed per protocol or on-treatment analysis to look at the effectiveness of treatments for those who actually use them. This is unfortunate because CACE analysis is relatively simple to undertake and is less likely to give us a biased estimate of the true likely treatment effect. For example, Kling et al. (2005) evaluated an initiative of giving families living in poor areas housing vouchers on the condition they moved to an affluent area. Some of those randomised to the intervention did not, for whatever reason, actually leave the poor neighbourhood. The authors quite correctly included them in their original randomised group. However, this will have diluted the effectiveness of the intervention. One outcome was the number of arrests for violence among the children of the families in the experiment. Using ITT the authors noted an average decline of 0.061 arrests for violence per person; however, using the instrumental variable approach the decline was much greater at 0.147 per person. Therefore, the people who chose to stay, despite being offered the voucher, were more likely to have had characteristics that put them at greater risk of being arrested for violent crime. The instrumental variable approach effectively controlled for this confounder and demonstrated that the children of those families who acted upon the offer of a voucher would have a 0.147 reduction in arrests, not the 0.061 implied by ITT analysis.

13.13   Discussion

Statistical analysis of trials should be relatively straightforward. Sample size estimation can be more complex in the sense that the most difficult part is not the arithmetical calculation; rather, it is agreeing on a difference that is important to detect: this is the main challenge of sample size estimation.

Prior sample size estimates can be informative when designing an RCT. It seems that, too often, sample sizes are chosen on the basis of logistics rather than on the need to ascertain an important difference. Trials in the social sciences and health care research often do not report the reasoning behind their sample size calculations. Many trials are too small to detect modest but worthwhile differences. It is important to consider the size of sample before we undertake a trial, as potentially useful interventions may be rejected due to a Type II error. Related to this is the issue of precision. Studies need to report with confidence intervals the likely range of estimates where the true effect will lie.

Randomised trial analysis is relatively straightforward compared with analysis of non-randomised data. If the trial has been conducted properly, and if there has been little or no loss to follow-up, relatively simple analytical methods are required to ascertain effectiveness. Non-randomised data are generally much more difficult to analyse.

13.14   Key points

- Sample size estimates can be important to ensure that the trial is large enough to detect important differences.
- Many trials, particularly in the social sciences, are too small.
- Statistical comparison of baseline characteristics is commonly undertaken; it is only necessary if subversion of subversion of allocation is suspected.
- Adjusted analysis is a useful technique for obtaining a more precise analysis.
- Instrumental variable analysis may be a useful technique in the presence of non-adherence.

14
Measuring Outcomes

14.1   Background

A crucial issue is how to measure whether or not something works using a good measure of outcome. The choice of outcome measure will clearly depend upon the research question. Because of the nature of this book we do not deal with specific measures of outcome; rather, we discuss some general rules.

An ideal outcome measure will be sensitive to important effects, reliable, in that it will return the same findings when participants are re-measured in the same circumstances, and valid, in that the outcome instrument will give us an accurate assessment of the actual outcome we wish to measure. This latter issue is important in that many outcomes that are measured are not 'true' outcome measures. For example, quality of life measurements do not truly measure a person's quality of life – they only give a general indication. 'Objective' measures of outcome, such as death, may not give us the complete picture. We may delay death by a statistically significant amount through a therapeutic intervention, but the quality of life lived may not be judged worthwhile. Consequently an intervention that merely prolongs life without improving its quality may be less desirable than a treatment that improves quality of life (assuming we can accurately measure this) but does not extend life.

14.2   Ceiling and floor effects

A good measure of effect will be valid and sensitive to important changes. If there is an improvement in outcome we need a measure that can reliably detect this. We also need a measure that can record the 'spread of effect' within our sample of participants. Some trials use outcome measures that suffer from ceiling and/or floor effects. For example, in education a ceiling effect may be due to a test that is too easy for the participants. Similarly, if we administer a test that is too difficult we will not observe a difference because the scores of the participants cannot fall below zero. In a randomised controlled trial designed to evaluate the effectiveness of computer-assisted instruction on the word recognition skills of students aged between seven and nine versus a traditional paper and pencil approach (Lin et al., 1991) ceiling effects can be observed in all of the post-tests. In a twenty-item multiple-choice test designed to measure word recognition accuracy the mean post-test scores were 19.06 for the intervention group and 19.51 for the control group. Therefore, this outcome measure was not appropriate because it could not measure a 'true' spread of outcomes in both groups. In this instance a moderate effect for the control group of −0.53 *was* statistically significant (95 per cent confidence intervals −0.12 to −0.95). But the 'true' measure of effect could have been much larger if the test had not suffered from ceiling effects. In a two-group study by Foster and colleagues (1994) evaluating a phonological awareness programme, there were 34 students in the intervention group and 35 in the control group. However, the authors found no effect of the intervention and this may have been partly due to the ceiling effect of their outcome measure, which they fully acknowledged in their write-up:

> The most obvious explanation for the lack of training effects on the STOPA in this experiment is the extremely high scores that were obtained by children in both groups on the posttests. Nineteen children in the experimental group and 17 children in the control group obtained either perfect or near perfect (29 or 30) scores on the posttest. (Foster et al., 1994)

In health care, quality of life measures, which are prone to ceiling and floor effects, are commonly used to measure outcome. Ideally, to gain the most statistical power we need a measure that has a mean of about 50 per cent so that there is no ceiling or floor effect of the test.

14.3   Surrogate outcomes

In addition to using tests with appropriate statistical properties, ideally we should use tests related to the most important outcome. For instance, a student may perform well in a spelling test of a list of words learned in a spelling intervention. However, the more educationally significant outcome would one that measured accurate spelling when writing text. Therefore, one could argue that to evaluate a method of spelling instruction, in addition to a spelling test one should also include a holistic writing score. Similarly, in health care research 'surrogate' markers of outcome are commonly used. For example, changes in blood pressure may be used to establish the effectiveness of a treatment for the prevention of stroke.

As a general rule it is best to choose a clinically, economically or educationally important measure of outcome rather than a proxy measure. Proxy or surrogate measures are those measures of outcome, such as blood pressure, that are not clinically important either to the patient or their physician. Having an elevated blood pressure is of little consequence to the patient: in contrast, having a stroke is of major importance. Using surrogates as a measure of outcome can be misleading (Fleming and DeMets, 1996). For example, changes in bone mineral density (BMD) are often used as surrogates to measure the effectiveness of treatments for the prevention of osteoporotic fractures. Some treatments, such as sodium fluoride, substantially increase BMD, but also increase fractures (Riggs et al., 1990). Similarly, those trials that used suppression of cardiac arrhythmia as a surrogate measure of benefit instead of mortality had literally fatal consequences for many thousands of patients who were subsequently exposed to this as a routine treatment (Silverman, 1997). In Table 14.1 some surrogates and their clinical outcomes are listed.

Table 14.1: Comparison of surrogate with true outcomes

Area	Surrogate outcome	'True' outcome
Cardiovascular	Changes in blood pressure Changes in lipid levels Restenosis	Stroke Heart attack Quality of life
Osteoporosis	Changes in bone density, markers of bone turnover	Fracture
Cancer screening	Tumours detected	Mortality from cancer
Vaccination	Antibody levels	Clinical symptoms of disease
Wounds	Debridement	Healing
Partner abuse	Feelings of anger or hostility to partner	Reduction in assaults
Literacy	Correct spellings in a list	Accurate spelling in written text

Surrogates are widely used in health care research because observing a difference in a surrogate measure requires much smaller sample sizes and shorter follow-up compared with clinical outcomes. Trials designed to observe changes in bone mineral density require only a few hundred participants, whereas trials designed to observe a fracture endpoint require many thousands of participants. A reliable surrogate of outcome can be invaluable as it allows a smaller and generally more rapid evaluation of a promising therapeutic agent to be undertaken with all of the attendant benefits that this will produce. In early evaluations surrogates can be used to confirm a biological hypothesis, but before the treatment is licensed a larger study should be undertaken to check that the changes in surrogate outcomes translate into changes in clinical events. Otherwise this can be misleading. Fleming and DeMets (1996) describe a small trial of interferon designed to examine its effect, using a surrogate, which was changed to a larger study looking at infection rates among children with chronic granulomatous disease. The original study sought to determine whether treatment with interferon would increase superoxide production (the surrogate), which it was believed would be reflected in a reduction in infections. However, the trial showed a 70 per cent reduction in infections, but did not show any effect on superoxide production. Had the trial continued as planned, looking at the surrogate, a highly effective treatment would not have been recognised. It is highly probable that effective treatments have been lost at an early stage because the mechanism of their effect was not fully understood and the inappropriate surrogates were selected.

In educational research surrogates can be misleading. An RCT was designed to evaluate the use of a spell-checker to aid students in identifying and correcting misspelled words in a pre-written story compared with students making spelling corrections by hand (Jinkerson and Baggett, 1993). The authors came to a positive conclusion about spell-checkers based on surrogate outcomes (the difference between the number of words spelled on the oral post-test and the number of misspelled words corrected in the story) although the study did not detect any effect on the primary outcome (post-test spelling accuracy). A statistically significant difference in the number of spelling errors corrected in relation to the children's spelling knowledge favoured the children in the computer group (who corrected more words than they were later able to spell), but no difference was detected between correction rates (number of words corrected divided by the number of words identified as errors) and spelling knowledge.

14.4 Qualitative outcomes

Generally trials use quantitative measures to assess outcome. However, it is possible to use qualitative data and compare the findings between the two groups. This has the advantage that any differences between the groups are likely to be due to the intervention. As an example, Leahy and colleagues undertook a pilot trial to ascertain the experiences of patients who had their heart surgery consultation audiotaped (Leahy et al., 2005). The intervention patients were given their audiotapes and the control patients were not given them. As this was a small pilot ($N = 20$) qualitative interviews were used in order to help plan the larger, definitive trial.

14.5 Discussion

Collecting the right outcome measures on as many trial participants as possible is a crucial element for the conduct of a rigorous study. It is important to collect outcomes that are as close as possible to the 'true' outcomes. This is because surrogate outcomes can mislead. Nevertheless surrogate outcome measures can be useful in helping to guide research at its earliest stages. For interventions that are likely to be delivered to vast numbers of people, it is important we evaluate such effects using outcomes that are relevant to the participant and society: not simply those of interest to the scientist.

14.6 Key points

- Most trials use 'surrogate' outcomes.
- Surrogates can mislead.
- It is important that important participant outcome measures are used.

15
Recruitment into Randomised Trials

15.1 Background

One of the most important aspects of undertaking an RCT is obtaining sufficient numbers of participants to allow us to demonstrate or exclude an important effect. Health care trials seem particularly vulnerable to under-recruitment, particularly trials that use 'trickle' or sequential recruitment, where we cannot identify all those in our sample of participants at the same time. For instance, if we want to recruit to a surgical trial for appendicitis we need to recruit participants as they arrive for surgery for the condition. Similarly, if we are recruiting to a study testing the effect of a court order on children absent from school, we need to recruit as the parents are referred to court. In contrast, other trials, such as a study of a school-based intervention means we can recruit the schools and then the children, achieve our sample and then randomise all the participants at the same time. Recruitment to this sort of trial tends to be easier and quicker as we can identify a list of schools, mail out to the schools and then the parents of the children in the schools, all of which can be undertaken relatively quickly and easily. In contrast, with sequential recruitment we have to estimate the numbers of potential participants arriving in a clinic, estimate how many are likely to be eligible and assume that this will remain constant. All of these estimates are subject to error, and often the numbers are over-estimated, leading to shortfalls in total recruitment and a lower sample size than is ideal.

Trials that do not achieve their target sample size run the risk of incurring a Type II error: that is, erroneously concluding there is no significant difference between the groups when there is. If recruitment is slow and difficult, research funders may erroneously conclude that they would get better value by using other, less rigorous, research designs. In this chapter we look at the issue of recruitment. Note, however, that most of the information in this chapter is based on expert opinion and experience. As trialists we know that this tends to form the lowest grade of evidence in any evidence-based decision-making. In this instance the issue of recruitment into randomised controlled trials has, ironically, rarely been addressed *using* a randomised controlled trial.

15.2   Recruitment difficulties

Recruitment into health care randomised trials is notoriously difficult. For other areas this may not be the case. In our experience, educational trials tend to find it relatively easier to recruit participants than health care trials. Few health care trials manage to recruit their target sample size within the specified time-frame. Many never make their prior sample size. In Table 15.1 Puffer and Torgerson (2003) undertook a survey of all individually randomised trials published in the *BMJ* and *Lancet* for the years 2000 and 2001: 41 per cent of trials experienced recruitment problems with significantly more multi-centred trials having problems. Indeed, if we also include trials that needed a time extension, 57 per cent of all studies had problems. It is worth noting that this is a biased sample leading to an underestimate of the size of the problem. Trials that collapsed due to poor recruitment and trials with poor recruitment would not have been published in these prestigious journals.

In another study of 122 trials funded by major UK grant agencies (i.e., Medical Research Council and NHS HTA programme) it was found that

Table 15.1:   Recruitment problems in a sample of trials

Trial characteristic	Number (%) or average
Conducted in primary care	28 (36)
Multi-centred trial	53 (67)
Experienced recruitment problems	32 (41)
Needed time extension	28 (35)
Need time extension or under-recruited.	45 (57)
Target recruitment time (mean, median IQR)	19, 12, 8–24
Needed extra funds for extension	15 (19)
Average age of participants (mean, median, IQR)	50, 57, 39–65
Target sample size (mean, median, IQR)	863, 296, 160–938
Achieved sample size (mean, median, IQR)	851, 303, 140–874
Average under-recruitment (mean, median, IQR)	171, 76, 6–336
Average time extension, months (mean, median, IQR)	6, 1, 0–9

IQR: interquartile range.

only 31 per cent of the trials achieved or exceeded their recruitment target (McDonald et al., 2006). Indeed about 45 per cent failed to achieve more than 80 per cent of their recruitment rate. More than half (54 per cent) of the trials in the sample required an extension to meet their recruitment target, and of these, thirteen trials achieved their target with the extension (McDonald et al., 2006). Note, in this study the prevalence of poor recruitment was worse than in the Puffer and Torgerson survey, as the latter was probably biased towards trials that recruited. Nevertheless, even this survey would have been biased towards the 'better' trials as the two funding agencies only tend to fund groups they consider likely to be able to undertake a scientifically satisfactory study.

Poor recruitment has the effect of reducing the power of the trial to find important differences, or if recruitment is slow, delaying the completion of the trial and increasing its expense. There are a number of reasons for poor or slow recruitment.

15.3   Administrative, bureaucratic barriers to recruitment

The sequence of planning and executing a trial starts with the submission of a trial protocol to a funding agency. Often this is a two-stage process. An outline application is submitted to, say, the Medical Research Council, which is sent out for peer review and then considered by a panel of trial experts. If the design is considered viable the MRC writes to the applicants asking for a full application. This first step can take about six months. If successful, the applicants are asked to re-submit a longer, more detailed, proposal. This again is peer reviewed and considered by a committee of trial experts. This process can take a further twelve months. Therefore, it is quite common for at least eighteen months to elapse before funding is confirmed and this is before a single patient has been recruited to the study.

Once funding has been agreed there are other hurdles to cross. The most important of these is ethics approval. Indeed, gaining ethics approval is usually a pre-requisite for trial funding being confirmed. Ethical approval can lead to considerable delay and postpone the start of the trial by several months. More recently another hurdle has been introduced into the NHS: research governance. After obtaining ethical approval, trialists in the UK now need to obtain research governance from the appropriate health care trust. If the trial is a multi-centred study then all the centres involved need to obtain research governance. Delay to the start of a trial because of this can be substantial. In a multi-centred trial we recently undertook, delays in approval ranged from two weeks to thirteen months! Therefore, once funding, ethical and now research governance approval have been gained it is likely to be at least two years before the trial can start.

15.4   Participant identification

Occasionally, trials compete with other studies for the same patients. Scientifically, it is usually valid for patients to participate in more than one trial, as the randomisation process will ensure that participants in one study will be evenly allocated across the various arms of the other study. On the other hand, ethics committees often object to patients being approached for inclusion into more than one trial. Nevertheless, careful collaboration between different trialists may mean that in some instances participants can be included in more than one trial and a convincing case may be put before an ethics committee. Indeed, in a factorial design participants are by definition taking part in more than one experiment.

Once the trial starts it is usual to find that the estimates of the numbers of eligible participants have been over-optimistic. If clinicians are asked for estimated numbers of eligible participants during the planning stage of the trial they usually over-estimate the numbers, due to several reasons. First, it may be that the clinician, who has an interest in the area, may see most of the eligible participants within his or her department and extrapolate those numbers to his colleagues, which leads to an over-estimation. Second, the total number of people with a given condition makes no allowance for the numbers that have to be excluded because they do not wish to take part or because they have a medical contra-indication.

The following scenario usually unfolds during a trial. Recruitment starts: it starts badly. Everyone working on the trial puts this down to 'teething' problems and they are hopeful it will improve. This is usually not the case as recruitment is often best during the early months of the trial, as this is where collaborators are at their most enthusiastic. Nevertheless, hope usually triumphs over experience and it is agreed to review the situation after a few months. At the next review the researchers discover that recruitment has worsened: this leads to panic. Remedial measures are taken, such as trying to get more centres on board, which requires ethical approval and leads to more delay. The measures taken may improve recruitment slightly but never enough, and the trial either closes or has to seek an extension of its funds to continue recruitment for longer or, commonly, a mix of the two.

There are several ways of trying to prevent this unhappy situation: these suggestions are based on experience and therefore are not strictly 'evidence-based'. First, before the trial starts *be* pessimistic and assume recruitment is going to be dire. Therefore, consider and implement all methods to improve recruitment at the start of the trial. Second, and extremely important, try to run a pilot phase before the main study. In a multi-centred trial this might mean getting local ethics committee approval for one centre ahead of the main trial in order to test out recruitment strategies and to gauge recruitment rates. Data from the pilot can be invaluable when assessing recruitment rates. Pilots are not always possible; indeed, in one trial ethical approval for the pilot phase of the study was only granted *after* the main trial was nearly completed. Apparently the ethics committee could not understand the concept of a pilot! Third, streamline the recruitment methods. One of the main barriers to recruitment is not that potential participants refuse to take part; it is that clinicians do not have the time to explain the trial to them and recruit them into the study. Therefore, anything that can remove some or all of the work of recruitment away from the clinician is likely to be beneficial. Fourth, if possible use 'database' recruitment, i.e., a list of potential participants. People on this list can be mailed at relatively low cost and high speed to ascertain whether they wish to take part in the trial. As long as the database is sufficiently large, recruitment is then merely mailing out to as many people as are needed in the trial. A frustrating recruitment problem occurs when participants have to be recruited from a clinic. Clinics can be cancelled due to various crises that erupt periodically in the health service and if they are cancelled participants cannot be recruited. Further, if the time of a research nurse is being paid for to recruit participants then this money is lost and cannot be reallocated.

In a multi-centred trial some centres always recruit better than others. As a rule of thumb with multi-centred trials 80 per cent of the participants tend to be recruited from 20 per cent of the centres. Unfortunately, it is nearly impossible to predict in advance which of the 20 per cent of centres will be good at recruitment.

If the financial arrangements of the trial are such that each centre receives an allocation of money to recruit participants this often means that those centres that do not or cannot recruit are a financial drain on the trial. To avoid this it is sensible to have contracts drawn up with specified targets. For example, the centres might have a target of recruiting 100 participants every six months for a half time research nurse's salary. After six months, if this target is not met, the funding can be either withdrawn or reduced and the savings reallocated to more successful centres.

There are various methods of improving recruitment, one of which is to involve the media. Depending on the intervention one can appeal directly to the public to contact the trial centre if they wish to take part in the study. An example of this was a randomised trial of hip protectors for the prevention of hip fractures (Birks et al., 2004). Hip protectors are used in specially developed underwear which protects the wearer's hip should they fall over. The start of this trial provoked a relatively large media interest due to mirth caused by the intervention. This interest was capitalised upon by appeals during television and newspaper interviews for those interested in taking part to contact the trial centre. This publicity enabled the trial to recruit several hundred participants in a relatively short space of time (Birks et al., 2004). Other approaches such as using posters or leaflets may be helpful although we have not noted that they have been very effective.

15.5   Financial incentives

Financial incentives will improve recruitment; however, ethically this can be problematic. Ethics committees will not usually allow direct payments to participants, unless it is to reimburse 'reasonable' travel expenses. Payments to clinicians or their employers to recruit participants may be more justified as it does take time out of normal clinical activities to recruit trial patients. Trials that rely on the goodwill of clinicians to recruit participants for no reimbursement are unlikely to recruit effectively. However, if reimbursement is used to help recruitment it is important to link this directly to recruitment targets. Funds should be withdrawn if targets are not met.

15.6   Evidence-based recruitment

A recent systematic review of recruitment methods (Watson and Torgerson, 2006) found fourteen papers describing twenty different interventions. In the following we summarise the main findings.

One trial of a patient preference design found no difference between that design and a normal recruitment approach (Cooper et al., 1997). As mentioned previously, two trials comparing placebos versus no placebos looked at recruitment rates. They found that recruitment was significantly greater among potential participants randomised to receive information about the 'open' version of the trial as compared with the placebo version. A trial undertaken in France randomised different centres to receive regular visits from the trial co-ordinator or simply have patient recruitment materials posted to the participating centres (Liénard et al., 2006). The trial did not detect a difference between the resource-intensive approach (i.e., trial co-ordinator visiting at regular intervals) versus the minimalist method. This trial was unable to show that 'accepted practice' in trial management of close support from the trial co-ordinators was more effective. Clearly, trial management methods need to be as rigorously evaluated as the treatments themselves. Two trials compared recruitment of participants using nurses compared with using doctors. Both trials found that doctors had slightly, but non-statistically significantly, greater recruitment than nurses and one of the trials found that nurses took longer and therefore recruitment was not significantly less expensive (Donovan et al., 2003; Aaronson et al., 1996). A cluster trial of training GPs and practice staff in the management of back pain led to significant increases in recruitment among the trained staff (i.e., more than double) (Farrin et al., 2005). Therefore, a training package for recruiting clinicians might be helpful.

An American trial looked at the use of Hispanic nurses to recruit Hispanic women in the Women's Health Initiative study of HRT: this was found to be helpful (Larkey et al., 2002). In contrast, African-American researchers were not more successful compared with non-African-American researchers in recruiting African-American men into a cancer screening trial, although the same study noted church-based methods did improve recruitment among African-Americans compared with non-church-based methods (Ford et al., 2004).

A study that used qualitative research methods of boosting trial recruitment claimed to show that recruitment rose after the introduction of enhanced recruitment methods that had been developed using qualitative research methods (Donovan et al., 2002). However, the quantitative evaluation was a simple before and after method and the before recruitment period was at the start of the trial, when recruitment is generally often low; therefore, this approach remains unproven.

Zelen's method is advocated as an approach to maximising recruitment: there is no randomised evidence to support this assertion as yet. However, some trials have used a mixture of Zelen's method and the normal consent method and have shown that recruitment is enhanced using Zelen's approach. For example, a trial by Andrew et al. showed that recruitment was better in the centre that used Zelen's method compared with the other centres (Andrew et al., 1993).

15.7   Discussion

Recruitment to clinical trials is extremely difficult. The challenges to recruitment must not be underestimated. Most trials probably do not recruit on time or reach their original target. Trial recruitment needs to be a key item for detailed discussion by the trial management team before recruitment starts. Prompt recruitment must be one of the key objectives for any trial, otherwise they will be underpowered and we may miss important effects. Little rigorous research has been undertaken to examine the most effective recruitment strategies. Many recruitment approaches are based on 'custom and practice' or expert opinion or best guesses. This evidence base for recruitment methods is unsatisfactory. Some trials of recruitment strategies have been undertaken (Watson and Torgerson, 2006) and the evidence from a review of these does encourage the use of educational interventions and the avoidance of placebos. However, the effectiveness of common recruitment approaches – such as sending trial co-ordinators on site visits – remains unproven.

In summary, the key messages on recruitment are: do a pilot; use database recruitment if possible; give some education to those doing the recruitment; and think carefully before using placebos.

15.8 Key points

- Recruitment is difficult in most health care trials.
- Trials using trickle recruitment are especially prone to the problem of poor recruitment.
- Trialists should plan for poor recruitment and take steps to avoid it.
- Effective interventions include: database recruitment; piloting recruitment; not using placebos; educating clinicians.

16
Systematic Reviews of Randomised Controlled Trials

16.1 Background

> The house of social science research is sadly dilapidated. It is strewn among the scree of a hundred journals and lies about in the unsightly rubble of a million dissertations. Even if it cannot be built into a science, the rubble ought to be sifted and culled for whatever consistency there is in it. (Glass et al., 1981)

In evidence-based public policy-making, for effectiveness questions, the highest level of evidence is widely considered to be a systematic review (research synthesis) of RCTs. A single RCT cannot always provide a definitive answer about the effectiveness of an intervention in all the circumstances where it may be applicable, i.e. in different settings or with participants with different characteristics. A notable exception is a single 'mega-trial', an example of which is the RCT of polio vaccine where 750 000 children were randomised.

A systematic review is essential as a prelude to an RCT, to assess whether another RCT is necessary and, if so, to inform its design. If relatively small and underpowered earlier RCTs are available, we should first review them to obtain an estimate of the anticipated effect size to inform the size of our trial. Similarly, on completion of a new trial we should add its results to any previous randomised evidence, to obtain a more precise overview of the relevant research. The best method of doing this is to undertake a systematic review of RCTs (Torgerson, 2003).

16.2   Systematic reviews

> The science of research synthesis – as in any other scientific research –
> implies that those who practice it will take steps to avoid misleading
> themselves and others by ignoring biases and the effects of chance.
> (Chalmers, 2003)

A systematic review employs a scientific approach to identifying and
synthesising all the RCTs in a given area. In the field of health care
research the Cochrane Collaboration was established in the early 1990s
to undertake, publish and disseminate high quality reviews of high quality
controlled studies, preferably those employing random allocation. The
world-wide success of the Cochrane Collaboration in turn led to the
establishment of its sister organisation, the Campbell Collaboration (in
2000), which aims to undertake systematic reviews of randomised trials
and quasi-experiments in the fields of education, crime and justice and
social welfare.

Although widespread interest in systematic reviews dates from
the mid-1990s, the concept has a much longer history. James Lind
(author of the scurvy experiment in the eighteenth century mentioned
earlier) gathered together all of the literature on scurvy to help
inform him about the best method for its treatment (see www.james-
lindlibrary.org).

Research synthesis can, in principle, be applied to studies of any design
(to address a range of questions); in this book we confine ourselves to its
application in the synthesis of RCTs.

A systematic review differs from a traditional 'narrative' review in respect
to the key principle of transparency in its methods in order to facilitate
replication. Other features of systematic reviews are important (for
example, systematic methods for searching exhaustively to locate all
potentially relevant studies, reasons for including studies established
a priori and methods for quantitative synthesis), but the defining principle
of the systematic review process is its explicit, transparent, potentially
replicable method.

In their systematic review of trials evaluating the use of human colloid
to replace fluid loss among injured patients Schierhout and Roberts
(1998) found a statistically significant increase in mortality associated
with the intervention. The review was disputed and replicated by Wilkes
and Navickis (2001), who also found an increase in mortality associated
with the intervention; however, by including a wider range of trials the
difference they found was no longer statistically significant. Eventually,

a large trial of nearly 7,000 critically ill patients comparing the use of human albumin with the use of saline for blood loss found little evidence for harm, *and* little evidence for benefit (SAFE Study Investigators, 2004).

In the field of education research, Ehri and colleagues (2001) undertook a systematic review of studies in the field of phonics instruction and concluded that systematic phonics instruction was more effective compared with non-systematic or no phonics instruction (pooled effect size of 0.41). A replication and update of this review supported the findings of the original review, but the overall effect size was substantially reduced to 0.27 (Torgerson et al., 2006).

In theory, a rigorously designed and conducted systematic review should minimise reviewer bias by making all the methods of the study explicit, for example decisions to include or exclude studies. However, even rigorously conducted systematic reviews can be susceptible to publication or design bias.

16.3   Publication bias

Any literature review may be susceptible to publication bias, where relevant studies are not included in the review because they have not been published. A number of steps can be used in the systematic review process to limit the potential for publication bias. Firstly, the systematic review search should be exhaustive. Secondly, published and unpublished literature should be included in the review. Randomised trials with positive intervention effects tend to be published more easily and rapidly than those showing a negative or null effect. Therefore limiting a systematic review to only published studies will tend to bias the combined effect size.

Studies of the prevalence of publication bias go back to the 1950s and 1960s. For an overview of the history of publication bias, see Torgerson (2006). For example, Smart (1964) noted that in the area of psychology unpublished studies were more likely to have negative results compared with published papers. He concluded that the neglect of negative studies was due to non-submission by authors or to greater critical examination of experiments containing negative results by journal editors and peer reviewers. These findings were confirmed in health care research by Dickersin (2002) and in psychological, educational and behavioural treatment research by Lipsey and Wilson (1993).

Sutton et al. (2000) and Egger et al. (1997) demonstrated that many meta-analyses in health care research did not consider the effect of publication bias on their results. For example, Sutton et al. (2000) analysed forty-eight systematic reviews; they estimated that twenty-three of these had some degree of publication bias. They then extrapolated from this to estimate that about half of meta-analyses may be subject to some level of publication bias and about a fifth will have a strong indication of missing trials.

Even when it is possible to access all of the publications there is a potential problem with time-lag bias (Hopewell et al., 2007). This occurs when positive trials are written up more quickly and accepted more rapidly by journals. Consequently a systematic review that includes very recent literature may bias the review towards a positive conclusion, as negative studies may still be going through the publication process.

Positive trials may be published in more prestigious, more easily accessed journals, and negative trials may be more likely to be published in more obscure outlets. For example, two trials that appeared to show that the use of hip protectors had a positive effect on the prevention of hip fractures were published in the leading medical journals (Lauritzen et al., 1993; Kannus et al., 2000). When two, larger, more rigorous trials that showed no benefit of hip protectors were undertaken, they were both published in lower impact journals (Birks et al., 2004; O'Hallaron et al., 2004).

16.4 Design bias

In addition to the potential problem of publication bias, a systematic review can produce biased findings if the primary studies included within the systematic review are, themselves, likely to be biased because they are of weak methodological quality. Collating several biased trials in a systematic review will produce a precise, but biased, result. Therefore, we need to assess the quality of the RCTs that we include in the review in order to limit the impact of design bias.

The quality of randomised controlled trials is variable, and poor quality trials may give misleading results. Clearly, inferences about the effectiveness of an intervention will be more reliable if they are drawn from good quality trials. Reviews in the health care literature have highlighted the methodological weaknesses of RCTs published in major medical journals (Pocock et al., 1987; Altman and Doré, 1990; Gore et al., 1992; Moher et al., 1994; Assman et al., 2000; Schulz and Grimes, 2002). Failure to conceal the randomisation process overestimates treatment effects compared with trials that use adequate concealment (Schulz and Grimes, 2002; Schulz et al., 1995; Egger et al., 2003; Hewitt et al., 2006). On the other hand, failure to *report* the randomisation process is not always an indicator that a rigorous approach was not used. For example, in a trial of bone density screening concealed allocation was undertaken (Torgerson et al., 1997). This was not reported in the published paper because, at that time, the problem of allocation subversion was not widely understood.

In educational research, it is sometimes difficult to know whether or not a controlled trial has been randomised. None of the published reports of two widely cited controlled trials comparing different approaches to phonics instruction (Johnston and Watson, 2004) describes methods of allocation. Correspondence with the lead author established that the allocation procedure for the first of the two experiments was researcher decision, while in the second experiment matching was followed by random allocation (Johnston, personal communication, 2005); thus the two trials were respectively non-randomised and randomised.

16.5   The CONSORT statement and trial quality

In an effort to improve the reporting of randomised trials in health care research many medical journals have adopted the CONSORT statement (Begg et al., 1996). A before and after evaluation of these guidelines appeared to show an improvement in the reporting of randomised studies (Moher et al., 2001). However, an evaluation of a larger number of randomised trials over a longer time frame indicated that the quality of trial reporting, in prestigious medical journals, was improving before the CONSORT guidelines were published and continued to improve at a similar rate after their adoption (Torgerson et al., 2005).

Evaluations comparing the effect sizes of 'good' quality trials compared with 'poor' quality trials demonstrate differences in effect (Kjaergaard et al., 2001). Indeed, the difference in effect sizes between small and large trials, so often explained by publication bias, was probably due to the fact that small trials tend to be of poorer quality. When compared with good quality large trials, good quality small trials yield similar estimates of effect.

Quality assurance scales to measure the quality of trials can give very different results depending on the items included and the weights given to individual items. If quality criteria use a system of 'weighting' or 'adding up' there is a risk of classifying a trial as being of 'good' quality simply because it performs well on many of the criteria. However, if the trial has a fatal flaw in one of the most important aspects of trial design, the results of the trial may be unreliable. On some scales studies can score highly if they are well reported rather than well conducted (Juni et al., 2001).

16.6   CONSORT, CLEAR NPT checklists

The CONSORT guidance is now widely accepted by medical journals and some psychological journals.

Table 16.1 gives the CONSORT checklist, modified to apply more widely than was originally intended (Torgerson, 2003), in this case to educational trials, but it could also be adapted for the reporting of trials in crime and justice, social welfare and other areas of public policy.

Some of the CONSORT researchers (Boutron et al., 2005) subsequently developed the CLEAR NPT checklist for non-pharmacological trials, which is a shortened version of CONSORT and focuses mainly on the aspects of trial quality that affect the internal validity of the study. This checklist can be applied to non-health care trials as well (see Table 16.2).

An important aspect of trial reporting is the use of the CONSORT flow diagram. In Figure 16.1 a diagram taken from an RCT of the use of ICT in the teaching of spelling is shown (Brooks et al., 2006).

The diagram includes the flow of participants through the trial. After allocation, four of the pupils left the school and could not be included in the pre-test. Some participants were not available for the post-test. Sensitivity analysis in the paper using post-test values only did not materially alter the findings of this study (Brooks et al., 2006).

Table 16.1:   Modified CONSORT quality criteria

Was the study population adequately described? (i.e., were the important characteristics of the participants described, e.g. age, gender, learner characteristics?)
Was the minimum important difference described? (i.e., was the smallest educationally important effect size described?)
Was the target sample size adequately determined?
Was intention to treat analysis (intention to teach analysis) used?
Was the unit of randomisation described (i.e., individuals or groups, e.g. classes, schools)?
Were the participants allocated using random number tables, coin flip, computer generation?
Was the randomisation process concealed from those who were involved in recruitment?
Were follow-up measures administered blind?
Was estimated effect on primary and secondary outcome measures stated?
Was precision of effect size estimated (confidence intervals)?
Were summary data presented in sufficient detail to permit alternative analyses or replication?
Was the discussion of the study findings consistent with the data?

166

Table 16.2: CLEAR NPT – checklist for non-pharmacological trials

Item		Possible answer
1	Was the generation of allocation sequences adequate?	Yes; No; Unclear
2	Was the intervention allocation concealed?	Yes; No; Unclear
3	Were details of the intervention administered to each group (e.g. class, school) made available?	Yes; No; Unclear
4	Were intervention providers' (e.g. teacher, instructor) experience or skill in each arm appropriate?	Yes; No; Unclear
5	Was participant adherence addressed quantitatively?	Yes; No; Unclear
6	Were participants adequately blinded?	Yes; No, because blinding is not feasible; No, although blinding is feasible; Unclear
6.1	If participants were not adequately blinded	
6.1.1	Were all other interventions and cointerventions the same in each randomised group?	Yes; No; Unclear
6.1.2	Were withdrawals and lost to follow-up the same in each randomised group?	Yes; No; Unclear
7	Were intervention providers adequately blinded?	Yes; No, because blinding was not feasible; No, although blinding was feasible; Unclear
7.1	If intervention providers were not adequately blinded	
7.1.1	Were all other interventions and cointerventions the same in each randomised group?	Yes; No; Unclear
7.1.2	Were withdrawals and lost to follow-up the same in each randomised group?	Yes; No; Unclear
8	Were outcome assessors adequately blinded to assess the primary outcomes?	Yes; No because blinding was not feasible; No, although blinding was feasible; Unclear
8.1	If outcome assessors were not adequately blinded, were specific methods used to avoid ascertainment bias?	Yes; No; Unclear
9	Was the follow-up schedule the same in each group?	Yes; No; Unclear
10	Were the main outcomes analysed according to the intention-to-treat (intention to teach) principle?	Yes; No; Unclear

(*Source*: Boutron et al., 2005). NB – wording slightly changed (e.g., treatment to intervention, patient to participant) to make it more applicable to all trials.

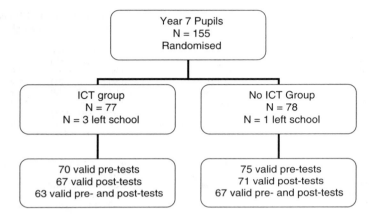

Figure 16.1: CONSORT flow diagram
Source: Brooks et al., 2006.

16.7 Trial quality

Compared with the field of health care research less methodological work on the quality of non-health care trials has been undertaken (Pocock et al., 1987; Altman and Doré, 1990; Gore et al., 1992; Moher et al., 1994; Assman et al., 2000). The quality of some health care RCTs is low, although, as noted above, in some cases this may be due to poor quality of reporting; however, much is due to low quality design and conduct.

In a comparison of the quality of RCTs between health care and education, in the sample of 84 education trials from a twelve-year period between 1990 and 2002 (Torgerson et al., 2005), no trial reported whether or not the randomisation process was concealed, and no trial reported the justification for sample size calculation. Only one trial reported the use of confidence intervals and only twelve (14 per cent) used blinded assessment of outcome. The same study did, however, note that the majority of health care trials – especially those published in relatively low impact journals – also had significant quality problems.

16.8 Meta-analysis

The main aim of a systematic review is to systematically locate either all the available evidence on a given subject or a representative sample of the evidence, which may then be combined in a synthesis, such as a meta-analysis, in order to give a precise overview of the existing literature within

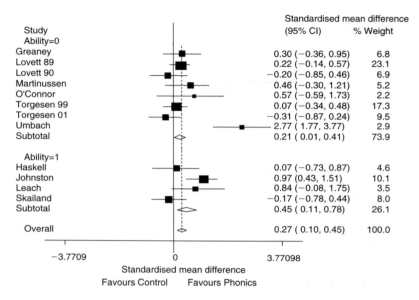

Figure 16.2:   Meta-analysis and Forest plot of systematic phonics teaching on reading skills
Source: Torgerson et al., 2006.

an area. A meta-analysis is a statistical method of combining similar studies to obtain a more precise estimate of effect, which is particularly valuable in areas that contain small, underpowered RCTs.

Glass (1976) and Glass et al. (1981) first proposed the term 'meta-analysis' to describe the method for aggregating the data from individual studies. The results from individual studies with similar conceptual underpinnings but with different measurement scales for outcomes are expressed in a standard metric: an effect size, which is the estimate of the size of a treatment effect. The effect size is usually the difference between the means of the experimental and control groups at post-test divided by the standard deviation of the control group (Glass, 1976). When the effect sizes are pooled into an aggregate effect size the individual studies are weighted by their sample sizes. In addition, subgroup analyses can be undertaken to explore the effect of moderator variables on the effect. Meta-analysis is also limited by the quality of its included studies.

In Figure 16.2 we show an example of a systematic review of RCTs evaluating systematic versus unsystematic or no phonics instruction, its meta-analysis and Forest plot (Torgerson et al., 2006). The results of the review are presented graphically and we can see the individual point estimates, depicted as a square with the 95 per cent confidence intervals.

The aggregate of all the twelve relatively small trials is a small effect size of 0.27, which is statistically significant (95 per cent confidence interval 0.10 to 0.45). Note that one, small trial is an obvious outlier with a positive effect size much greater than any other study in the meta-analysis. If we remove this small study, then the re-calculated effect size of the meta-analysis is no longer statistically significant.

When a number of trials have been undertaken in a given area we can undertake a 'meta-regression'. This is a statistical analysis where we use study level variables to explain differences in effect. In Figure 16.2 the effect of phonics instruction seems to be consistent among children with different learner characteristics (children with learning difficulties or normally attaining children).

16.9   Quality of systematic reviews

Because the robustness of the findings of systematic reviews is underpinned by the quality of their design, conduct and reporting, it is important that these should be rigorous. Important quality issues include, for example, whether or not the reviewers examined the effect sizes by method of allocation (random or other method); the degree to which bias was limited in the review; whether the searching was exhaustive (including a search of 'fugitive' or 'grey' literature in order to limit the possibility of publication bias) and transparent; and whether the variability in the quality of included trials was assessed and taken into consideration in the synthesis.

The importance of the quality appraisal of systematic reviews was recognised in the field of health care research in the QUOROM (Quality of Reporting of Meta-analyses) statement (Moher et al., 1999; Shea et al., 2001). Like the CONSORT statement (Altman, 1996) for the reporting of RCTs, the QUOROM statement was developed by methodologists as a consensus statement for the quality of reporting of meta-analyses in health care research. It is believed that the quality of reporting of meta-analyses is a reasonably good (though not perfect) indicator of the quality of the review (Shea et al., 2001). The stages of a meta-analysis in which the QUOROM standards should be adopted are: the rationale for the meta-analysis; the methods and results for the search; the inclusion/exclusion criteria; the coding of the primary studies; the meta-analysis; quality assurance procedures; and the interpretation of the results.

Other quality appraisal checklists are available, particularly in the area of health care research. For example, a systematic review on the reporting of RCTs in health care research found thirty-four checklists (Shea et al., 2001). More recently, the Campbell Collaboration has developed guidelines for the writing of protocols for systematic reviews in the fields of education, criminal justice and other social sciences; and in the UK the EPPI Centre has developed similar guidelines specifically in the field of education. The QUOROM checklist (Table 16.3) is specifically designed for the quality appraisal of reporting of meta-analyses of experimental research and has been modified for educational meta-analyses using educationally appropriate terminology to describe participants and interventions.

As well as the QUOROM guidelines for reporting systematic reviews guidance has also been developed for the quality appraisal of systematic reviews (Shea et al., 2007). In health care research it has been estimated that there are at least twenty-four instruments for the assessment of the quality of systematic reviews (Shea et al., 2001). A tool that attempts to bring together widely agreed criteria for the quality of systematic reviews is the AMSTAR measurement tool (Shea et al., 2004), which contains eleven items to assess the quality of systematic reviews (Table 16.4).

Table 16.3:   Key features of the QUOROM statement (adapted for systematic reviews in research in the wider social sciences)

Introduction: Explicitly state problem and rationale for review.

Methods: searching: State sources of information (e.g., names of databases, hand searching of key journals), search restrictions (e.g., year, publication language, published and/or unpublished).

Selection: Inclusion and exclusion criteria.

Validity assessment: Quality assessment (e.g., blinded follow-up).

Data abstraction: Process used (e.g., double data extraction).

Study characteristics: Type of study design, student characteristics, details of intervention, outcomes, how was educational heterogeneity assessed?

Data synthesis: How were data combined? Measures of effect, statistical testing and confidence intervals, handling of missing data, sensitivity and subgroup analyses, assessment of publication bias.

Results: trial flow: Provide a profile of trials identified and reasons for inclusion/exclusion.

Study characteristics: Provide descriptive data for each trial (e.g., age, setting, class size, intervention).

Quantitative data synthesis: Report agreement between reviewers on selection and validity assessment, present summary results, report data needed to calculate effect sizes and confidence intervals (i.e., number, mean, standard deviations by group).

Discussion: Summarise key findings and educational inferences. Interpret results in light of all the evidence, acknowledge potential biases in review and suggest areas for future research.

Source: adapted from Shea et al. (2001).

Table 16.4: AMSTAR quality appraisal tool for systematic reviews

1. Was an 'a priori' design provided? The research question and inclusion criteria should be established before the conduct of the review	Yes No Can't answer Not applicable
2. Was there duplicate study selection and data extraction? There should be at least two independent data extractors and a consensus procedure for disagreements should be in place.	Yes No Can't answer Not applicable
3. Was a comprehensive literature search preformed? At least two electronic sources should be searched. The report must include years and databases used. Key words and/or MESH terms must be stated and where feasible the search strategy should be provided. All searches should be supplemented by consulting current contents, reviews, textbooks, specialised registers, or experts in the particular field of study, and by reviewing the references in the studies found.	Yes No Can't answer Not applicable
4. Was the status of the publication (i.e., grey literature) used as an inclusion criterion? The authors should state that they searched for reports regardless of their publication type. The authors should state whether or not they excluded any reports (from the systematic review) based on the publication status, language etc.	Yes No Can't answer Not applicable
5. Was a list of studies (included and excluded) provided? A list of included and excluded studies should be provided.	Yes No Can't answer Not applicable
6. Were the characteristics of the included studies provided? In an aggregated form such as a table, data from the original studies should be provided on the participants, interventions and outcomes. The range of characteristics in all the studies analysed, e.g., age, race, sex, relevant socio-economic data, should be reported.	Yes No Can't answer Not applicable

(*Continued*)

Table 16.4: (Continued)

7. Was the scientific quality of the included studies assessed and documented? 'A priori' methods of assessment should be provided (e.g., for effectiveness studies if the author(s) chose to include only randomised, double-blind, placebo controlled studies, or allocation concealment as inclusion criteria); for other types of studies alternative items will be relevant.	Yes No Can't answer Not applicable
8. Was the scientific quality of the included studies used appropriately in formulating conclusions? The results of the methodological rigour and scientific quality should be considered in the analysis and the conclusions of the review, and explicitly stated in formulating recommendations.	Yes No Can't answer Not applicable
9. Were the methods used to combine the findings of the studies appropriate? For the pooled results, a test should be done to ensure the studies were combinable, to assess their homogeneity (i.e., Chi-squared test for homogeneity, I^2). If heterogeneity exists a random effects model should be used and/or the clinical appropriateness of combining should be taken into consideration (i.e., is it sensible to combine?)	Yes No Can't answer Not applicable
10. Was the likelihood of publication bias assessed? An assessment of publication bias should include a combination of graphical aids (e.g., funnel plot, other available tests) and or statistical tests (e.g., Egger regression test).	Yes No Can't answer Not applicable
11. Was the conflict of interest stated? Potential sources of support should be clearly acknowledged in both the systematic review and the included studies.	Yes No Can't answer Not applicable

Source: Shea et al., 2007.

16.10   Using systematic reviews to develop an RCT

As noted previously, a systematic review is an invaluable tool for informing the design of an RCT. For instance, if we want to undertake the 'definitive' trial of systematic phonics teaching versus other forms of reading instruction we could use the results of a systematic review to inform the calculation of the required sample size. From Figure 16.2 we can see that the systematic review of RCTs suggested an effect size of 0.27 favouring systematic phonics teaching over other phonics approaches. As a minimum we ought to make our trial sufficiently large to detect at least a 0.27 difference in effect size. To detect this difference with 80 per cent power and using individual randomisation (see Chapter 13) we would need about 440 children in the trial. Such a trial would be much larger than any of those that were included in the meta-analysis: the largest trial only included 121 children. Note, however, the difference of 0.27 may be exaggerated through the possibility of publication bias or because a small trial with an extreme result was included. Therefore, to be conservative we would probably want to detect 0.25 or 0.20 of an effect size. An effect size of 0.20 would require about 800 participants for an individually randomised trial: a cluster randomised trial would require several times more participants.

From Figure 16.2 we can see that the meta-analysis of trials has been divided into two groups: children experiencing learning difficulties and normally attaining children. The effect size of phonics instruction among children experiencing difficulties is 0.21 whereas the effect size among normally attaining children is 0.45: there is insufficient evidence to focus our study on children with learning difficulties. Therefore, we should probably include children with all learner characteristics.

A single summary graph of our systematic review has informed us about the potential size of the trial and the kind of participants we should include. Without having undertaken the review we might have either underpowered our trial or selected too narrow a range of participants. The review might also help in the selection of outcome measures. For example, we might avoid tests that appear to have poor performance characteristics, or we might decide to include a test that was widely used in previous research in order to enhance the credibility of our findings.

16.11   Discussion

A systematic review of good quality RCTs is the highest level of evidence in effectiveness research. An individual RCT may, by chance or through weak design, produce a biased result. Combining trials in an overview – even if the trials cannot be formally synthesised in a meta-analysis – is usually more informative than relying on the results of a single trial. The exception to this may be if there is a large, definitive study that overrides the evidence from a series of small trials. The definitive trial of human albumin was probably more robust in its conclusions than the preceding systematic reviews that included a more heterogeneous sample of studies.

16.12   Key points

- Systematic reviews of high quality RCTs are the best method of informing effectiveness questions.
- The statistical summary of different trials (meta-analysis) improves precision.
- Graphical displays of trials help inform future RCT design as well as policy.
- All reviews are susceptible to publication and design biases; systematic reviews are less susceptible, due to exhaustive searching, and quality appraisal of included trials.
- New trials contribute to updated systematic reviews.

17
Economic Evaluation Alongside Randomised Trials

17.1 Background

Economic evaluation is of key importance in rational decision-making. Most interventions have a cost, and some effective interventions are simply too expensive to be implemented. Unless economic evaluations are included alongside randomised trials we run the risk of introducing effective, but cost-ineffective interventions. In this chapter we discuss some of the basic concepts and issues surrounding the use of economic evaluations in trial settings. Economic evaluation is a complex discipline and we do not attempt to do full justice to it here. There are numerous textbooks solely concerned with economics and economic evaluation. In this book we cover some of the key issues and introduce some key concepts which are important to bear in mind when planning an economic aspect to a trial. Ideally, however, one should include an economist in the trial team.

17.2 Establishing the need for an RCT

One role that economics can fulfil is to ascertain whether or not it is worthwhile to undertake a given RCT. Any research has an opportunity cost. If we fund a trial to evaluate the use of a treatment for heart failure this means we cannot use the resources to fund a trial evaluating novel therapies for breast cancer treatment. It is argued that economic techniques can be used to help with the prioritisation of research (Fleurence and Torgerson, 2004). There are a number of approaches that can be used to help research prioritisation. One method is to establish the burden of the problem and its costs to society. In health care we would try to count the lives or Quality Adjusted Life Years (QALYs) lost and the costs of a list of diseases. In its most naive form research is directed to those areas that

175

have the greatest burden and/or cost. The problem with this approach is that it takes no account of whether a disease is amenable to treatment by current or incipient technologies. Many illnesses, whilst prevalent, may not be curable – whatever treatment is used. Furthermore, this approach does not take into account the cost of any potential treatments or their likely impact. Consequently if we depend upon this method we may not invest in researching an intervention that is relatively inexpensive but deals with a less common disease. Also this approach takes no account of the cost of the research. A single trial dealing with a prevalent disease might cost £20 million but doing this study could displace twenty smaller studies addressing twenty other disease areas. Whilst the single, large, expensive study may be worthwhile, more sophisticated analyses than merely looking at total disease burden are required to assess whether the opportunity lost or cost is worthwhile.

Another approach to identifying research priorities is to undertake prior modelling exercises of different treatments and then select those that are likely to be most cost effective. For example, in the mid-1990s there was discussion about which treatments should be evaluated for the prevention of fractures in older people. In a simple modelling exercise it was shown that, given assumptions of effectiveness derived from observational data, vitamin D appeared to be a good buy in terms of further evaluation (Torgerson et al., 1996). However, there was more robust evidence for the effectiveness of calcium. Therefore, a sensible approach was to use a factorial design evaluating both calcium and vitamin D together or independently: this trial design was put forward to the MRC and funded (RECORD Trial Group, 2005).

In the example above of research prioritisation, choices were only made between several treatments within the same disease area. The question of whether any evaluation within that disease area was worthwhile compared to, say, cardiac care was not established.

Using economics to prioritise research efforts is rarely undertaken; however, given constrained research budgets it probably should be done more often. Economic modelling techniques try to combine all the likely costs and benefits of undertaking a research programme in order to make research prioritisation more rational. Such modelling techniques can also be used to inform aspects of the trial design, such as sample size and the appropriate treatment comparator.

One role for pilot trials might be to help inform whether or not it is cost effective to undertake the definitive trial. Usually a pilot trial is undertaken simply to check assumptions of recruitment, adherence and other practicalities of undertaking a trial. However, a pilot could also produce some fairly robust cost data that could then be used to assess whether it is actually worthwhile investing a large amount of scarce resources in doing the definitive evaluation.

As well as helping to establish the need for a trial, economic techniques can also be used to help choose the most efficient trial design. For instance, as noted previously, simple economic techniques can be used to establish the most efficient allocation ratio. Prior economic evaluation can also determine the likely size of a trial: a trial can be powered to detect an effect size that is too small to be cost-effective; consequently we might choose a smaller trial to detect a larger size as we are uninterested in small differences because they will not be cost effective.

17.3   Economic evaluations alongside an RCT

The RCT is often the best vehicle for providing unbiased estimates of both effects and costs. Whilst it is generally true that an RCT is the best method to provide unbiased estimates of costs this may not always be the case. Sometimes, due to the design of the RCT, the costs profile of participants or the costs of the trial intervention may not reflect actual practice when the intervention is implemented. For instance, the cost of an intervention may be relatively high when being used in an RCT, but fall when economies of scale reduce the costs when implemented. Therefore, it is important to bear in mind that RCT data may need to be supplemented by data generated from other means. It is important, however, to choose an RCT design that is optimum to inform decision-making about the best treatment option. As noted in previous chapters, trials can be explanatory or pragmatic. Pragmatic trials are the best design for an economic evaluation as this design more closely resembles routine clinical practice and it is this we wish to cost and evaluate.

17.4   Perspective of the evaluation

It is important for any economic evaluation to specify the perspective. Ideally the widest perspective – the societal perspective – should be adopted. The societal perspective measures all the costs and benefits of any intervention. If, for instance, an intervention increases or decreases employment then this cost and benefit should be measured and included in the analysis even if the intervention does not directly aim to change this. Many economic evaluations, however, use a narrower perspective – usually the perspective of the organisation that pays for the intervention. For instance, a health care treatment will result in an increase in health care costs to deliver the intervention but may also reduce downstream costs, such as admissions to hospital or consultations by a primary care physician. There are likely to be other costs. A patient may have to take time off work (which includes unpaid work) to attend a doctor's appointment – this cost ought be measured and included, but often it is not. The disadvantage of not adopting a wide perspective is that there is an incentive to 'cost-shift' from one sector of society to another. For example, if we want to evaluate a policy of caring for people in the community who previously resided in an institution then adopting a narrow perspective could be misleading. Such a policy change would reduce costs in the health sector but increase costs to the families caring for the person, as well as other costs such as social welfare. Adopting a health care perspective could lead to the adoption of a policy that increases overall costs to society and reduces utility because, within the health care sector, the costs are lowered and the utility is increased. But, in the non-health care sector, costs are increased and there may be a reduced utility among carers and so the overall effect may lead to societal inefficiencies.

Nevertheless, many evaluations do adopt a narrow perspective – for instance the UK's National Institute for Clinical Effectiveness (NICE), which uses health economics to inform its decisions, only uses a health care perspective. This tends to increase the cost effectiveness of interventions that mainly impact on the health sector relative to treatments that impact on the non-health sector. Economists often use a narrow perspective because it can be quite time consuming and difficult to identify and value the multitude of costs and effects involved. Given limited researcher resources, identification of what is perceived *a priori* as the main costs may be the most efficient use of researcher resources. Often some of the wider impacts of an intervention may have little impact on the wider evaluation. The main drivers tend to be the cost of delivering the intervention and the immediate benefits. The additional costs and benefits may add little to the conclusions. Obviously without measuring these we cannot always be sure that this is the case.

17.5   Cost ascertainment

Costs comprise resource quantity weighted by price. It is important to gather and report actual resource quantities used, for example, number of GP visits, class size and grade and experience of staff. This is because prices change, not least with inflation, and the results of the evaluation may be different with different prices. If we know the quantity of resources we can look at the results with different prices (i.e., a sensitivity analysis).

There are several sources of cost data in health care evaluations: the participant, routine records, hospital purchases etc. Generally the participant is the easiest source of cost data as collecting cost data from participant questionnaires is relatively easy. The relevant cost questions can be added to participant questionnaires. Economists, however, often collect large amounts of detailed data, such as the length of a visit, its type as well as how many visits take place. This data collection can be onerous for the participant and jeopardise the response rates to the trial as a whole or there can be large amounts of missing data. Consequently it is best to try to obtain the key data, such as the number of visits, and make some assumptions about their length. It is better to have some data, which are relatively accurate, than no data or worse, inaccurate data. It is not necessarily the case that routinely collected data from medical records, for example, are more accurate than self-reported data. Some medical treatments, such as drugs that trigger a prescription, are accurate; however, other events are not. For example, analysis of routine medical records suggests that some individuals suffer dozens of hip fractures when it is unlikely for them to ever have more than two fractures. This is because a single event is often re-recorded as a new event. For instance a patient who has had a hip fracture may consult for pain relief and this may then be coded on the computer, erroneously, as a new hip fracture.

17.6   Measurement of non-monetary outcomes

Ideally we would like to measure both the inputs and outputs of a novel programme in money. As noted previously, this is sometimes possible but often it is not. Physical or mental incapacity can sometimes be translated into monetary values by looking at average compensation payments that courts award for similar problems caused by industrial accidents, for example. The increased benefit of education can sometimes be measured in terms of lifetime increases in income identified from longitudinal or cohort studies that have followed up groups of people with different educational qualifications and examined average salary differences. This latter approach, however, will tend to inflate the value of improved education as some of the value of a better education is signalling to the market that the person is a relatively scarce resource. If an intervention leads to an across-the-board increase in educational attainment then the value of that education in terms of compensation from the employment market will tend to be less.

When it is simply not possible to measure output in monetary terms we can state the quantity of the output in terms of the natural units. We can look at the number of lives saved, cancers averted or the numbers of children passing a certain threshold test. The problem with this approach is that it is difficult to generalise between different interventions. If we have one treatment that reduces hip fractures by 20 per cent and another treatment that reduces breast cancer recurrence by 10 per cent which should we choose, given similar costs? Or if we have to choose between investing in an intervention that boosts average literacy levels by 10 per cent or one that improves numeracy levels by a similar amount, which one should we choose?

One way around this problem is to convert the outcomes into a common measure of utility (or well-being). In health care this is commonly done by converting improvements in health into Quality Adjusted Life Years (QALYs). A QALY is where we measure the length of life and weight it by its quality. Consequently a year of life that is 70 per cent of perfect health is 0.7 of a QALY. Typically people are given several health care scenarios and asked to give these a weighting: is living with painful arthritis requiring a walking aid 70 per cent or 80 per cent of full health? Using a sample of people we can calculate an average value for different health states. Similarly, we can ask people to rate a utility scenario for an educational intervention. For example, Fletcher et al. (1990) gave educational policy-makers different scenarios regarding mathematics achievement. They were asked to rate these different outcomes on a rating scale to give a utility of improved mathematics outcomes. In principle such an approach could be applied across different educational outcomes allowing economists to undertake a cost utility analysis between different educational interventions as is done routinely for health care evaluations.

17.7   Analysing costs and benefits

A key issue when considering both costs and benefits concerns those which occur at the margin. When we are changing to a new programme or a new intervention we may be gaining some additional costs with some additional benefit. It is the additional or incremental costs and benefits that are important, not the total costs and benefits. A common analytical mistake when undertaking an economic evaluation is to measure the total costs and the total benefits and calculate an average cost effectiveness or cost benefit ratio. This approach is incorrect and misleading (Torgerson and Spencer, 1996). Let us suppose that an existing intervention costs $100 and our new, alternative, intervention costs $150. The incremental cost of this is $50. The existing intervention leads to a benefit of 10 units. The cost per unit achieved for the existing intervention is calculated by simply dividing the cost by the number of units, which in this case results in a cost effectiveness ratio of $10 per unit. Now our RCT has shown that the new treatment improves outcome by 12 units in the intervention group compared with 10 units in the control group at a cost of $150 versus a cost of $100. Commonly the average cost effectiveness ratio is calculated by dividing $150 by 12, which in turn results in a cost per unit of $12.50. This appears to be a relatively small increase in cost per unit outcome. However, the outcome of interest is the incremental cost effectiveness ratio, which is estimated by dividing the extra $50 cost of the novel intervention by the extra 2 units of output. Consequently the incremental cost effectiveness ratio is $25 per unit, not $12.5. For a policy-maker the key question should be: if I invest an extra $50 for this programme what additional benefit do I get? We might conclude that at $25 per unit, which is double the average cost effectiveness ratio, the new investment is not worth it.

The incremental cost effectiveness ratio is the most common method of informing decision-making. The problem that arises in interpreting this ratio is the question of when something is cost effective. In some instances the decision is very clear. If the new intervention is more expensive and less effective than the old intervention then we are in a situation of 'dominance'. We do not need to undertake complex analyses to conclude that we should retain the older intervention. Similarly, if the new intervention is less expensive and more effective, we should choose this as the new intervention is dominant. The more complex decision arises when either the new intervention is better at increased cost or worse at lower cost. At what cost per unit of benefit should we decide to purchase the intervention?

In health care a cost per QALY of around £20 000 to £30 000 ($50 000) seems to be a widely accepted threshold. In other words, society would be willing to pay up to about £20 000 to gain one more life year for a person in full health. This threshold is arbitrary, however, and is not based upon any fundamental economic theory or paradigm as to what the correct amount is.

17.8   Sensitivity analysis

Cost ascertainment is not straightforward. As noted previously, the costs may vary by place and time. Consequently it is always good practice to challenge the results of the economic analysis using a sensitivity analysis. In a sensitivity analysis we may change the prices of costs to reflect different settings or different expectations. If, for example, an intervention appears to be cost effective only if the costs are half those ascertained in the trial, then we might recommend that further work needs to be done to reduce the costs of the programme before it is implemented. Alternatively, if our base analysis suggests something *is* cost effective, we might test this finding by increasing the costs to see at what point the intervention will no longer be cost effective. If we only need a small increase in costs then we might adopt the intervention more cautiously or again recommend further research to increase our certainty. On the other hand, if we double our costs and it is still cost effective we might then consider the intervention should be implemented without further ado.

17.9   Discounting

When an intervention has effects that extend out into time we need to weight these future effects, both costs and outcomes, to reflect this time difference. This is known as discounting, which reflects time preference: society prefers benefits now rather than in the future. Consider this scenario. We have two interventions: one will improve the pass rate of 16-year-old children for their national maths test this year; the other is aimed at younger children but will also improve their pass rate in five years' time? Which one is preferred? Assuming equal costs and equal numbers of children passing the exam we would prefer the programme that is aimed at 16-year-olds rather than 11-year-olds. The next question that arises is how much better must the programme aimed at 11-year-olds be for us to prefer it to the one aimed at 16-year-olds – again assuming equal costs. The difference between the groups in terms of numbers passing the exam will form the basis of a discount rate. For example we might demand that the intervention among 11-year-old children will get 120 children through the standard in five years' time compared with investing the same resources to get 100 16-year-old children through the standard now.

17.10   Modelling

Many trials are not long enough to capture all the long-term costs and benefits of an intervention. Consequently economists often supplement trial data with computer models. These enable us to assess whether, by making assumptions of future benefits, the intervention is cost effective in the longer term. Modelling is probably most useful for interventions that are of doubtful cost effectiveness in the short term. If an intervention is cost effective in the time frame of a typical trial then, unless we expect longer-term costs or harms, modelling beyond the trial will only confirm what we already know.

17.11   Reporting results

Most economic evaluations report their results in terms of cost effectiveness ratios. For example, the incremental cost per QALY may be reported. Uncertainty around this estimate can be expressed as confidence intervals as is normal for effectiveness outcomes. Another approach for reporting uncertainty is the cost effectiveness acceptability curve (CEAC). This is a graphical technique where the cost per unit of output is plotted on the x-axis whilst the probability of attaining a given cost per unit is plotted in the y-axis. The point estimate of the cost effectiveness ratio is usually the point of 50 per cent probability. Because economic evaluations have to inform decisions that need to be made, even if it is a 'do nothing' option, the CEAC represents the range of willingness to pay values and is really an indication for more research. For instance, we might observe a cost per unit of outcome with a 51 per cent probability of $10 000 or less. In other words, there is a 49 per cent chance that the cost per unit is greater than $10 000. If we are willing to pay $10 000 we should adopt the intervention even if the upper 95 per cent probability may be $100 000, which is too much. Despite there being a lot of uncertainty we still need to act, and adopting the programme is the one most likely to be efficient. However, we still might need more research to reduce our uncertainty.

17.12   Discussion

Economic evaluations are an important component of many pragmatic trials. We do not just want to know whether something works; we also want to know whether it is cost effective or not. Sometimes prior modelling can tell us whether or not something is worthwhile before we do a trial. There is little value in evaluating whether something works or not if it is too expensive to implement even if effective. For example, the Tennessee class size experiment, whilst effective, was too expensive to implement widely.

Economic evaluations are not widely used outside of health care (Levin, 2001), which is a pity as many social science programmes have large cost implications. Interestingly the first *known* economic evaluation alongside a randomised controlled trial was actually undertaken in the field of education. The first known educational RCT (Walters, 1931) also included a basic economic evaluation. 'If the cost of educating a student one year be placed at $385, or $192.50 per semester, the annual saving to the University would have been $891' (Walters, 1931). Unfortunately, educational researchers do not usually conduct economic evaluations alongside their RCTs at the present time. This lack of interest means that economic evaluation tools have not been as widely developed as they should have been in the wider social sciences. For example, little work has been done on the development of a utility tool for the measurement of non-health outcomes of interventions. Such measurement is vital to inform decision-making within a given social science area.

17.13   Key points

- Economics is not just about cost.
- Economics seeks to prioritise scarce resources to maximise societal benefit or utility.
- Economics alongside trials can help inform decision-makers with respect to whether or not an intervention should be implemented.

18
Conclusions

18.1 Background

Arguably the most significant contribution to health care research in the last century was the development of the methodology and methods of the randomised controlled trial. This development has led to the rejection of harmful treatments and the more rapid adoption of beneficial therapies. Other evaluative methods cannot be used to judge the effectiveness of interventions with the same degree of certainty as the RCT.

However, other fields, such as education and crime and justice, have not capitalised on an earlier interest in RCTs (Walters, 1931, 1932; Lindquist, 1940) and now undertake relatively few studies using an RCT design (Oakley, 2000).

18.2 Alternatives to RCTs

Trials are often perceived as being difficult and expensive to undertake, and non-randomised controlled studies are thought to be less expensive or less complex alternatives. The latter argument is not convincing, because a high quality quasi-experiment requires intensive baseline data collection in order to enable adjustment for observable confounders. Some potential confounders, such as age and gender, are easy to measure and correct for; with others it is more difficult. For example, in the study by Luellen et al. (2005), which looked at the use of propensity scores to eliminate confounding, the authors recorded twenty-five key variables in order to try to eliminate selection bias. The choice of variables for ensuring baseline comparability must predict treatment group or outcome. It is ineffective to simply use variables which are easily available but are not necessarily associated with group membership or outcome (such as gender). Therefore, in contrast to a well-conducted RCT, a well-conducted quasi-experiment makes greater demands on the researcher in terms of accurately measuring as many potential confounders as possible. Although it is often helpful to obtain good measurements of important covariates at the beginning of a trial, such as pre-test score, this is not a prerequisite; we know that the random allocation process will produce unbiased distribution of covariates between the groups. The main reason for measuring baseline test scores, for example, is in order to increase the power of the experiment, and guard against chance effects. If pre-test measurement is difficult or impractical, we can address the power issues by increasing the sample size. For those researchers wishing to conduct a rigorous quasi-experiment the luxury of not measuring baseline covariates is not possible. Quasi-experimenters may encounter problems with matching. In order to locate matched controls in a case control study, researchers may need to use a different geographical area, which can potentially introduce geographical confounds. Regression discontinuity designs do not require as much detailed data collection as other quasi-experiments, but they encounter other problems, including lack of power, as larger sample sizes are required when using this design. In addition, poor adherence to the cut-off point may threaten internal validity.

Quasi-experimenters are limited by all the problems also faced by trialists. Loss to follow-up can potentially bias quasi-experiments, just as it can true experiments. Similarly, blinded follow-up is important in a quasi-experiment because ascertainment bias can as easily be introduced into a quasi-experiment as it can in an RCT. Indeed, it could be argued that the deterministic approach of allocating participants to a study in a quasi-experiment could make it more difficult to blind the observer.

18.3   Ethical constraints

Participants taking part in RCTs sometimes do not benefit from participating in the study. Further, if they are randomised to receive a treatment that ultimately proves to be hazardous then they are likely to be more disadvantaged than if they had refused participation. The only way of addressing this question, robustly, is to randomise potential participants to be recruited or not recruited into a trial. Another approach, which is more feasible, is to compare participants who are eligible for a study but refuse trial enrolment. Hallstrom and colleagues (2003) undertook such an observational study, and found that mortality was reduced among trial participants compared with non-participants. This mortality benefit was even apparent among participants who received the active treatment in the CAST trial, which you may recall from Chapter 1 was a treatment that increased overall mortality. There are several explanations for this phenomenon, not least the potential for selection bias – that is, trial volunteers were healthier in some unmeasured way compared with trial refusers. Other explanations include more diligent treatment when participating in a trial due to the need to carefully audit trial participants. Therefore, from an ethical standpoint, taking part in many health care trials may be advantageous to the participant rather than the opposite (there are clearly exceptions to this).

In some circumstances using an RCT is clearly impossible. For example, it is clearly not possible to randomise people to take up smoking in order to ascertain whether or not smoking increases morbidity. Indeed, because the evidence for the harmful effects of smoking is not derived from randomised trials, it has been claimed that the association between smoking and harmful effects is possibly due to confounding (Fisher, 1958). The argument is as follows: smokers may, for example, be more likely to have a genetic predisposition that makes them take up smoking, which also puts them at increased risk of cancer; or smokers may have a lifestyle (a poor diet, for example) that puts them at elevated risk. Nevertheless we can 'prove' that smoking is harmful through the use of an RCT, by, for example randomising smokers to receive or not receive a smoking cessation programme. If the RCT demonstrates that the programme is effective at reducing the prevalence of smoking then we can follow both groups up to monitor the incidence of other outcomes. Anthonisen and colleagues (2005) randomised 5900 smokers to either a smoking cessation programme or to normal care to test if the enhanced programme would enable smokers to quit in the longer term. After five years 22 per cent of the intervention group had ceased smoking compared with 6 per cent of the control group. Nevertheless, after fourteen years there were significant differences between the groups in terms of cardiovascular and cancer mortality. Consequently, we can be confident that smokers who stop smoking enjoy a lower risk of adverse health events.

An earlier trial confirmed observational data that pregnant women who smoke are likely to give birth to babies with low birth weight. MacArthur and colleagues (1987) randomised about 1000 pregnant smokers to receive or not receive an anti-smoking health education package. In the intervention group, 9 per cent stopped smoking compared with 6 per cent of the control group, and 28 per cent of the intervention group reduced tobacco consumption compared with 19 per cent of the control group. This relatively small difference led to the women in the health education group having babies that were heavier and longer than babies in the control group. Note that in this trial the majority of the mothers in the intervention group remained smokers and the analysis was by intention to treat, which would underestimate the truly harmful effects of smoking on birth weight.

Observational data have shown that breast-fed babies have fewer health problems than bottle-fed babies. These data could be confounded, like the observations on smoking, as women who breast-feed are likely to be from a different socio-economic class than bottle-feeding women, and the associated lifestyle factors and income levels may be responsible for the differences in health outcomes. However, we can test the benefits of breast-feeding in an RCT. As with the examples above, we can take women from an area that has low breast-feeding rates and offer education and support to encourage breast-feeding. Two studies in Mexico and the Ukraine have done this (Morrow et al., 1999; Kramer et al., 2001). In one study the rates of breast-feeding increased from 6 per cent to 43 per cent, and in the other they increased from 12 per cent to 60 per cent. The infants from both groups were followed up, and the children from the breast-fed group were less likely to develop eczema and diarrhoea compared with children in the control group. Note, this was an intention to treat analysis and the majority of the intervention group used bottle-feeding. Again these data support the observational studies that found breast-feeding is best for children.

These examples demonstrate that it is possible to use the RCT to indirectly evaluate the impact of certain factors where it is unethical or impractical to make a direct comparison.

18.4 Interventions that may be ineffective

Whilst RCTs are generally thought of as providing evidence for what works, equally important is their role in providing evidence for what does not work or what is harmful. Usually ineffective interventions use up resources, therefore even ones that do no direct harm 'crowd out' alternative productive uses of resources. In Table 18.1, we present a sample of randomised trials that have demonstrated interventions are ineffective or harmful.

The table shows a range of interventions that affect large sections of the population. For instance, many millions of women have used hormone replacement therapy over the years. Synthetic phonics instruction was introduced as the first method for teaching reading to all children starting school in the UK during 2006 and 2007.

Table 18.1: Selected interventions which are ineffective, harmful or no different to alternative interventions, as demonstrated by RCTs

Year, Study	Intervention	Outcome
2007, Bjelakovic et al.	Systematic review of trials of antioxidant supplements (beta carotene, vitamin A & E).	Increased mortality.
2006, Shennan et al.	Trial of antibiotics for a symptomatic vaginal infection for pregnant women.	Increased risk of giving premature birth.
2004, CRASH trial	Trial of high dose steroids for head injured patients.	Increased mortality at one month.
2002, WHI trial	Trial of hormone replacement therapy.	Increased risk of stroke.
2001, Achara et al.	Systematic review of trials of driver education.	Increased risk of accidents and deaths.
2006, Torgerson et al.	Systematic review of trials of synthetic versus analytic phonics instruction.	No difference detected between the two methods.
2004, Rouse et al.	Trial of computer supported literacy teaching.	No additional benefit detected.
1978, Berg et al.	Social work support for truants.	Increases truancy and juvenile crime.

18.5   An inconvenient truth

Even when a rigorous RCT has been completed, it is part of the human condition to ignore unpalatable or unacceptable results. Kaptchuk (2003) has described a range of interpretive biases that people use to explain away inconvenient findings. For instance, if the findings from a trial, irrespective of its quality, support a prior belief then its results are often perceived as being more credible. However, if the results of a trial run counter to existing belief systems they are sometimes doubted and the reader tends to look more strenuously for methodological faults in the study. Kaptchuk (2003) describes a randomised trial of evaluating two 'fake' trials being shown to trial participants, the only difference being that one evaluated a credible treatment and the other evaluated a less credible treatment. The results were believed more often in the trial with a credible intervention than in the trial with the less credible treatment. There are many examples of 'real life' trials that have shown an intervention to be either harmful or ineffective and for researchers to disbelieve their findings. It is important, however, to resist the impulse to disbelieve the results of a well-conducted trial that gives results that are counter-intuitive. A historical example of this is the James Lind scurvy experiment (www.jameslindlibrary.org/).

18.6   Role of theory in developing RCTs

When designing a trial there is often some well-defined theoretical rationale for why an intervention may or may not be effective. The MRC framework (2002) for designing 'complex' interventions describes an early stage of trial development which includes a theoretical component. A problem with over-reliance on theory to guide RCT development is that the theory may simply be wrong. The use of HRT for the prevention of stroke in women was based on incorrect biological theory, as was the widespread use of vitamin supplements to improve health. Whilst virtually all interventions that are evaluated using a trial design are underpinned with some kind of theoretical basis, it is important to remember that the most important issue is what works; the issue of why or how it works is of less importance. We can be completely erroneous in the theoretical base and still identify the correct solution. For instance, typhus, which is spread by body infestation, was originally believed to be caused by filthy clothes and dirty bodies. Consequently, in the seventeenth and eighteenth centuries the navy adopted a practice of removing and burning the dirty clothes of new recruits, then hosing down the recruits, which removed body infestation and reduced typhus (Rodger, 2005): the wrong theory but the correct solution.

18.7   Concluding remarks

Health care research routinely uses randomised controlled trials to test the effectiveness of interventions. Other areas of public policy, such as education and criminal justice, have not capitalised on their earlier interest in RCTs and now undertake few randomised studies, some of which are poorly designed (Torgerson et al., 2005). However, many health care professionals are still resistant to the wider usage of trials (e.g., Penston, 2007) or object to the use of trials in their specialist field because they claim that they are either inappropriate or cannot be undertaken. For example, an editorial in the *British Medical Journal* commenting on the fact that a meta-analysis of controlled trials found no evidence that problem-based learning in continuing medical education was more effective than didactic teaching methods felt that the method, the RCT, was inappropriate for its evaluation (Prideaux, 2002). Whilst some trials can be rightly criticised as being too small or too badly designed to evaluate an intervention, it is not the method itself that is at fault, but rather the implementation of the approach. The correct response to a null finding, based on a weak study, is to undertake a robust RCT, whilst the correct response to a null finding from a robust RCT is to reconsider the intervention.

Unfortunately, both health care research and social science research far too often rely on the weakest evaluative method (the before and after study) and place credence on observational data as opposed to randomised trials. In all areas of the social sciences we need more randomised trials.

References

Aaronson, N. K., Visser-Pol, E., Leenhouts, G. H., Muller, M. J. et al. (1996) 'Telephone based nursing intervention improves the effectiveness of the informed consent process in cancer clinical trials', *Journal of Clinical Oncology* 13: 984–96.

Achara, S., Adeyemi, B., Dosekun, E., Kelleher, S., Lansley, M., Male, I., Muhialdin, N., Reynolds, L., Roberts, I., Smailbegovic, M. and van der Spek, N., The Cochrane Injuries Group Driver Education Reviewers (2001) 'Evidence based road safety: the Driving Standards Agency's schools programme', *Lancet*, 358: 230–2.

Adamson, J., Cockayne, S., Puffer, S. and Torgerson, D. J. (2006) 'Review of randomised trials using the post-randomised consent (Zelen's) design', *Contemporary Clinical Trials* 27: 305–19.

Adamson, S. J., Sellman, J. D. and Doré, G. M. (2005) 'Therapy preference and treatment outcome in clients with mild to moderate alcohol dependence', *Drug and Alcohol Review* 24: 209–16.

Altman D. G. (1991) *Practical Statistics for Medical Research*. London: Chapman and Hall.

Altman, D. G. (1996) 'Better reporting of randomised controlled trials: the CONSORT statement', *British Medical Journal* 313: 570–1.

Altman, D. G. and Doré, C. J. (1990) 'Randomisation and baseline comparisons in clinical trials', *Lancet* 335: 149–53.

Altman, D. G. and Doré, C. J. (1991) 'Baseline comparisons in randomized clinical trials', *Statistics in Medicine* 10: 797–802.

Altman, D. G., Whitehead, J., Parmar, M. K. B., Stenning, S. P., Fayers, P. M. and Machin, D. (1995) 'Randomised consent designs in cancer clinical trials', *European Journal of Cancer* 31A: 1934–44.

Andrew, M., Vegh, P., Cacao, C. et al. (1993) 'A randomized controlled trial of platelet transfusions in thrombocytopenic premature infants', *Journal of Pediatrics* 123: 285–91.

Anthonisen, N. R., Skeans, M. A., Wise, R. A., Manfreda, J., Kanner, R. E. and Connett, J. E. for the Lung Health Study Research Group (2005) 'The effects of a smoking cessation program on long-term survival in smokers with mild lung disease', *Annals of Internal Medicine* 42: 1–12.

Assman, S. F., Pocock, S. J., Enos, L. E. and Kasten, L. E. (2000) 'Subgroup analysis and other (mis)uses of baseline data in clinical trials', *Lancet* 355: 1064–9.

Atkin, W. S., Edwards, R., Wardle, J., Northover, J. M. A., Sutton, S., Hart, A. R., Williams, C. B. and Cuzick, J. (2001) 'Design of a multicentre randomised trial to evaluate flexible sigmoidoscopy in colorectal cancer screening', *Journal of Medical Screening* 8: 137–44.

Avenell, A., Grant, A. M., McGee, M., McPherson, G., Campbell, M. K. and McGee, M. A. for the RECORD Trial Management Group (2004) 'The effects of an open design on trial participant recruitment, compliance and retention: a randomized controlled trial comparison with a blinded, placebo-controlled design', *Clinical Trials* 1: 1–9.

Aveyard, P., Cheng, K. K., Almond, J. et al. (1999) 'Cluster randomised controlled trial of expert system based on the transtheoretical (stages of change) model of smoking prevention and cessation in schools', *British Medical Journal* 319: 948–53.

Baker, S., Gersten, R. and Keating, T. (2000) 'When less may be more: a 2-year longitudinal evaluation of a volunteer tutoring program requiring minimal training', *Reading Research Quarterly* 35: 494–519.

Banerjee, A., Cole, S., Duflo, E. and Linden, L. (2005) 'Remedying education: evidence from two randomized experiments in India', *NBER Working Paper* No. 11904.

Barrett-Connor, E., Grady, D., Sashegyi, A., Anderson, P. W., Cox, D. A., Hoszowski, K., Rautaharju, P. and Harper, K. D. (2002) 'Raloxifene and cardiovascular events in osteoporotic postmenopausal women', *Journal of the American Medical Association* 287: 847–57.

Barrett-Connor, E., Mosca, L., Collins, P., Geiger, M. J., Grady, D., Kornitzer, M., McNabb, M. A. and Wenger, N. K. (2006) 'Effects of raloxifene on cardiovascular events and breast cancer in postmenopausal women', *New England Journal of Medicine* 355: 125–37.

Batchelder, J. S. and Rachal, J. R. (2000) 'Efficacy of a computer-assisted instruction program in a prison setting: an experimental study', *Adult Education Quarterly* 50: 120–33.

Bech, B. H., Obel, C., Henriksen, T. B. and Olsen, J. (2007) 'Effect of reducing caffeine intake on birth weight and length of gestation: randomised controlled trial', *British Medical Journal* 334: 409–12.

Begg, C. B., Cho, M. K., Eastwood, S. et al. (1996) 'Improving the quality of reporting of randomised controlled trials: the CONSORT statement', *Journal of the American Medical Association* 276: 637–9.

Belsky, J., Melhuish, E., Barnes, J., Leyland, A. H. and Romaniuk, H. (2006) 'Effects of sure start local programmes on children and families: early findings from a quasi-experimental, cross sectional study', *British Medical Journal* 332: 1476.

Berg, I., Consterdine, M., Hullin, R., McGuire, R. and Tyrer, S. (1978) 'The effect of two randomly allocated court procedures on truancy', *British Journal of Criminology* 18: 232–44.

Berger, V. W. (2005) *Selection Bias and Covariate Imbalances in Randomized Clinical Trials*. Chichester, UK: Wiley.

Berk, R. A. (2005) 'Randomized experiments as the bronze standard', *Journal of Experimental Criminology* 1: 417–33.

Berninger, V., Abbott, R., Rogan, L., Reed, E., Abbott, S., Brooks, A., Vaughan, K. and Graham, S. (1998) 'Teaching spelling to children with specific learning difficulties: the mind's ear and eye beat the computer or pencil', *Learning Disability Quarterly* 21: 106–22.

Birks, Y. F., Porthouse, J., Addie, C., Loughney, K., Saxon, L., Baverstock, M. et al. (2004) 'Randomized controlled trial of hip protectors among women living in the community', *Osteoporosis International* 15: 701–6.

Bjelakovic, G., Nikolova, D., Gluud, L. L., Simonetti, R. G. and Gluud, C. (2007) 'Mortality in randomized trials of antioxidant supplements for primary and secondary prevention', *Journal of the American Medical Association* 297: 842–57.

Bland, M. J. (2000) *An Introduction to Medical Statistics*. Oxford: Oxford University Press.

Bland, M. J. (2004) 'Cluster randomised trials in the medical literature: two bibliometric surveys', *BMC Medical Research Methodology* 4, 21.

Borm, G. F., Melis, R. J. F., Teerenstra, S. and Peer P. G. (2005) 'Pseudo cluster randomization: a treatment allocation method to minimize contamination and selection bias', *Statistics in Medicine* 24: 3535–47.

Boruch, R. F. (1997) 'Randomized experiments for planning and evaluation: a practical approach', *Applied Social Research Methods Series* 44, Sage Publications London.

Bourduin, C. M., Mann, B. J., Cone, L. T., Henggeler, S. W., Fucci, B. R., Blaske, D. M. and Williams, R. A. (1995) 'Multisystemic treatment of serious juvenile offenders: long-term prevention of criminality and violence', *Journal of Consulting and Clinical Psychology* 63: 569–78.

Boutron, I., Moher, D., Tugwell, P., Giraudeau, B., Poiraudeau, S., Nizard, R. and Ravaud, P. (2005) 'A checklist to evaluate a report of a nonpharmcological trial (CLEAR NPT) was developed using consensus', *Journal of Clinical Epidemiology* 58: 1233–40.

Brewin, C. R. and Bradley, C. (1989) 'Patient preferences and randomised clinical trials', *British Medical Journal* 299: 313–15.

Brooks, G., Burton, M., Coles, P., Miles, J., Torgerson, C. and Torgerson, D. (2008) 'Randomised controlled trial of incentives to improve attendance at adult literacy classes', *Oxford Review of Education* 34, 4 (August, in press).

Brooks, G., Miles, J. N. V., Torgerson, C. J. and Torgerson, D. J. (2006) 'Is an intervention using computer software effective in literacy learning? A randomised controlled trial', *Educational Studies* 32: 133–43.

Brown, S., Thorpe, H., Hawkins, K. and Brown, J. (2005) 'Minimization – reducing predictability for multi-centre trials whilst retaining balance with centre', *Statistics in Medicine* 24: 3715–27.

Browne, R. H. (1995) 'On the use of a pilot sample for sample size determination', *Statistics in Medicine* 14: 1933–40.

Burnand, B., Kernan, W. N. and Feinstein, A. R. (1990) 'Indexes and boundaries for "quantitative significance" in statistical decisions', *Journal of Clinical Epidemiology* 43: 1273–84.

Campbell, D. T. and Ross, H. L. (1968) 'The Connecticut crackdown on speeding: time-series data in quasi-experimental analysis', *Law and Society Review* 3: 33–53.

Cardiac Arrhythmia Suppression Trial (CAST) Investigators (1991) 'Preliminary report: effect of encainide and flecainide on mortality in a randomised trial of arrhythmia suppression after myocardial infaction', *New England Journal of Medicine* 321: 406–12.

Carlton, M. B., Litton, F. W. and Zinkgraf, S. A. (1985) 'The effects of an intraclass peer tutoring program on the sight-word recognition ability of students who are mildly mentally retarded', *Mental Retardation* 23: 74–8.

Carr, J. L., Klaber-Moffett, J. A., Howarth, E., Richmond, S. J., Torgerson, D. J., Jackson, D. A. and Metcalfe, C. J. (2006) 'A randomized trial comparing group exercise programme for back pain patients with individual physiotherapy in a severely deprived area', *Disability and Rehabilitation* 27: 929–37.

Castle, J. M., Riach, J. and Nicholson, T. (1994) 'Getting off to a better start in reading and spelling: the effects of phonemic awareness instruction within a whole language program', *Journal of Educational Psychology* 86: 350–9.

Chalmers, I. (2001) 'Comparing like with like: some historical milestones in the evolution of methods to create unbiased comparison groups in therapeutic experiments', *International Journal of Epidemiology* 30: 1156–64.

Chalmers, I. (2003) 'Trying to do more good than harm in policy and practice: the role of rigorous, transparent, up-to-date evaluations', *Annals of the American Academy of Political and Social Science* 589: 22–40.

Chattopadhyay, R. and Duflo, E. (2004) 'Women as policy makers: evidence from a randomized policy experiment in India', *Econometrica* 72: 1409–43.

Clement, S., Sikorski, J., Wilson, J. and Candy, B. (1998) 'Merits of alternative strategies for incorporating patient preferences into clinical trials must be considered carefully', *British Medical Journal* 317: 78.

Cochrane Injuries Group Driver Education Reviewers (2001) 'Evidence based road safety: the Driving Standards Agency's schools programme', *Lancet* 358: 230–2.

Cochrane, T., Davey, R. C. and Matthes Edwards, S. M. (2005) 'Randomised controlled trial of the cost-effectiveness of water-based therapy for lower limb osteoarthritis', *Health Technology Assessment* 9: 31.

Comparative Obstetric Mobile Epidural Trial (COMET) Study Group UK (2001) 'Effect of low-dose mobile versus traditional epidural techniques on mode of delivery: a randomised controlled trial', *Lancet* 358: 19–23.

Cook, T. D. (2005) 'Emergent principles for cluster-based experiments', *Annals of the American Academy of Political and Social Science* 599: 176–98.

Cook, T. D. and Campbell, D. (1979) *Quasi-Experimentation: Design and Analysis Issues for Field Settings*. Boston: Houghton Mifflin.

Cook, T. D. and Wong, V. (2007) 'Empirical tests of the validity of the regression discontinuity design', *Annales d'Economie et de Statistique* (in press).

Cooper, K. G., Grant, A. M. and Garratt, A. M. (1997) 'The impact of using a partially randomised patient preference design when evaluating managements for heavy menstrual bleeding', *British Journal of Obstetrics and Gynaecology* 104: 1367–73.

CRASH Trial Collaborators (2004) 'Effect of intravenous corticosteroids on death within 14 days in 10 008 adults with clinically significant head injury (MRC CRASH trial): randomised placebo-controlled trial', *Lancet* 365: 1321–8.

Craven, R. G., Marsh, H. W., Debus, R. L. and Jayasinghe, U. (2001) 'Diffusion effects: control group contamination threats to the validity of teacher-administered interventions', *Journal of Educational Psychology* 93: 639–45.

Daniels, J., Wheatley, K. and Gray, R. (2004) 'Pairwise randomisation to balance within centres without possible foreknowledge of allocation', *Controlled Clinical Trials*, 24, 3S: 104–105S.

Davis, R. G. and Taylor, B. G. (1997) 'A proactive response to family violence: the results of a randomized experiment', *Criminology* 35: 307–33.

Dickersin, K. (2002) 'Reducing reporting biases', in I. Chalmers, I. Milne and U. Trohler (eds), *The James Lind Library* (www.jameslindlibrary.org).

Donner, A. and Klar, N. (2000) *Design and Analysis of Cluster Randomization Trials in Health Research*. London: Arnold.

Donovan, J., Mills, N., Smith, M., Brindle, L., Jacoby, A., Peters, T., Frankel, S., Neal, D., Hamdy, F. and Little, P. (2002) 'Improving design and conduct of randomised trials by embedding them in qualitative research: ProtecT (prostate testing for cancer and treatment) study', *British Medical Journal* 325: 766–70.

Donovan, J. L., Peters, T. J., Noble, S., Powell, P., Gillatt, D., Oliver, S. E., Lane, J. A., Neal, D. E. and Hamdy, F. C. (2003) 'Who can best recruit to randomized trials?

Randomized trial comparing surgeons and nurses recruiting patients to a trial of treatments for localized prostate cancer (the ProtecT study)', *Journal of Clinical Epidemiology* 56: 605–9.

Downing, J. and Jones, B. (1966) 'Some problems of evaluating IT: a second experiment', *Educational Research*, 100–14.

Dumville, J. C., Hahn, S., Miles, J. N. V. and Torgerson, D. J. (2006a) 'The use of unequal randomisation ratios in clinical trials: a review', *Contemporary Clinical Trials* 27: 1–12.

Dumville, J. C., Torgerson, D. J. and Hewitt, C. E. (2006b) 'Reporting attrition in randomised controlled trials', *British Medical Journal* 332: 969–71.

Duncan, D., Beck, S. J., Hood, K. and Johansen, A. (2006) 'Using dietetic assistants to improve the outcome of hip fracture: a randomised controlled trial of nutritional support in an acute trauma ward', *Age and Ageing* 35: 148–53.

Dunford, F. W. (2000) 'The San Diego navy experiment: an assessment of interventions for men who assault their wives', *Journal of Consulting and Clinical Psychology* 68: 468–76.

Durelli, L., Verdun, E., Barbero, P., Bergui, M., Versino, E., Ghezzi, A. et al. (2002) 'Every-other-day interferon beta-1b versus once-weekly interferon beta-1a for multiple sclerosis: results of a 2-year prospective randomised multicentre study (INCOMIN)', *Lancet* 359: 1453–60.

Edwards, P., Roberts, I., Clarke, M. et al. (2002) 'Increasing response rates to postal questionnaires: systematic review', *British Medical Journal* 324: 1183–92.

Egger, M., Davey Smith, G., Schneider, M. and Minder, C. (1997) 'Bias in meta-analysis detected by a simple graphical test', *British Medical Journal* 315: 629–34.

Egger, M., Juni, P., Bartlett, C., Holenstein, F. and Sterne, J. (2003) 'How important are comprehensive literature searches and the assessment of trial quality in systematic reviews?' *NHS Health Technology Assessment* 7: 1–76.

Ehri, L. C., Nunes, S. R., Willows, D. M., Schuster, B. V., Yaghoub-Zadeh, S. and Shanahan, T. (2001) 'Phonemic awareness instruction helps children learn to read: evidence from the National Reading Panel's meta-analysis', *Reading Research Quarterly* 36: 250–87.

Evans, H. M. (2004) 'Should patients be allowed to veto their participation in clinical research?' *Journal of Medical Ethics* 30: 198–203.

Farrin, A., Russell, I., Torgerson, D. J. and Underwood, M. (2005) 'Differential recruitment in a cluster randomized trial in primary care: the experience of the UK Back pain, Exercise, Active management and Manipulation (UK BEAM) feasibility study', *Clinical Trials* 2: 119–24.

Farrington, D. P. and Walsh, B. C. (2005) 'Randomized experiments in criminology: what have we learned in the last two decades?' *Journal of Experimental Criminology* 1: 9–38.

Feder, L. and Dugan, L. (2002) 'A test of the efficacy of court-mandated counseling for domestic violence offenders: the Broward Experiment', *Justice Quarterly* 19: 343–75.

Feldman, S. C. and Fish, M. C. (1991) 'Use of computer-mediated reading supports to enhance reading comprehension of high school students', *Journal of Educational Computing Research* 7: 25–36.

Fergusson, D., Cranley Glass, K., Waring, D. and Shapiro, S. (2004) 'Turning a blind eye: the success of blinding reported in a random sample of randomised, placebo controlled trials', *British Medical Journal* 328: 432.

Field, D. J., Davis, C., Elbourne, D., Grant, A., Johnson, A. and Macrae, D. (1996) 'UK collaborative randomised trial of neonatal extracorporeal membrane oxygenation', *Lancet* 348: 75–82.

Finkelstein, J. S., Hayes, A., Hunzelman, J. L., Wyland, J. J., Lee, H. and Neer R. M. (2003) 'The effects of parathyroid hormone, alendronate, or both in men with osteoporosis', *New England Journal of Medicine* 349: 1216–26.

Finsen, V. and Storeheier, A. H. (2006) 'Scratch lottery tickets are a poor incentive to respond to mailed questionnaires', *BMC Medical Research Methodology* 6, 19. doi:10.1186/1471-2288-6-19.

Fisher, R. A. (1958) 'Cancer and smoking', *Nature* 182: 596.

Fisher, R. A. (1971) *The Design of Experiments*. New York: Hafner Publishing Company.

Fleming, T. R. and DeMets, D. L. (1996) 'Surrogate end points in clinical trials: are we being misled?' *Annals of Internal Medicine* 125: 605–13.

Fletcher, J. D., Hawley, D. E. and Piele, P. K. (1990) 'Costs, effects and utility of microcomputer assisted instruction in the classroom', *American Educational Research Journal* 27: 783–806.

Fleurence, R. and Torgerson, D. J. (2004) 'Setting priorities for research', *Health Policy* 69: 1–10.

Ford, M. E., Havstad, S. L. and Davis, S. D. (2004) 'A randomized trial of recruitment methods for older African American men in the prostate, lung, colorectal and ovarian (PLCO) cancer screening trial', *Clinical Trials* 1: 343–51.

Forsetlund, L., Chalmers, I. and Bjørndal, A. (2007) 'When was random allocation first used to generate comparison groups in experiments to assess the effects of social interventions?' *Economics of Innovation and New Technology* 16: 371–84.

Foster, K. C., Erickson, G. C., Foster, D. F., Brinkman, D. and Torgesen, J. K. (1994) 'Computer administered instruction in phonological awareness: evaluation of the Daisyquest program', *Journal of Research and Development in Education* 27: 126–37.

Freiman, J. A., Chalmers, T. C., Smith, H. Jr. and Kuebler, R. R. (1978) 'The importance of beta, type II error and sample size in the design and interpretation of the randomised clinical trial. Survey of 71 negative trials', *New England Journal of Medicine* 299: 690–4.

Friedman, M. (1992) 'Communication: do old fallacies ever die', *Journal of Economic Literature* 30: 2129–32.

Gavgani, A. S. M., Hodjati, M., Hohite, H. and Davies, C. (2002) 'Effect of insecticide impregnated dog collars on incidence of zoonotic visceral leishmaniasis in Iranian children: a matched cluster randomised trial', *Lancet* 360: 374–9.

Glass, G. V. (1976) 'Integrating findings: the meta-analysis of research', in L. Shulman (ed.), *Review of Research in Education*, 5: 351–79. Itasca, Il: Peacock.

Glass, G. V., McGaw, B. and Smith, M. L. (1981) *Meta-Analysis in Social Research*. Beverly Hills, CA: Sage.

Glasziou, P., Chalmers, I., Rawlins, M. and McCulloch, P. (2007) 'When are randomised trials unnecessary? Picking signal from noise', *British Medical Journal* 334: 349–51.

Gluud, C. and Nikolova, D. (2007) 'Likely country of origin in publications on randomised controlled trials and controlled clinical trials during the last 60 years', *Trials* 8, 7.

Goodman, S. N. and Berlin, J. A. (1994) 'The use of predicted confidence intervals when planning experiments and the misuse of power when interpreting results', *Annals of Internal Medicine* 121: 200–6.

Gore, S. M., Jones, G. and Thompson, S. G. (1992) 'The *Lancet*'s statistical review process: areas for improvement by authors', *Lancet* 340: 100–2.

Gøtzsche, P. C. and Olsen, O. (2000) 'Is screening for breast cancer with mammography justifiable?' *Lancet* 355: 129–34.

Gosnell, H. F. (1926) 'An experiment in the stimulation of voting', *American Political Science Review* 20: 869–74.

Grady, D., Rueben, S. B., Pettiti, D. B. et al. (1992) 'Hormone therapy to prevent disease and prolong life in postmenopausal women', *Annals of Internal Medicine* 117: 1016–37.

Gratt, J. M., Schouten, E. G. and Kok, F. J. (2002) 'Effect of daily vitamin E and multivitamin-mineral supplementation on acute respiratory tract infections in elderly persons: a randomized controlled trial', *Journal of the American Medical Association* 288: 715–21.

Gray, A. R., Topping, K. J. and Carcary, W. B. (1998) 'Individual and group learning of the Highway Code: comparing board game and traditional methods', *Educational Research* 40: 45–53.

GRIT Study Group (2004) 'Infant wellbeing at 2 years of age in the Growth Restriction Intervention (GRIT): multicentred randomised controlled trial', *Lancet* 364: 513–20.

Grossman, D. C., Neckerman, H. J., Koepsall, T. D., Liu, P. Y., Asher, K. N., Frey, K., Beland, K. and Rivara, F. P. (1997) 'Effectiveness of a violence prevention curriculum among children in elementary school', *Journal of the American Medical Association* 277: 1605–11.

Hahn, S., Puffer, S., Torgerson, D. J. and Watson, J. (2005) 'Methodological bias in cluster randomised trials', *BMC Medical Research Methodology* 5: 10.

Hardcastle, J. D., Chamberlain, J. O., Robinson, M. H. E., Moss, S. M., Amar, S. S., Balfour, T. W. et al. (1996) 'Randomised controlled trial of faecal-occult-blood screening for colorectal cancer', *Lancet* 348: 1472–7.

Harlow, T., Greaves, C., White, A., Brown L., Hart, A. and Ernst, E. (2004) 'Randomised controlled trial of magnetic bracelets for relieving pain in osteoarthritis of the hip and knee', *British Medical Journal* 329: 1450–4.

Hatcher, P., Hulme, C. and Ellis, A. (1994) 'Ameliorating early reading failure by integrating the teaching of reading and phonological skills: the phonological linkage hypothesis', *Child Development* 65: 41–57.

Hemminiki, E., Hovi, S. L., Veerus, P., Sevon, T., Tuimala, R., Rahu, R. and Hakama, M. (2004) 'Blinding decreased recruitment in a prevention trial of postmenopausal hormone therapy', *Journal of Clinical Epidemiology* 57: 1237–43.

Henshaw, R. C., Naji, S. A., Russell, I. T. and Templeton, A. A. (1993) 'Comparison of medical abortion with surgical vacuum aspiration: women's preferences and acceptability of treatment', *British Medical Journal* 307: 714–17.

Hewitt, C., Hahn, S., Torgerson, D. J., Watson, J. and Bland, J. M. (2005) 'Adequacy and reporting of allocation concealment: review of recent trials published in four general medical journals', *British Medical Journal* 330: 1057–8.

Hewitt, C., Miles, J. N. V. and Torgerson, D. J. (2006) 'Taking account of non-compliance in randomised controlled trials', *Canadian Medical Association Journal* 175: 347–8.

Hewitt, C. and Torgerson, D. J. (2006) 'Restricted randomisation: is it necessary?' *British Medical Journal* 332: 1506–8.

Hirschel, J. D., Hutchinson, I. W. and Dean, C. W. (1992) 'The failure of arrest to deter spouse abuse', *Journal of Research in Crime and Delinquency* 29: 7–33.

Hollis, S. and Campbell, F. (1999) 'What is meant by intention to treat analysis? Survey of published randomised controlled trials', *British Medical Journal* 319: 670–4.

Hopewell, S., Clarke, M., Stewart, L. and Tierney, J. (2007) 'Time to publication for results of clinical trials', Cochrane Database of Systematic Reviews 2.

Howden-Chapman, P., Mattheson, A., Carne, J., Viggers, H. et al. (2007) 'Effect of insulating existing houses in health inequality: cluster randomised study in the community', *British Medical Journal* 334: 460.

Hrobjartsson, A. and Gotzsche, P. C. (2001) 'Is the placebo powerless? An analysis of clinical trials comparing placebo with no treatment', *New England Journal of Medicine* 344: 1594–602.

Hundley, V. A., Cruickshank, F. M., Lang, G. D. et al. (1994) 'Midwife managed delivery unit: a randomised controlled comparison with consultant led care', *British Medical Journal* 309: 1400–4.

Hutchings, J., Bywater, T., Daley, D., Gardner, F., Whitaker, C., Jones, K., Eames, C. and Edwards, R. T. (2007) 'Parenting intervention in Sure Start services for children at risk of developing conduct disorder: pragmatic randomised controlled trial', *British Medical Journal*, Doi 10.1136/bmj.39126.620799.55.

International Collaborative Ovarian Neoplasm (ICON) Group (2002) 'Paclitaxel plus carboplatin versus standard chemotherapy with either single-agent carboplatin or cyclophosphamide, doxorubicin, and cisplatin in women with ovarian cancer: the ICON3 randomised trial'. *Lancet* 360: 505–15.

ISIS-2 Collaborative Group (1988) 'Randomised trial of intravenous streptokinase, oral aspirin, both, or neither among 17 187 cases of suspected acute myocardial infarction', *Lancet* 2: 349–60.

Jacob, B. A. and Lefgren, L. (2004) 'Remedial education and student achievement: a regression-discontinuity analysis', *Review of Economics and Statistics* 86: 226–44.

Jellema, P., van der Windt, D. A. W. M., van der Horst, H. E., Twisk, J. W. R., Stalman, W. A. B. and Bouter, L. M. (2005) 'Should treatment of (sub) acute low back pain be aimed at psychosocial prognostic factors? Cluster randomised clinical trial in general practice', *British Medical Journal* 331: 84.

Jinkerson, L. and Baggett, P. (1993) 'Spell checkers: aids in identifying and correcting spelling errors', *Journal of Computing in Childhood Education* 4: 291–306.

Johnson, R. E., Jones, G. T., Wiles, N. J., Chaddock, C., Potter, R. G., Roberts, C., Symmons, D. P. M., Watson, P. J., Torgerson, D. J. and Macfarlane, G. J. (2007) 'Randomised controlled trial of active exercise, education and cognitive behavioural therapy for persistent disabling low back pain', *Spine* (in press).

Johnston, R. S. and Watson, J. E. (2004) 'Accelerating the development of reading, spelling and phonemic awareness skills in initial readers', *Reading and Writing: an Interdisciplinary Journal* 17: 327–57.

Jones, L. P., Harris, R. and Finnegan, D. (2002) 'School attendance demonstration project: an evaluation of a program to motivate public assistance teens to attend and complete school in an urban school district', *Research on Social Work Practice* 12: 222–37.

Juni, P., Altman, D. G. and Egger, M. (2001) 'Assessing the quality of randomised controlled trials', in M. Egger, G. Davey-Smith and D. Altman (eds), *Systematic Reviews in Health Care: Meta-analysis in Context*, 2nd edn. London: BMJ Publishing Group.

Juni, P., Witschi, A., Bloch, R. and Egger, M. (1999) 'The hazards of scoring quality of clinical trials for meta-analyses', *Journal of the American Medical Association*, 135: 982–9.

Kannus, P., Parkkari, J., Niemi, S., Pasanen, M., Palvanen, M., Järvinen, M. and Vuori, I. (2000) 'Prevention of hip fracture in elderly people with use of a hip protector', *New England Journal of Medicine* 343: 1506–13.

Kaptchuk, T. J. (2003) 'Effect of interpretive bias on research evidence', *British Medical Journal* 326: 1453–5.

Kaptchuk, T. J., Stason, W. B., Davis, R. B., Legedza, A. R. T., Schnyer, R. N., Kerr, C. E., Stone, D. A., Nam, B. H., Kirsch, I. and Goldman, R. H. (2006) 'Sham device *v* inert pill: randomised controlled trial of two placebo treatments', *British Medical Journal* 332: 391–7.

Karlberg, J., Mattsson, L. A. and Wiklund, I. (1995) 'A quality of life perspective on who benefits from estradiol replacement therapy', *Acta Obstet Gynecol Scan* 74: 367–72.

Kennedy, A. and Grant, A. (1997) 'Subversion of allocation in a randomised controlled trial', *Controlled Clinical Trials* 18 (Supplement 3): 77–88.

Kendrick, D., Marsh, P., Fielding, P. and Miller, P. (1999) 'Preventing injuries in children: cluster randomised controlled trial in primary care', *British Medical Journal* 318: 980–3.

Khaw, K. T., Bingham, S., Welch, A. et al. (2001) 'Relation between plasma ascorbic acid and mortality in men and women in EPIC-Norfolk prospective study: a prospective population study', *Lancet* 357: 657–63.

Kinley, H., Czoski-Murray, C., George, S., McCabe, C. et al. (2001) 'Extended scope of nursing practice: a multicentre randomised controlled trial of appropriately trained nurses and pre-registration house officers in pre-operative assessment in elective general surgery', *Health Technology Assessment* 5: 20.

Kinley, H., Czoski-Murray, C., George, S., McCabe, C. et al. (2002) 'Effectiveness of appropriately trained nurses in preoperative assessment: randomised controlled equivalence/non-inferiority trial', *British Medical Journal* 325: 1323.

Kitchener, H. C., Dunn, G., Lawton, V., Reid, F., Nelson, L. and Smith, A. R. B. (2006) 'Laparoscopic versus open colposuspension: results of a prospective randomised controlled trial', *British Journal of Obstetrics and Gynaecology* 113: 1007–13.

Kjaergaard, L. L., Villumsen, J. and Cluud, C. (2001) 'Reported methodologic quality and discrepancies between large and small randomized trials in meta-analyses', *Annals of Internal Medicine* 135: 982–9.

Klaber-Moffett, J. A., Richmond, S., Jackson, D., Coulton, S., Hahn, S., Farrin, A., Manca, A. and Torgerson, D. J. (2005) 'Randomised trial of a brief physiotherapy intervention compared with usual physiotherapy for neck pain patients: outcomes, costs and patient preference', *British Medical Journal* 330: 75.

Klaber-Moffett, J., Torgerson, D. J., Bell-Syer, S., Jackson, D. A., Llewlyn-Phillips, H., Farrin, A. and Barber, J. (1999) 'A randomised trial of exercise for primary care back pain patients: clinical outcomes, costs and preferences', *British Medical Journal* 319: 279–83.

Kling, J. R., Ludwig, J. and Katz, L. F. (2005) 'Neighborhood effects on crime for female and male youth: evidence from a randomized housing voucher experiment', *Quarterly Journal of Economics* Feb: 87–130.

Kramer, M. S., Barr, R. G., Dagenais, S., Yang, H., Jones, P., Ciofani, L. and Jane, F. (2001) 'Pacifier use, early weaning, and cry/fuss behaviour: a randomized controlled trial', *Journal of the American Medical Association* 286: 322–6.

Krueger, A. B. and Zhu, P. (2002) 'Another look at the New York City school voucher experiment', *NBER Working Paper*, 9418.

Kumar, A., Soares, H., Wells, R., Clarke, M., Hozo, I., Bleyer, A., Reaman, G., Chalmers, I. and Djulbegovic, B. (2005) 'Are experimental treatments for cancer in children superior to established treatments? Observational study of randomised controlled trials by the Children's Oncology Group', *British Medical Journal* 331: 1295.

Lancaster, G. A., Dodd, S. and Williamson, P. R. (2004) 'Design and analysis of pilot studies: recommendations for good practice', *Journal of Evaluation in Clinical Practice* 10: 307–12.

Larkey, L. K., Staten, L. K., Ritenabugh, C., Hall, R. A. et al. (2002) 'Recruitment of Hispanic women to the Women's Health Initiative: the case of Embajadoras in Arizona', *Controlled Clinical Trials* 23: 289–98.

Lauritzen, J. B., Petersen, M. M. and Lund, B. (1993) 'Effect of external hip protectors on hip fractures', *Lancet* 341: 11–13.

Leahy, M., Douglas, J., Barley, V., Jarman, M. and Cooper, G. (2005) 'Audiotaping the heart surgery consultation: qualitative study of patients' experiences', *Heart* 91: 1469–70.

Lehr, R. (1992) 'Sixteen S-squared over D-squared: a relation for crude sample size estimates', *Statistics in Medicine* 11: 1099–1102.

Leigh-Brown, A. P., Kennedy, A. D. M., Campbell, J., Torgerson, D. J., Webb, J. A. G. and Grant, A. M. (2001) 'The OMENS Trial: opportunistic evaluation of musculo skeletal physician care among outpatients unlikely to require surgery', *Health Bulletin* 59: 198–210.

Levin, H. M. (2001) 'Waiting for Godot: cost-effectiveness analysis in education', *New Directions for Evaluation* 90: 55–68.

Liénard, J. L., Quinaux, E., Fabre-Guillevin, E., Piedbois, P. et al. (2006) 'Impact of on-site initiation visits on patient recruitment and data quality in a randomized trial of adjuvant chemotherapy for breast cancer', *Clinical Trials* 3: 486–92.

Lin, A., Podell, D. M. and Rein, N. (1991) 'The effects of CAI on word recognition in mildly mentally handicapped and non-handicapped learners', *Journal of Special Education Technology* 11: 16–25.

Linden, A., Adams, J. L. and Roberts, N. (2006) 'Evaluating disease management programme effectiveness: an introduction to the regression discontinuity design', *Journal of Evaluation in Clinical Practice* 12: 124–31.

Lindquist, E. F. (1940) *Statistical Analysis in Educational Research*. Boston: Houghton Mifflin.

Lipsey, M. W. and Wilson, D. B. (1993) 'The efficacy of psychological, educational and behavioural treatment: confirmation from meta-analysis', *American Psychologist* 48: 1181–1209.

Little, P., Gould, C., Williamson, I., Warner, G., Gantley, M. and Kinmonth, A. L. (1997) 'Reattendance and complications in a randomised trial of prescribing strategies for sore throat: the medicalising effect of prescribing antibiotics', *British Medical Journal* 315: 350–2.

Luellen, J. K., Shadish, W. R. and Clark, M. H. (2005) 'Propensity scores: an introduction and experimental test', *Evaluation Review* 29: 530–58.

MacArthur, C., Newton, J. R. and Knox, E. G. (1987) 'Effect of anti-smoking health education on infant size at birth: a randomized controlled trial', *British Journal of Obstetrics and Gynaecology* 94: 295–300.

MacDonald, G. (1997) 'Social work: beyond control?' in A. Maynard and I. Chalmers (eds), *Non-random Reflections on Health Services Research*. London: BMJ Publishing Group.

Majeed, A. W., Troy, G., Nicholl, J. P., Smythe, A., Reed, M. W. R., Stoddard, C. J. et al. (1996) 'Randomised, prospective, single blind comparison of laparoscopic versus small-incision cholecystectomy', *Lancet* 347: 989–94.

Marchant, P. (2005) 'Evaluating area-wide crime-reduction measures', *Significance*, June: 63–5.

Martinson, K. and Friedlander, D. (1994) *GAIN: Basic Education in a Welfare-to-Work Program. California's Greater Avenues for Independence Program*. Manpower Demonstration Research Corp, US, New York.

Martinussen, R. L. and Kirby, J. R. (1998) 'Instruction in successive and phonological processing to improve the reading acquisition skills of at-risk kindergarten children', *Developmental Disabilities Bulletin* 26: 19–39.

McAlister, F. A., Straus, S. E., Sackett, D. L. and Altman, D. G. (2003) 'Analysis and reporting of factorial trials: a systematic review', *Journal of the American Medical Association* 289: 2545–53.

McDonald, A. M., Knight, R. C., Campbell, M. K., Entwistle, V. A., Grant, A. M., Cook, J. A., Elbourne, D. R., Francis, D., Garcia, J., Roberts, I. and Snowdon, C. (2006) 'What influences recruitment to randomised controlled trials? A review of trials funded by two UK funding agencies', *Trials* 7: 9.

Medical Research Council (1944) 'Clinical trial of patulin in the common cold', *Lancet* 2: 370–2.

Medical Research Council (1948) 'Steptomycin treatment of pulmonary tuberculosis: a Medical Research Council investigation', *British Medical Journal* 2: 769–82.

Medical Research Council (2000) *A Framework for Development and Evaluation of RCTs for Complex Interventions to Improve Health*. London: MRC.

Miller, E. R., Pastor-Barriuso, R., Dalal, D., Riemersma, R. A., Appel, L. J. and Guallar, E. (2005) 'Meta-analysis: high-dosage vitamin E supplementation may increase all cause mortality', *Annals of Internal Medicine* 142: 37–46.

Milne, I. and Chalmers, I. 'Hamilton's report of a controlled trial of bloodletting, 1816', The James Lind Library (www.jameslindlibrary.org). Accessed 2 June 2006.

Moher, D., Cook, D. J., Eastwood, S., Olkin, I., Rennie, D. and Stroup, D. F. (1999) Improving the quality of reports of meta-analyses of randomized controlled trials: the QUOROM statement. Quality of reporting of meta-analyses', *Lancet* 354: 1896–1900.

Moher, D., Dulberg, C. S. and Wells, G. A. (1994) 'Statistical power, sample size, and their reporting in randomised controlled trials', *Journal of the American Medical Association* 272: 122–4.

Moher, D., Jones, A. and Lepage, L. (2001) 'Use of the CONSORT statement and quality of reports of randomised trials', *Journal of the American Medical Association* 285: 1992–5.

Morton, V. and Torgerson, D. J. (2003) 'Regression to the mean: effects on health care decision making', *British Medical Journal* 326: 1083–4.

Morrow, A. L., Guerrero, M. L., Shults, J., Calva, J. J., Lutter, C., Bravo, J., Ruiz-Palacios, G., Morrow, R. C. and Butterfoss, F. D. (1999) 'Efficacy of home-based peer counselling to promote exclusive breastfeeding: a randomised controlled trial', *Lancet* 353: 1226–31.

MRC/BHF (2002) 'Heart Protection Study of antioxidant vitamin supplementation in 20 536 high-risk individuals: a randomised placebo-controlled trial', *Lancet* 360: 23–33.

MRC Laparoscopic Groin Hernia Repair Group (1999) 'Laparoscopic versus open repair of groin hernia: a randomised comparison', *Lancet* 354: 183–8.

Murray, D. M. (1998) *Design and Analysis of Group-Randomized Trials*. Oxford: Oxford University Press.

Newton, K. M., Reed, S. D., LaCroix, A. Z., Grothaus, L. C., Ehrlich, K. and Guiltinan, J. (2006) 'Treatment of vasomotor symptoms of menopause with black cohosh multibotanicals, soy, hormone therapy or placebo', *Annals of Internal Medicine* 145: 869–79.

Noseworthy, J., Ebers, G. C., Vandervoot, M. K., Farquhar, R. E., Yetisir, E. and Roberts, R. (1994) 'The impact of blinding on the results of a randomized, placebo-controlled multiple sclerosis clinical trial', *Neurology* 44: 16–20.

Nutbeam, B., Macaskill, P., Smith, C., Simpson, J. and Catford, J. (1993) 'Evaluation of two school smoking education programmes under normal classroom conditions', *British Medical Journal* 306: 102–7.

Oakley, A. (2000) *Experiments in Knowing: Gender and Method in the Social Sciences*. Cambridge: Polity Press.

O'Halloran, P. D., Cran, G. W., Beringer, T. R., Kernohan, G., O'Neill, C., Orr, J. et al. (2004) 'A cluster randomised controlled trial to evaluate a policy of making hip protectors available to residents of nursing homes', *Age & Ageing* 33: 582–8.

O'Rourke, P. P., Crone, R. K., Vacanti, J. P., Ware, J. H., Lillehli, C. W., Parad, R. B. et al. (1989) 'Extracorporeal membrane oxygenation and conventional medical therapy in neonates with persistent pulmonary hypertension of the newborn: a prospective randomized study', *Paediatrics* 84: 957–63.

Pablos-Mendez, A., Barr, G. and Shea, S. (1998) 'Run-in periods in randomized trials: implications for the application of results in clinical practice', *Journal of the American Medical Association* 279: 222–5.

Penston, J. (2007) 'The urge to sprinkle statistics is irresistible', *British Medical Journal* 334: 440.

Petrosino, A., Turpin-Petrosino, C. and Buehler, J. (2002) '"Scared straight" and other juvenile awareness programmes for preventing juvenille delinquency', Campbell Collaboration website: www.campbellcollaboration.org/doc-pdf/ssr.pdf.

Pockaj, B. A., Loprinzi, C. L., Sloan, J. A., Novotny, P. J., Barton, D. L., Hagenmaier, A., Zhang, H., Lambert, G. H., Reeser, K. A. and Wisbey, J. A. (2004) 'Pilot evaluation of black cohosh for the treatment of hot flushes in women', *Cancer Investigation* 22: 515–21.

Pocock, S. J. (1983) *Clinical Trials: a Practical Approach*. Chichester: Wiley.

Pocock, S. J., Hughes, M. D. and Lee, R. J. (1987) 'Statistical problems in the reporting of clinical trials', *New England Journal of Medicine* 317: 426–32.

Porthouse, J., Cockayne, C., King, C., Saxon, L., Steele, E., Aspray, T., Baverstock, M., Birks, Y., Dumville, J., Francis, R. M., Iglesias, C., Puffer, S., Sutcliffe, A., Watt, I. and Torgerson, D. J. (2005) 'Randomised controlled trial of calcium and vitamin D supplementation for fracture prevention in primary care', *British Medical Journal* 330: 1003.

Prideaux, D. (2002) 'Researching the outcomes of educational interventions: a matter of design', *British Medical Journal* 324: 126–7.

Puffer, S. and Torgerson, D. J. (2003) 'Recruitment difficulties in randomised controlled trials', *Controlled Clinical Trials* 3S: 214S–215S.

Puffer, S., Torgerson, D. J. and Watson, J. (2003) 'Evidence for risk of bias in cluster randomised trials: a review of recent trials published in three general medical journals', *British Medical Journal* 327: 785.

Purdon, S., Stratford, N., Taylor, R., Natarajan, L., Bell, S. and Wittenburg, D. (2006) 'Impacts of the Job Retention and Rehabilitation Pilot', *Department for Work and Pensions* Research Report, 342.

RECORD Trial Group (2005) 'Randomised placebo-controlled trial of daily oral vitamin D_3 and/or calcium for the secondary prevention of low-trauma fractures in the elderly', *Lancet* 365: 1621–8.

Riggs, B. L., Hodgson, S. F., O'Fallon, W. M. et al. (1990) 'Effect of fluoride treatment on the fracture rate in postmenopausal women with osteoporosis', *New England Journal of Medicine* 322: 802–9.

Rimm-Kaufman, S. E., Kagan, J. and Byers H. (1999) 'The effectiveness of adult volunteer tutoring on reading among "at risk" first grade children', *Reading Research and Instruction* 38: 143–52.

Roberts, P. J., Roberts, C., Sibbald, B. and Torgerson, D. J. (2000) 'The effect of a direct payment or lottery on questionnaire response rates: a randomised controlled trial', *Journal of Epidemiology and Community Health* 54: 71–2.

Rodger, N. A. M. (2005) *The Command of the Ocean*. Harmondsworth Penguin Books Ltd.

Rosenberger, W. F. and Lachin, J. M. (2002) *Randomization in Clinical Trials: Theory and Practice*. New York: Wiley.

Rouse, C. E., Krueger, A. B. and Markman, L. (2004) 'Putting computerized instruction to the test: a randomized evaluation of a "scientifically based" reading program', NBER Working Paper Series, 10315.

Rutter, M. (2006) 'Is Sure Start an effective preventive intervention?' *Child and Adolescent Mental Health* 11: 135–41.

SAFE Study Investigators (2004) 'A comparison of albumin and saline for fluid resuscitation in the intensive care unit', *New England Journal of Medicine* 350: 2247–56.

Salter, G. C., Roman, M., Bland, M. J. and MacPherson, H. (2006) 'Acupuncture for chronic neck pain: a pilot for a randomised controlled trial', *BMC Musculoskeletal Disorders* 7: 99.

Sauerland, S. and Maegele, M. (2004) 'A CRASH landing in severe head injury', *Lancet* 364: 1291–2.

Schierhout, G. and Roberts, I. (1998) 'Fluid resuscitation with colloid or crystalloid solutions in critically ill patients: a systematic review of randomised trials', *British Medical Journal* 316: 961–4.

Schwartz, D. and Lellouch, J. (1967) 'Explanatory and pragmatic attitudes in therapeutic trials', *Journal of Chronic Diseases* 20: 637–48.

Schulz, K. F., Chalmers, I., Hayes, R. J. and Altman, D. G. (1995) 'Empirical evidence of bias: dimensions of methodological quality associated with estimates of treatment effects in controlled trials', *Journal of the American Medical Association* 273: 408–12.

Schulz, K. F. and Grimes, D. A. (2005) 'Sample size calculations in randomised trials: mandatory and mystical', *Lancet* 365: 1348–53.

Senn, S. (2004) 'Turning a blind eye: authors have blinkered view of blinding', *British Medical Journal* 328: 1135–6.

Shadish, W. R., Cook, T. D. and Campbell, T. D. (2002) *Experimental and Quasi-experimental Designs for Generalized Causal Inference*. Boston: Houghton Mifflin.

Shea, B., Dube, C. and Moher, D. (2001) 'Assessing the quality of reports of systematic reviews: the QUOROM statement compared to other tools', in M. Egger, G. Davey-Smith and D. Altman (eds), *Systematic Reviews in Healthcare: Meta-analysis in Context* (2nd edn). London: BMJ Publishing Group.

Shea, B., Grimshaw, J. M., Wells, G. A., Boers, M., Andersson, N., Hamel, C., Porter, A. C., Tugwell, P., Moher, D. and Bouter, L. M. (2007) 'Development of AMSTAR: a measurement tool to assess the methodological quality of systematic reviews', *BMC Medical Research Methodology* 7: 10.

Sheldon, T. A. and Oakley, A. (2002) 'Why we need randomised trials', in *Clinical Trials*. London: BMJ Publishing.

Shennan, A., Crawshaw, S., Briley, A., Hawken, J., Seed, P., Jones, G. and Poston, L. (2005) 'A randomised controlled trial of metronidazole for the prevention of preterm birth in women positive for cervicovaginal fetal fibronectin: the PREMET study', *BJOG* 113, 1: 65–74.

Shennan, A., Crawshaw, S., Briley, A., Hawken, J., Seed, P., Jones, G. and Poston, L. (2006) 'A randomised controlled trial of metronidazole for the prevention of preterm birth in women positive for cervicovaginal fetal fibronectin: the PREMET study', *BJOG* 113, 7: 850–1.

Sherman, K. J., Cherkin, D. C., Erro, J., Miglioretti, D. L. and Deyo, R. A. (2005) 'Comparing yoga, exercise, and a self-care book for chronic low back pain: a randomized, controlled trial', *Annals of Internal Medicine* 143: 849–56.

Sherman, L. W. and Weisburd, D. (1995) 'General deterrent effects of police patrol in crime "hot spots": a randomized controlled trial', *Justice Quarterly* 12: 625–48.

Silverman, W. A. (1977) 'The lesson of retrolental fibroplasia', *Scientific American* 236: 100–7.

Silverman, W. (1997) 'Equitable distribution of the risks and benefits associated with medical innovations', in A. Maynard and I. Chalmers (eds), *Non-random Reflections on Health Services Research*. London: BMJ Publishing Group.

Silverman, W. A. (1998) *Where's the Evidence: Debates in Modern Medicine*. Oxford: Oxford University Press.

Silverman, W. (2004) 'Personal reflections on lessons learned from randomized trials involving newborn infants from 1951 to 1967', *Clinical Trials* 1: 179–84.

Silverman, W. A. and Altman, D. G. (1996) 'Patients' preferences and randomised trials', *Lancet* 347: 171–4.

Sinclair, M. F., Christenson, S. L. and Thurlow, M. L. (2005) 'Promoting school completion of urban secondary youth with emotional or behavioural disabilities', *Exceptional Children* 71: 465–82.

Smart, R. G. (1964) 'The importance of negative results in psychological research', *Canadian Psychologist* 5: 225–32.

Snowdon, C., Garcia, J. and Elbourne, D. (1997) 'Making sense of randomization: responses of parents of critically ill babies to random allocation of treatment in a clinical trial', *Social Science and Medicine* 45: 1337–55.

Spencer, M. B., Noll, E. and Cassidy, E. (2005) 'Monetary incentives in support of academic achievement', *Evaluation Review* 29: 199–222.

Steptoe, A., Doherty, S., Rink, E., Kerry, S., Kendrick, T. and Hilton, S. (1999) 'Behavioural counselling in general practice for the promotion of healthy behaviour among adults at increased risk of coronary heart disease: randomised trial', *British Medical Journal* 319: 943–8.

Sterne, J. A. C. and Davey-Smith, G. (2001) 'Sifting the evidence – what's wrong with significance tests?' *British Medical Journal* 322: 226–31.

Sutton, A. J., Duval, S. J., Tweedie, R. L., Abrams, K. R. A. and Jones, D. R. (2000) 'Empirical assessment of the effect of publication bias on meta-analyses', *British Medical Journal* 320: 1574–7.

Thomas, E., Croft, P. R., Paterson, S. M., Dziedzic, K. and Hay, E. M. (2004) 'What influences participants' treatment preference and can it influence outcome? Results from a primary care-based randomised trial for shoulder pain', *British Journal of General Practice* 54: 93–6.

Torgerson, C. J. (2001) 'The evidence for misleading statistics in local education authority league tables', *Curriculum* 22: 26–9.

Torgerson, C. J. (2003) *Systematic Reviews*. London: Continuum.

Torgerson, C. J. (2006) 'Publication bias: the Achilles' heel of systematic reviews?' *British Journal of Educational Studies* 54: 89–102.

Torgerson, C. J., Brooks, G. and Hall, J. (2006) *Literature Review of Phonics Use*. London: DfES.

Torgerson, C. J. and Elbourne, D. (2002) 'A systematic review and meta-analysis of the effectiveness of information and communication technology (ICT) on the teaching of spelling', *Journal of Research in Reading* 35: 129–43.

Torgerson, C. J., King, S. E. and Sowden, A. J. (2002) 'Do volunteers in schools help children to learn to read? A systematic review of randomised controlled trials', *Educational Studies* 28: 433–44.

Torgerson, C. J. and Torgerson, D. J. (2001) 'The need for randomised controlled trials in educational research', *British Journal of Educational Studies* 49: 316–28.

Torgerson, C. J., Torgerson, D. J., Birks, Y. F. and Porthouse, J. (2005) 'A comparison of randomised controlled trials in health and education', *British Educational Research Journal* 31: 761–85.

Torgerson, D. J. (2001a) 'Contamination in trials: is cluster randomisation the answer?' *British Medical Journal* 322: 355–7.

Torgerson, D. J. (2001b) 'Commentary: problems with randomised consent', *British Medical Journal* 322: 459.

Torgerson, D. J. and Campbell, M. K. (1997) 'Unequal randomisation can improve the economic efficiency of clinical trials', *Journal of Health Services Research and Policy* 2: 81–5.

Torgerson, D. J. and Campbell, M. K. (2000) 'Cost effectiveness calculations and sample size', *British Medical Journal* 321: 697.

Torgerson, D. J., Klaber-Moffett, J. A. and Russell, I. T. (1996) 'Patient preferences in randomised trials: threat or opportunity', *Journal of Health Services Research and Policy* 1: 194–7.

Torgerson, D. J. and Roland, M. (1998) 'Understanding controlled trials: what is Zelen's design?' *British Medical Journal* 316: 606.

Torgerson, D. J. and Spencer, A. (1996) 'Marginal costs and benefits', *British Medical Journal* 312: 35–6.

Torgerson, D. J., Thomas, R. E., Campbell, M. K. and Reid, D. M. (1997) 'Randomised trial of osteoporosis screening: HRT uptake and quality of life results', *Archives of Internal Medicine* 157: 2121–5.

Torgerson, D. J. and Torgerson, C. J. (2003) 'Avoiding bias in randomised controlled trials in educational research', *British Journal of Educational Studies* 51: 36–45.

Treasure, T. and MacRae, K. D. (1998) 'Minimisation: the platinum standard for trials?' *British Medical Journal* 317: 362–3.

Trowman, R., Dumville, J. C., Hahn, S. and Torgerson, D. J. (2006) 'A systematic review of the effects of calcium supplementation on body weight', *British Journal of Nutrition* 95: 1033–8.

Trowman, R., Dumville, J. C., Cranney, G. and Torgerson, D. J. (2007) 'Identifying and rectifying baseline imbalances in systematic reviews: a methodological case-study', *Journal of Clinical Epidemiology and Endocrinology* (in press).

Tucker, C. M., Herman, K. C., Reid, A. C., Keefer, N. L. and Vogel, D. L. (1998) 'The research-based model partnership education program: a 4-year outcome study', *Journal of Research and Development in Education* 32: 32–7.

Tunis, S. R., Stryer, D. B. and Clancy, C. M. (2003) 'Practical clinical trials: increasing the value of clinical research for decision making in clinical and health policy', *Journal of the American Medical Association* 290: 1624–32.

Turner, J., Edwards, A. E., Gemmell, L. W., Mbako, A., Russell, D., Wilkinson, C., Edmonson, C., Wotton, J. R. and Russell, I. (2006) 'Does a high dependency unit enhance the post-operative care of fracture neck of femur patients? Pragmatic randomised trial', *Care of the Critically Ill* 22: 1–4.

Tversky, A. and Kahneman, D. (1974) 'Judgement under uncertainty: heuristics and biases', *Science* 185: 1124–31.

UK Flexible Sigmoidoscopy Screening Trial Investigators (2002) 'Single flexible sigmoidoscopy screening to prevent colorectal cancer: baseline findings of a UK multicentred randomised trial', *Lancet* 359: 1291–1300.

Verstappen, W. H. J. M., Weijden, T., Sijbrandij, K., Smeele, I., Hermsen, J., Grimshaw, J. and Grol, R. T. M. (2003) 'Effect of practice-based strategy on test ordering performance of primary care physicians: a randomized trial', *Journal of the American Medical Association* 289: 2407–12.

Verstappen, W. H. J. M., Weijden, T., Sijbrandij, K., Smeele, I., Hermsen, J., Grimshaw, J. and Grol, R. T. M. (2004) 'Block design allowed for control of the Hawthorne effect in a randomized controlled trial of test ordering', *Journal of Clinical Epidemiology* 57: 1119–23.

Walters, J. E. (1931) 'Seniors as counsellors', *Journal of Higher Education* 2: 446–8.

Walters, J. E. (1932) 'Measuring effectiveness of personnel counseling', *Personnel Journal* 11: 227–36.

Watson, J. M. and Torgerson, D. J. (2006) 'Increasing recruitment to randomised trials: a review of randomised trials', *BMC Medical Research Methodology* 6: 34.

Wilkes, M. M. and Navickis R. J. (2001) 'Patient survival after human albumin administration: a meta-analysis of randomized, controlled trials', *Annals of Internal Medicine* 135: 149–64.

Wittes, J., Schabenberger, O., Zucker, D., Brittain, E. and Proschan, M. (1999) 'Internal pilot studies I: type I error rate of the Naïve t-Test', *Statistics in Medicine* 18: 3481–91.

Wood, D. A., Kinmouth, A. L., Davies, G. A. et al. (1994) 'Randomised controlled trial evaluating cardiovascular screening and intervention in general practice: principal results of British family heart survey', *British Medical Journal* 308: 313–20.

Wortman, P. M. (1995) 'An exemplary evaluation of a program that worked: the High/Scope Perry Preschool Project', *Evaluation Practice* 16: 257–65.

Writing Group for the Women's Health Initiative Investigators (2002) 'Risks and benefits of oestrogen plus progestin in healthy postmenopausal women: principal results from the Women's Health Initiative randomised controlled trial', *Journal of the American Medical Association* 288: 321–33.

Zelen, M. (1979) 'A new design for randomized clinical trials', *New England Journal of Medicine* 300: 1242–5.

Index